MENTORING TEACHER
IN THE PRIMARY SCH(

Mentoring Teachers in the Primary School helps mentors of trainee and newly qualified primary school teachers to both develop their own mentoring skills and provide the essential guidance their beginning teachers need as they navigate the roller-coaster of the first years in the classroom. Offering tried and tested strategies based on the best research, it covers the knowledge, skills and understanding every mentor needs.

Together with tools for self-evaluation, this book is a vital source of support and inspiration for all those involved in developing the next generation of outstanding teachers. Key topics for primary mentors include:

- the role of the mentor,
- mentoring relationships,
- mentoring in specialist areas,
- mentoring development.

Filled with guidance to support mentors' own development, as well as the development of beginning primary teachers, *Mentoring Teachers in the Primary School* is a vital guide for mentors of primary school teachers, both trainee and newly qualified, with ready-to-use strategies that support and inspire mentors.

Kristy Howells is a Reader in Physical Education and Sport Pedagogy at Canterbury Christ Church University.

Julia Lawrence was until recently a Senior Lecturer in Education at the University of Hull.

Judith Roden recently retired from her role as Principal Lecturer in Primary Education at Canterbury Christ Church University.

MENTORING TRAINEE AND NEWLY QUALIFIED TEACHERS

Series edited by: Susan Capel, Trevor Wright, Julia Lawrence and Sarah Younie

The **Mentoring Trainee and Newly Qualified Teachers** Series are subject-specific, practical books designed to reinforce and develop mentors' understanding of the different aspects of their role, as well as exploring issues that mentees encounter in the course of learning to teach. The books have two main foci: first, challenging mentors to reflect critically on theory, research and evidence, on their own knowledge, their approaches to mentoring and how they work with beginning teachers in order to move their practice forward; and second, supporting mentors to effectively facilitate the development of beginning teachers. Although the basic structure of all the subject books is similar, each book is different to reflect the needs of mentors in relation to the unique nature of each subject or age phase. Elements of appropriate theory introduce each topic or issue, with emphasis placed on the practical application of material. The chapter authors in each book have been engaged with mentoring over a long period of time and share research, evidence and their experience.

We hope that this series of books supports you in developing into an effective, reflective mentor as you support the development of the next generation of teachers.

For more information about this series, please visit: https://www.routledge.com/Mentoring-Trainee-and-Newly-Qualified-Teachers/book-series/MTNQT

Titles in the series

Mentoring Physical Education Teachers in the Secondary School
Edited by Susan Capel and Julia Lawrence

Mentoring Design and Technology Teachers in the Secondary School
Edited by Suzanne Lawson and Susan Wood-Griffith

Mentoring English Teachers in the Secondary School
Edited by Debbie Hickman

Mentoring Science Teachers in the Secondary School
Edited by Saima Salehjee

Mentoring Teachers in the Primary School
Edited by Kristy Howells and Julia Lawrence, with Judith Roden

MENTORING TEACHERS IN THE PRIMARY SCHOOL

A Practical Guide

Edited by Kristy Howells and Julia Lawrence, with Judith Roden

LONDON AND NEW YORK

First published 2021
by Routledge
2 Park Square, Milton Park, Abingdon, Oxon OX14 4RN

and by Routledge
52 Vanderbilt Avenue, New York, NY 10017

Routledge is an imprint of the Taylor & Francis Group, an informa business

British Library Cataloguing-in-Publication Data
A catalogue record for this book is available from the British Library

Library of Congress Cataloging-in-Publication Data
Names: Howells, Kristy, editor. | Lawrence, Julia Clare, editor. | Roden, Judith, editor.
Title: Mentoring teachers in the primary school: a practical guide/
Edited by Kristy Howells and Julia Lawrence with Judith Roden.
Description: Abingdon, Oxon; New York: Routledge, 2021. |
Includes bibliographical references and index.
Identifiers: LCCN 2020037731 (print) | LCCN 2020037732 (ebook) |
ISBN 9781138389069 (hardback) | ISBN 9781138389076 (paperback) |
ISBN 9780429424199 (ebook)
Subjects: LCSH: Mentoring in education-Great Britain. |
Primary school teachers-Training of-Great Britain. |
Primary school teachers-In-service training-Great Britain. |
Education, Primary-Great Britain.
Classification: LCC LB1731.4 .M472 2021 (print) |
LCC LB1731.4 (ebook) | DDC 371.1020941-dc23
LC record available at https://lccn.loc.gov/2020037731
LC ebook record available at https://lccn.loc.gov/2020037732

ISBN: 978-1-138-38906-9 (hbk)
ISBN: 978-1-138-38907-6 (pbk)
ISBN: 978-0-429-42419-9 (ebk)

Typeset in Interstate
by Newgen Publishing UK

CONTENTS

ILLUSTRATIONS

Figures

Tables

TASKS

CASE STUDIES

CONTRIBUTORS

Editors

Dr Kristy Howells is a Reader in Physical Education and Sport Pedagogy at Canterbury Christ Church University. She has written on a number of subjects relating to primary education including physical education, teaching and coaching, reflective practice, physical development, physical activity and mental wellbeing as well as diet and nutrition.

Dr Julia Lawrence was until recently a Senior Lecturer in Education at the University of Hull. She has written on a number of subjects relating to primary education including physical education, mentoring, reflective practice and becoming a teacher educator.

Judith Roden recently retired from her role as Principal Lecturer in Primary Education at Canterbury Christ Church University. She has written extensively about primary science education, curriculum development and mentoring. She has edited a number of books and is series editor of popular books across the primary curriculum.

Contributors

Victoria Blake works at Teach First and specialises in developing beginning teachers and their mentors on a teacher training programme. She is currently qualifying as a counsellor. Her particular interests are in building effective relationships and creating an environment in which people can flourish.

Wendy E. Cobb is a Senior Lecturer and behaviour lead in the Faculty of Education at Canterbury Christ Church University. Wendy facilitates an emotional health network for students and education practitioners in partnership with the charity Family Links and leads mentor development training.

Dr Gina Donaldson is a Senior Lecturer in primary education at Canterbury Christ Church University, specialising in primary mathematics. She leads the provision for primary mathematics specialist student teachers and works with mentors in supporting their progress in school.

Dr Sandra Eady is a Senior Lecturer in Education at Queen Margaret University, Edinburgh. Sandra has written on a number of subjects relating to professional education, including mentoring, professional learning and education partnership.

Gill Golder is Director of Teacher Education, Department Head for Education and Programme Leader for Secondary Education at the University of St Mark and St John, Plymouth.

Sarah Goodwin is a primary school teacher and lead mentor at St Peter's Church of England Primary School, Folkestone. She has mentored students from Canterbury Christ Church University, beginning teachers, early career teachers and middle leaders. Sarah is also trained as a Specialist Leader of Education for art and drama.

Jessica Harley is a Senior Lecturer in primary and early years at Canterbury Christ Church University. She has led on the expansion of the early years programme and leadership development within the Teach First programme in the South Coast region.

Rebecca Heaton is a Deputy Head Teacher at an outstanding coastal primary school in Kent, situated in an area of high deprivation. Her specialisms include primary mathematics, information technology and curriculum development.

Dr Lindsay Joyce is a Chartered Psychologist working with schools, charities and businesses on topics such as wellbeing and coaching. Her work is based in Acceptance and Commitment Therapy (ACT) and Compassion Focused Therapy, and she particularly enjoys supporting frontline practitioners such as teachers, social workers and prison officers to apply evidence-based psychology to support themselves and others.

Alison Keyworth is a Senior Lecturer in postgraduate and professional development at the University of St Mark and St John, Plymouth.

Hazel King is a Senior Lecturer in primary education at Canterbury Christ Church University. Hazel has written about mentoring student teachers and about her own journey to become a teacher educator from a career as a primary school teacher and mathematics subject lead.

Cornelia Lucey is a Positive Psychologist and Leadership expert. She works independently for education institutions, charities and across sectors to support the development of wellbeing and positive leadership for individuals, teams and organisations and is co-founder of LIVEWISE (www.livewise.how).

Dr Lorele Mackie is a Lecturer in Education at the University of Stirling. Her research interests include professional learning and innovative pedagogies. She is currently undertaking research in two areas: the use of formative assessment in the mentoring of primary student teachers; and learning and teaching in second and subsequent languages.

Claire March is a Senior Lecturer in Education at Canterbury Christ Church University. Claire has previously written on art and design, in particular linked to the practice of sketchbooks and the development of technology to assist the creative process.

Gill Rowland is a Senior Lecturer in Education at Canterbury Christ Church University. She works extensively with school mentors and has contributed to the design and delivery of a mentor development programme run by the university.

Clare Shaw is a Senior Lecturer in primary initial teacher education at the University of St Mark and St John, Plymouth.

Sarah St. John is a Senior Lecturer in primary education at Canterbury Christ Church University. Her research interests include the role of mentors and coaches and how they can be used to facilitate learning.

Bea Stevenson is the Head of Education at the emotional health charity Family Links. From a background in primary teaching, Bea led the Teach First strategy for working effectively with mentors across the country. She works with schools to develop good emotional and mental health for the learning community.

Dr Rachael Stone is a Senior Lecturer at Canterbury Christ Church University. Her research includes collaborative research with a focus on what teachers understand about the teaching of reading.

Dr d'Reen Struthers is a Lecturer in Education at UCL-Institute of Education. Drawing from her experience in teacher education and higher education, she has written on music education, resilience, the nature of school-university partnerships, and the Connected Curriculum for Higher Education. She has also developed mentoring programmes for schools and universities drawing on critical reflective practices, resilience and approaches to practitioner research.

Sonia Tomlinson is a Senior Lecturer in primary education at Canterbury Christ Church University. She has written about mentoring trainees and newly qualified teachers in primary mathematics to support them in becoming effective teachers of mathematics in primary education.

Karen Vincent is a Senior Lecturer in early years and primary education at Canterbury Christ Church University. She has written on a number of subjects relating to early years and primary initial teacher education, including pedagogies of play, play and mathematics, literacy transition from EYFS to KS1 and mentoring.

Dr Hellen Ward is a Principal Lecturer and the Director of the STEM Hub of the South East of England. Hellen has written on a range of science-related subjects and hopes everyone will engage with inspirational role models in the future.

Penny Webb is a Senior Lecturer at Canterbury Christ Church University and specialises in primary initial teacher education (ITE) and special educational needs and disability. Penny takes a lead in special educational needs and disability across the ITE programmes.

AN INTRODUCTION TO THE SERIES: MENTORING TRAINEE AND NEWLY QUALIFIED TEACHERS

Mentoring is a very important and exciting role. What could be better than supporting the development of the next generation of teachers? A mentor is almost certainly an effective teacher, but this doesn't automatically guarantee that he or she will be a good mentor, despite similarities in the two roles. This series of practical workbooks covers primary mentoring and most subjects in the secondary curriculum. They are designed specifically to reinforce mentors' understanding of different aspects of their role, for mentors to learn about and reflect on their role, to provide support for mentors in aspects of their development and to enable them to analyse their success in supporting the development of beginning teachers (defined as trainee, newly qualified and early career teachers). This book has two main foci: first, the focus is on challenging mentors to reflect critically on theory, research and evidence, on their own knowledge, how they work with beginning teachers, how they work with more experienced teachers and on their approaches to mentoring in order to move their practice forward. Second, the focus is on supporting mentors to effectively facilitate the development of beginning teachers. Thus, some of the practical activities in the books are designed to encourage reflection, whilst others ask mentors to undertake activities with beginning teachers. This book can be used alongside generic and subject books designed for student and newly qualified teachers. These books include Capel, Leask and Younie's (2019) *Learning to Teach in the Secondary School: A Companion to School Experience,* which deals with aspects of teaching and learning applicable to all subjects, and Cremin and Burnett's (2018) *Learning to Teach in the Primary School*. Further, the generic books are complemented by three series: Learning to Teach [subject] in the Secondary School: A Companion to School Experience; A Practical Guide to Teaching [subject] in the Secondary School; and Learning to Teach in the Primary School. These books are designed for student teachers on different types of initial teacher education programmes (and indeed a beginning teacher with whom you are working may have used or is currently using them). However, these books are proving equally useful to tutors and mentors in their work with student teachers, both in relation to the knowledge, skills and understanding the student teacher is developing and some tasks that mentors might find it useful to support a beginning teacher to do. They are also supported by a book designed for newly qualified teachers, *Surviving and Thriving in the Secondary School: The NQT's Essential Companion* (Capel et al., 2019). These titles cover material not generally needed by student teachers on an initial teacher education course, but which is needed by newly qualified teachers in their school work and early career.

The information in this book should link with the information in the generic text and relevant book in the three series in a number of ways. For example, mentors might want to refer a beginning teacher to read about specific knowledge, understanding and skills they are focusing on developing, or to undertake tasks in the book, either alone or with their support, then discus the tasks. It is recommended that you have copies of these books available so that you can cross-reference when needed.

In turn, the books complement a range of resources on which mentors can draw (including other mentors of beginning teachers in the same or other subjects or age phase, other teachers and a range of other resources including books, research articles and websites).

The positive feedback on *Learning to Teach* and the related books above, particularly the way they have supported the learning of student teachers in their development into effective, reflective teachers, encouraged us to retain the main features of that book in this series. Like teaching, mentoring should be research- and evidence-informed. Thus, this series of books introduces theory, research and professional evidence-based advice and guidance to support mentors as they develop their mentoring to support beginning teachers' development. The main focus is the practical application of material. Elements of appropriate theory introduce each topic or issue, and recent research into mentoring and/or teaching and learning is integral to the presentation. Tasks are provided to help mentors identify key features of the topic or issue and reflect on and/or apply them to their own practice of mentoring beginning teachers. Although the basic structure of all the books is similar, each book is different to reflect the needs of mentors in relation to the unique nature of each subject.

The chapter authors in the books have been engaged with mentoring over a long period of time and are aiming to share research/evidence and their experience. We, as series editors, are pleased to extend the work in initial teacher education to the work of mentors of beginning teachers. We hope that this series of books supports you in developing into an effective, reflective mentor as you support the development of the next generation of subject teachers.

Susan Capel, Julia Lawrence, Trevor Wright and Sarah Younie

ACKNOWLEDGEMENTS

We would like to recognise and acknowledge the contribution of each author to this book and thank them for their continued support and patience as the book developed through various formats. As a team, we would like to thank Judith Roden and Professor Susan Capel for their inspiration and initial development of the book.

We would also like to acknowledge all the mentors and teacher educators as well as beginning teachers who contributed to the authors' discussions, tasks, illustrations, case studies, thoughts, ideas and chapter development.

We would also like to thank JD and Helen for the fabulous support they have given us throughout our writing and editing of this book.

We dedicate this book to Paddy Grinter, who always had a smile on his face and a glint in his eye whenever we saw him, who inspired so many beginning teachers through his mentoring and especially through the power of dance. Paddy is sadly missed.

Introduction

Teacher training has changed rapidly over the last few years, and will no doubt continue to change/evolve. Most notably, numbers on predominantly university-based teacher training courses have decreased as the government has encouraged more school-led and school-based teacher training. With this change, there are now more teachers than ever acting as mentors in school-led teacher training, in addition to those mentoring on university-led programmes. Consequently, the quality and quantity of support available to supporting mentors of beginning teachers varies considerably. Additionally, as well as mentoring trainee teachers, many school-based mentors may also have other mentoring responsibilities - for example, acting as a mentor for newly qualified teachers, early career teachers or teachers new to the school. Supporting this wide variety of mentees in a primary school presents a significant challenge for mentors who are often generalist teachers themselves. The role of a mentor in primary schools is multifaceted and goes beyond support for the development of generic aspects of teaching. Mentors are often required to act as 'subject'-specific and specialist mentors across the broad range of subjects taught within the primary education setting.

The range of expertise required to be an effective mentor potentially places huge demands on the mentor, who is usually the first 'port of call' for both a trainee primary teacher and those in the early stages of their teaching career. Research suggests that the role of the mentor is both vital and highly influential to a beginning teacher. For the purpose of this book, beginning teachers are defined as trainees, newly qualified, early career teachers or those new to the school setting and in need of support and guidance - indeed, all those who would benefit hugely from a mentor. This book is designed to help support the gap in both training for and support of school-based mentors to enable them to be confident in effectively supporting beginning primary teachers.

This book's authors are drawn from both those who currently train and educate teachers within universities throughout the United Kingdom, as well as practitioners who are based within schools. The aim is to offer a wide range of experience, expertise and advice to support the mentor workforce within our primary schools. You will hear the different voices of the experts within their own chapters throughout the book. The book has been purposefully written in this style to allow key experts to contribute and share their work in order to support all mentors and their mentees.

It is anticipated that, as more teacher training becomes school-led in England, there will be an increasing need for support from such texts, to support primary school-based mentors and the teachers they are mentoring. The book is designed as a practical workbook with tasks throughout the chapters. Tasks have been designed in a number of ways and include:

- reflexive pause moments for mentors to consider their current practice and mentoring
- mentoring ideas and suggestions for the mentor to trial with their mentee/beginning teachers
- problem-based scenarios to prompt thinking and discussions
- case study examples to illustrate practice as well as policy.

The practical aspects of each chapter are designed to be used in an ongoing way throughout each chapter to help mentors develop themselves. These should provide support and ideas for mentors to aid in their support in beginning teacher development. Authors within each chapter have drawn explicitly on research and evidence to ensure that the book provides evidence-based practice in mentoring beginning primary teachers. Within each chapter, authors provide examples and strategies, including templates that you could use to observe and assess. They also include selections of mentor/mentee dialogue, question and answer sessions, coaching sessions and other learning activities designed as solutions to help mentors in problem-solving exercises. The aim of the book is to help you, as mentors, to analyse your own practice, to reflect upon your approaches to mentoring and how, through engagement with this book, you may move your own practice forward as well as the practice of the mentee, a beginning teacher whom you are mentoring.

The book is divided into four sections. Section 1 focuses on the role of the mentor, exemplifying what it means to be a mentor. It focuses specifically on:

- models of mentoring
- becoming a mentor
- successful mentoring in action
- managing your role as a mentor.

Section 2 focuses on mentoring relationships, examines the whole interrelated process of mentoring and considers:

- the importance of working with beginning teachers
- working with beginning teachers
- developing a relationship with your mentees
- developing learning conversations with your mentees
- making accurate assessments of your mentees
- supporting the wellbeing and additional needs of your mentees
- supporting resilience in practice
- mentoring to enable others to 'thrive' in teaching.

Section 3 focuses on mentoring in specialist areas, and reveals how you, as a mentor, can support particular subject areas:

- mentoring for art and design
- mentoring for mathematics
- mentoring for physical education
- mentoring for reading
- mentoring for science, technology, engineering and mathematics (STEM).

Section 4 focuses on particular aspects of continued professional development, designed to support mentor development:

- the role of research in mentoring
- developing a community of mentoring and coaching in a school
- developing successful partnership working for mentors.

Although the book is divided into chapters, a similar approach is taken within all the chapters. Each chapter is laid out as follows:

- *introduction* to the content of the chapter
- *objectives*, presented to outline what will be achieved, known, understood by the end of the chapter
- *main content of the chapter*, which includes research and evidence that underpins the focus of the chapter. Each chapter contains practical activities in the form of tasks to support the development of the mentors' knowledge and understanding. These include personal reflections about mentors' own practice, or critically evaluating case studies
- *a summary* of the chapter that reviews the key points
- *further reading*, publications selected to help mentors to continue to extend their knowledge and understanding following completion of the chapter.

The book has been written with the mentor as the main reader, although it may also be useful for a mentor to use parts of the book with a beginning teacher so they understand the process of mentoring and how the mentor is supporting them within their journey.

The term 'learning journey' is used in several places in this book. This term could be applied to a beginning teacher on the journey to become a more skilled practitioner. It could equally be applied to the mentor involved in the journey towards becoming a more effective mentor. Ultimately, of course, although this is often implicit, the book fundamentally aims to improve the learning journey and progress of the children with whom mentors and mentees work in school. Never should it be forgotten that at the heart of the work of mentoring a mentee is pupil progress across the whole spectrum of learning in the primary school.

With this perspective in mind, we hope that Figure 0.1, designed by Jessica Harley, may help you as a mentor to develop the learning journey of your mentee by engaging them in reflection on their pupils' learning journey. Listening to your mentee explaining planning the essential elements of pupil learning in the diagram may also provide you, as a mentor, with the opportunity to develop your own personal learning journey.

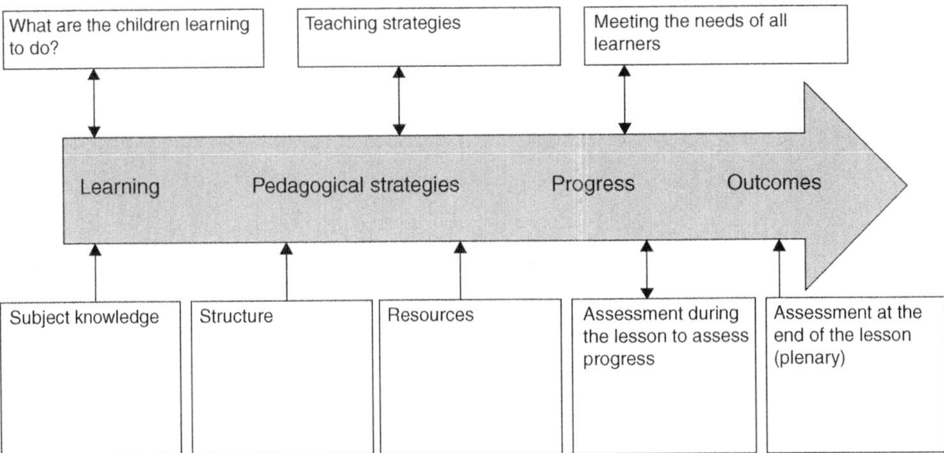

Figure 0.1 Template of lesson learning journey
Source: Jessica Harley.

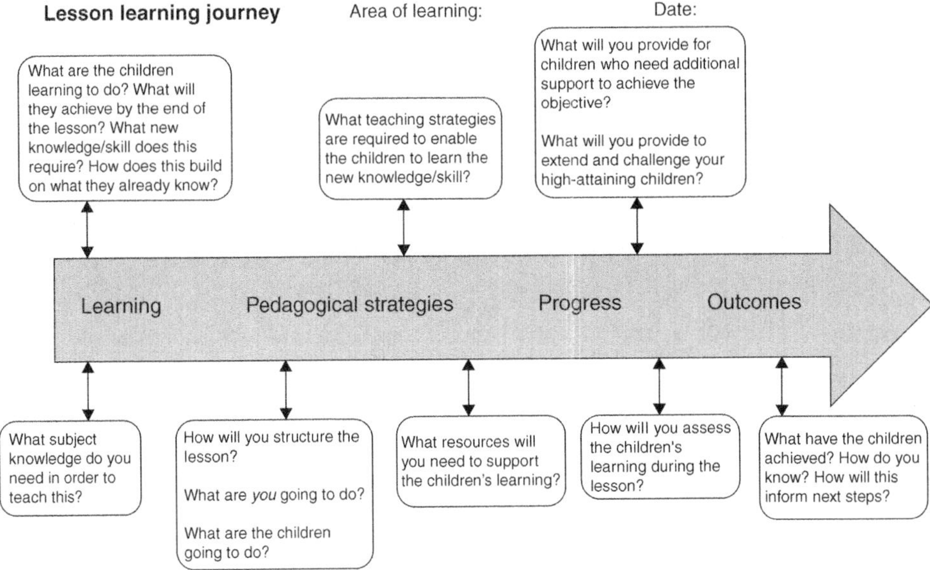

Figure 0.2 Completed lesson learning journey

We hope you will find this book a useful resource to support you in your role as a mentor, and we welcome any comments you would like to share with us.

Kristy Howells
Julia Lawrence
Judith Roden
October 2020

SECTION 1

The role of the mentor

1 Models of mentoring

Gill Golder, Alison Keyworth and Clare Shaw

Introduction

Your job as a mentor is to develop a positive working relationship with a beginning teacher to enable them to grow and develop, both professionally and personally. How you go about this will be influenced by a number of factors, such as your own experience of being mentored in the past and your commonsense opinions of the role. These are important starting points, but you are likely to grow as an effective mentor when you also base your approaches on evidence. This book is designed to support you in considering the evidence that will underpin your practice.

This chapter starts by looking at different definitions of mentoring. It then examines the importance of the context in which you are working as a mentor, highlighting a number of documents from England and other countries that impact your mentoring practice. The chapter then considers three potential mentoring models a mentor could adopt to inform their practice. These models underpin various roles you undertake and hence the other chapters in this book.

Objectives

At the end of this chapter, you should:

- Have a greater understanding of what is meant by the term 'mentoring' for a beginning teacher
- Have an appreciation of the key context in which you work that may influence the manner in which you act as a mentor in school
- Have an awareness of the plethora of mentoring models that exist
- Be able to compare and contrast three developmental mentoring models and how these could be used to support your role as a mentor.

Before reading further, undertake Task 1.1.

Task 1.1 Mentor reflection: Reflecting on your understanding of mentoring

Reflect on what you understand by mentoring by considering the following questions

- How would you define mentoring?
- How does your definition inform your practice as a mentor?
- How do the various policy and guidance documents relevant to your context influence your mentoring practice?
- Do you base your mentoring practice on personal experience or on a model(s) of mentoring? If a model, which one(s)? Why?

Definitions of mentoring

Mentoring is widely used in many contexts for the purpose of helping people to learn and develop, both professionally and personally. There are numerous and frequently contradictory definitions of mentoring, with accompanying models of how mentoring is best approached (Haggard, Dougherty, Turban and Wilbanks, 2011). While different models might utilise different terminology and vary in emphasis regarding the role of a mentor, what remains consistent is the view that mentoring is a supportive learning relationship. The mentor, with their more extensive experience, is there to support the learner's development. The quality of the relationship between mentor and mentee is extremely important.

The terms 'mentoring' and 'coaching' are at times used interchangeably. Both aim to develop the professional or professional competencies of the client or colleague. Although mentoring and coaching have much in common, an important difference between the two is the focus of developmental activities. In mentoring, the focus is on development at significant career transitions, whereas in coaching the focus is on the development of a specific aspect of a professional learner's practice (CUREE, 2005).

Montgomery (2017) suggested that definitions of mentoring often involve the concept that advice and guidance to a novice, or person with limited experience, is given by an experienced person. In this way, mentoring can be seen to be hierarchical; a top-down approach largely based on a one-way flow of information.

> Mentoring involves the use of the same models and skills of questioning, listening, clarifying and reframing associated with coaching. Traditionally, however, mentoring in the workplace has tended to describe a relationship in which a more experienced colleague uses his or her greater knowledge and understanding of the work or workplace to support the development of a more junior or inexperienced member of staff.
>
> (CIPD, 2012, p.1)

In contrast, other definitions of mentoring follow a less hierarchal structure. These include peer mentoring (Driscoll, Parkes, Tilley-Lubbs, Brill and Pitts Bannister, 2009) and group mentoring (Kroll, 2016). In these approaches to mentoring, the flow of information is more bidirectional. Montgomery (2017) suggested they are more personalised as mentoring is more effectively adapted to an individual mentee's goals and needs. Higgins and Thomas (2001) suggest that top-down mentoring has greater impact on short-term career outcomes and individually driven mentoring supports long-term career development more effectively. Whether the focus is on short- or long-term tailored development of a mentee, there are common aspect to all forms of mentoring. CIDP (2012, p. 1) identifies four characteristics of mentoring:

- It is essentially a supportive form of development.
- It focuses on helping a person manage their career and improve skills.
- Personal issues can be discussed productively.
- Mentoring activities have both organisational and individual goals.

In education, school-based mentors play a vital role in the development of student teachers and the induction of newly qualified teachers. They also support other staff at various points of career development. As with mentoring in other contexts, there is a focus on learning, development and the provision of appropriate support and encouragement. The definition of a mentor outlined in the National Standards for School-based Initial Teacher Training (ITT) Mentors in England (Department for Education (DfE), 2016b, p. 11) is someone who 'is a suitably experienced teacher who has formal responsibility to work collaboratively within the ITT partnership to help ensure the trainee receives the highest quality training'. However, in initial teacher education in many countries, including England, assessment of the beginning teacher is integral to the mentor's role. This is supported by Pollard (2014), who suggests that the role of the mentor in ITT has developed because of three aspects: the complexity of the capabilities teachers need to meet, the focus on high professional standards in school and the transfer of knowledge from one generation to another. Before reading any further, undertake Task 1.2.

Task 1.2 Mentoring reflection: Understanding the term 'mentoring'

- Research the terms 'mentoring' and 'coaching'.
- List a variety of terms that you associate with coaching and mentoring.
- Make a list of common and unique characteristics for both.

The context in which you are working, which underpins your mentoring practice

Mentoring is increasingly important in a range of fields, both in the United Kingdom and internationally, as a tool to support recruitment into a profession, retention in that profession, professional learning, networking and career development. In teaching, it is widely recognised that there is a strong relationship between professional learning, teaching knowledge and practices, educational leadership and pupil results (Cordingly et al., 2015). There has been an increase in the development of policy and guidance documents as well as frameworks, toolkits and factsheets over the past few years to support educators and others in fulfilling their roles as mentors.

As a mentor, it is important to recognise and embed current policy and statutory guidance into your mentoring practice. A number of key documents underpin the mentoring process in initial teacher education and beyond in England and elsewhere. These constitute the key external drivers in shaping mentoring practice in school. Being aware of these is important, but knowing how to use them to support your work with a beginning teacher can add purpose and validity to what you do. (There are examples of how to do this in other chapters in this book.) They also enable you to recognise the value of being a mentor in school, as 'effective professional development for teachers is a core part of securing effective teaching' (DFE 2016b, p. 3).

Table 1.1 highlights policy and guidance documents that influence the work you do in school with a beginning teacher in England, but also signposts you to examples of international equivalence documents to enable you to make comparisons internationally.

Now complete Task 1.3.

Task 1.3 The context in which you carry out your mentoring duties

Reflect on the context in which you carry out your mentoring duties. Ensure you are familiar with the relevant documents above (or, if you are working outside England, documents specific to your own context). What aspects of these documents do you identify as being of most use to your work and why?

Effective mentoring models

As alluded to above, there are a number of mentoring models that a mentor could adopt in order to support the growth and development of a beginning teacher. Attempts have been made to categorise different approaches to mentoring – for example, Maynard and Furlong (1995) suggest there are three categories of mentoring: the apprentice model, the competence model and the reflective model. The apprenticeship model argues that the skills of being a teacher are best learned by supervised practice, with guidance from imitation of experienced practitioners. The competence model suggests that learning to teach requires learning a predefined list of competences. (The current Teachers Standards in England (DFE, 2011) could be described as a competence model.) In this model, the mentor becomes a systematic trainer supporting a beginning teacher to meet the competences. In the reflective model, the promotion of reflective practice through mentoring is key. This requires a beginning teacher to have some mastery of the skills of teaching to be able to reflect upon their own practice and for the mentor to be a co-inquirer and facilitator rather than instructor. Task 1.4 asks you to look at three different mentoring models.

Table 1.1 Key external drivers influencing mentoring work

	Policy/guidance document	*Author and date introduced*	*Key purpose*
Teacher Standards documents	Teachers' Standards (England)	DFE (2011)	Used to assess all student teachers working towards qualified teacher status (QTS) as well as newly qualified teachers completing their statutory induction period. 'Providers of ITT should assess trainees against the standards in a way that is consistent with what could reasonably be expected of a trainee teacher prior to the award of QTS' (DFE, 2011, p. 6).
	The Australian Professional Standards for teachers (Australia)	Australian Institute for Teaching and School Leadership (AITSL) (2011)	The Standards are designed so that teachers know what they should be aiming to achieve at every stage of their career; to enable them to improve their practice inside and outside of the classroom. 'The Standards do this by providing a framework which makes clear the knowledge, practice and professional engagement required across teachers' careers' (AITSL 2011, p. 2).
Core content requirements for initial teacher education	Framework of Core Content for Initial Teacher Training (England)	DFE (2016a)	The aim of this framework is to improve the consistency and quality of ITT courses by supporting those involved in training teachers and student teachers themselves to have a better understanding of the key elements of good ITT content.
	Differentiated Primary and Lower Secondary Teacher Education Programmes for Years 1-7 and Years 5-10 (Norway)	Ministry of Education and Research (2010)	These regulations apply to universities and university colleges that provide primary and lower secondary teacher education. They aim to ensure that teacher education institutions provide integrated, professionally oriented and research-based primary and lower secondary teacher education programmes of high academic quality.
National or regional standards for educators acting as mentors	National Standards for School-based Initial Teacher Training (ITT) Mentors (England)	DFE (2016b)	The standards were developed to bring greater coherence and consistency to school-based mentoring arrangements for student teachers. They set out the minimum level of practice expected of mentors. They are used to foster consistency in the practice of mentors, raise the profile of mentoring and build a culture of mentoring in schools
	The New York State Mentoring Standards Albany (USA)	The State Education Department/The University of The State Of New York (2011)	A set of standards that guide the design and implementation of teacher mentoring programmes in New York State through teacher induction.

(*continued*)

Table 1.1 (Cont.)

	Policy/guidance document	*Author and date introduced*	*Key purpose*
National or regional guidelines for general coaching and mentoring practice	National Framework for Mentoring and Coaching (England)	Centre for the Use of Resource and Evidence in Education (CUREE) (2005)	The framework was developed in order to help schools implement mentoring and coaching to assist with continuing professional development and other activities. It sets out ten principles based on evidence from research and consultation which are recommended to inform mentoring and coaching programmes in schools. The framework provides a tool for reflection on existing practice and further development and assists a mentor in self-regulation and monitoring of their own practice.
	NTC Continuum of Mentoring Practice (USA)	New Teacher Centre (NTC) (2011)	Designed to assist programme leaders as they seek to implement mentoring to support induction programmes that are capable of accelerating the development of beginning teacher effectiveness, improving teacher retention, strengthening teacher leadership and increasing pupil learning. 'It presents a holistic view of mentoring, based on six professional standards ... The continuum of mentoring practice describes three levels of development, labelled Exploring/Emerging, Applying, Integrating/Innovating' (NTC 2011, p. 2).
Professional development expectations for teachers	Standards for Teachers' Professional Development (England)	DFE (2016c)	This is intended for 'all those working in and with, schools in order to raise expectations for professional development, to focus on achieving the best improvement in pupil outcomes and also to develop teachers as respected members of the profession' (DFE 2016b, p. 4). There is an emphasis on using the standards to support regular reflection on existing practice and discussion between all members of the teaching community. There are five parts to the standard which, when acted upon together, ensure effective professional development.
	Ohio Standards for Professional Development (USA)	Ohio Department for Education (2015)	These define the essential elements of a strong professional learning system, which is one way school systems can support all educators and encourage improved teaching and learning.

Task 1.4 Three different mentoring models

- What are the features of practice for each of these models: apprentice, competence and reflective?
- Which features of these models do you use/want to use in your mentoring?
- When do/would you use each model of mentoring?

Maynard and Furlong (1995, p. 18) acknowledge that these three models exist but suggest that they should be taken together, in order to contribute to 'a view of mentoring that responds to the changing needs of trainees'. It is this recognition that mentoring practices and approaches evolve as a beginning teacher develops, and the need for an examination of different stages of development that lead to us exploring three models of mentoring in more detail. We explore three well-known models (Clutterbuck, 2004; Daloz, 2012; Katz, 1995), all of which focus on the need for the mentor to be flexible in their style and approach to best fit the needs of a beginning teacher at any given stage of their development, in initial teacher education and/or their teaching career.

Daloz's (2012) developmental model identifies two key aspects that need to be present in order for optimal learning to take place: *challenge* and *support*. The challenge aspect refers to your ability as a mentor to question a beginning teacher to enable them to reflect critically on their own beliefs, behaviours and attitudes. The support aspect relies on you being able to offer an empathetic ear, actively listen and encourage a beginning teacher to find solutions in order to continue to develop and progress.

Daloz (2012) argues that a combination of high challenge and high support need to be offered by you as the mentor for a beginning teacher to learn effectively and to 'grow' (high challenge + high support = growth). At the opposite end of this spectrum is what Daloz refers to as 'stasis'. A beginning teacher's learning in this zone is very limited indeed as a result of their mentor offering low levels of challenge and support (low challenge + low support = stasis). Where challenge is high but support is low, a beginning teacher is likely to 'retreat' from development (high challenge + low support = retreat). However, where challenge is low but support is high, a beginning teacher is unlikely to move beyond their present situation despite their potential for growth being on the increase. Daloz refers to this as 'confirmation' (low challenge + high support = confirmation). You therefore need to be aware of both the level of challenge you offer and the level of support needed by the beginning teacher.

The second model is Katz's (1995) stages of development model, which describes a model for professional growth in four stages:

1. survival stage
2. consolidation stage
3. renewal stage
4. maturity stage.

During the first stage, *survival*, a beginning teacher is likely to show signs of being very self-focused and just 'getting by' or coping from day to day. They are likely to experience their practice from a position of doubt and to ask questions such as 'Can I get to the end of the week?' or 'Can I really do this day after day?' During this initial stage, a beginning teacher may show a reluctance to take responsibility for things, and instead look to blame others - for example, the pupils, their colleagues, the school. As a mentor observing a beginning teacher during the survival stage, you are likely to see elements of confusion and a lack of any clear rules and routines in their lessons. The beginning teacher may also demonstrate little, if any, consistency in their approach to managing behaviour. Their teaching style is often very teacher-centric and they show a reluctance to deviate from their 'script' in any way.

By the second stage, *consolidation*, it is likely that a beginning teacher will have begun to implement clearer rules and routines into their classrooms. There is evidence of them starting to question their own practice and being more open to alternative ways of doing things. While observing a beginning teacher at this stage, you are likely to notice that their classes are generally well managed and that the needs of the average pupil are predominantly well catered for. In addition, the beginning teacher is likely to demonstrate a greater awareness of individual pupils and their learning needs. However, they are unlikely to have gained a true grasp of how to support and cater for the needs of pupils within specific subgroups - for example, special educational needs and disability (SEND), English as an additional language (EAL) and gifted and talented (GandT).

The *renewal* stage is the point at which a beginning teacher is becoming much more self-aware and self-critical. They have generally mastered the basics and are now striving for ways in which they can improve their practice. They are looking for strategies and ideas to introduce more creative and innovative activities into their lessons. As a general rule of thumb, at the renewal stage beginning teachers are often at their most self-motivated and are eager to contribute to departmental discussions, offer suggestions, design additional resources and/or become involved in the running of lunchtime and after-school clubs.

The final stage of Katz's model, *maturity*, is where a beginning teacher is demonstrating signs of developing their own beliefs, teaching style and strategies. They regularly ask themselves a number of questions that support deeper levels of reflection, both in and on practice (Schön, 1983). They are still looking to improve their practice and are still interested in new ideas and resources. However, their focus has shifted from an inwards perspective to a much broader one. They are now very much interested in the impact of their teaching on their pupils' learning and progress. Task 1.5 focuses on the responsibilities of the mentor and beginning teacher at each stage of Katz's (1995) stages of development model.

Task 1.5 Responsibilities of the mentor and beginning teacher at each stage of Katz's stages of development model

In each of Katz's (1995) stages, there are responsibilities for both the mentor and beginning teacher. Identify what you would do to support a beginning teacher at each stage.

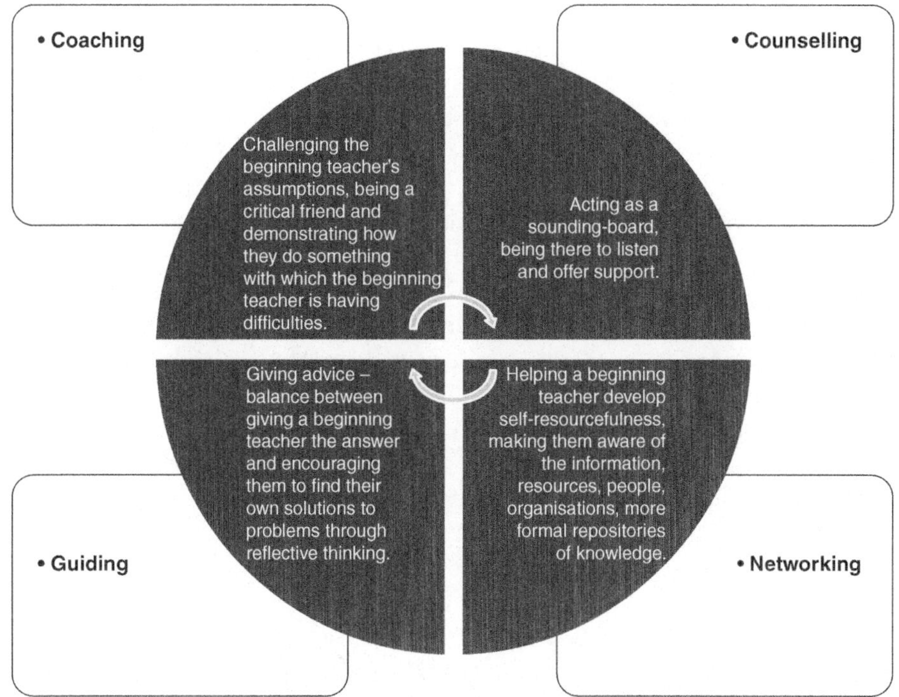

Figure 1.1 Model of developmental mentoring
Source: Adapted from Clutterbuck (2004, p. 9).

Finally, Clutterbuck's (2004) model of developmental mentoring suggests that an effective mentor wants to draw on all four of the 'helping to learn' styles (guiding, coaching, counselling and networking) (see Figure 1.1). Figure 1.1 shows that in any given mentoring relationship, a mentor may need to adopt a different style and/or approach to challenge and support a beginning teacher at various stages of their development. In developmental mentoring the beginning teacher sets the agenda based on their own development needs and the mentor provides insight and guidance to support the beginning teacher to achieve the desired goals. A more expert mentor will be able to select the right 'helping to learn' style for a beginning teacher's needs. Now complete Task 1.6, which looks at Clutterbuck's model.

Task 1.6 Helping a beginning teacher to learn using Clutterbuck's model

- Consider which of the four 'helping to learn' styles you feel most comfortable with and why.
- Which do you use the least often and/or feel the least comfortable with and why?
- What could they do to overcome this?

Your ability to assess and identify the developmental stage in which a beginning teacher is operating at any given point is a significant aspect of your role in becoming an effective mentor and ensuring growth takes places. Of equal importance, however, is your skill in adapting your own approach to fit the developmental needs of a beginning teacher. It is worth remembering that none of the three models - Daloz (2012, Katz (1995) or Clutterbuck (2004) - is linear in structure, so it is likely that a beginning teacher will move 'to and fro' between stages/zones - for example, if teaching different aspects of the curriculum in which they have greater or lesser knowledge and/or confidence or starting at a new school. With each of the models considered above, it is possible to see elements of all three approaches to mentoring described by Maynard and Furlong (1995). Regardless of the mentoring model on which you prefer to base your practice, the attributes of the mentor play a crucial role in making decisions about the approach to mentoring.

There have been a number of attempts to characterise attributes of mentors. For example, Child and Merrill (2005) sought to generate an understanding of the attributes of a mentor in initial teacher education. Cho et al. (2011) describe personal qualities that lie at the core of the mentor's identity and professional traits that relate to success in work-related activities. The DFE (2016) describes four separate, but related, areas in the National Standards for School-based Initial Teacher Training (ITT) Mentors - that is, personal qualities, teaching, professionalism and self-development, and working in partnership. Ragins (2016) describes the attributes of a mentor as an antecedent to high quality mentoring; as something that needs to be in place before a mentor-mentee relationship begins. Task 1.7 asks you to consider the attributes of an effective mentor (see also Chapter 2).

Task 1.7 Attributes of an effective mentor

- Considering the context and models of mentoring outlined in this chapter, reflect upon what you think the attributes of an effective mentor are. Attach a level of significance to each attribute, using three categories of significance: *essential*, *desirable* and *highly desirable*.
- Having identified the attributes and the levels of significance, place five of the attributes in a prioritised list that best captures the ideal profile of a mentor of a beginning teacher.
- Reflect on your own practice as a mentor and how you might develop the attributes that you have prioritised.

Finally, Task 1.8 asks you to reflect again on your mentoring practice after having read this chapter.

Task 1.8 Mentor reflection: Reflecting on your mentoring practice

After having read this chapter, reflect how your understanding of definitions of mentoring, relevant policy and guidance documents, and models of mentoring have impacted or will impact on your practice.

Summary

Effective mentoring is a complex and demanding task but, as with any role that enables you to have a positive impact on the development of others, it is hugely rewarding. In this chapter, we have considered the importance of:

- being aware of different definitions of mentoring
- understanding the content in which you are carrying out your role and what moral, political or theoretical drivers might influence the education system in which you work and/or your work as a mentor
- having a broad understanding of different models of, or approaches to, mentoring in order to make decisions about how to carry out your role as a mentor.

Further reading

Cordingley, P., Higgins, S., Greany, T., Buckler, N., Coles-Jordan, D., Crisp, B., Saunders, L. and Coe, R. (2015) *Developing Great Teaching: Lessons from the International Reviews into Effective Professional Development*, London: Teacher Development Trust.

Maynard, T. and Furlong, J. (1995) 'Learning to teach and models of mentoring', in T. Kerry and A. Shelton-Mayes (eds), *Issues in Mentoring*, London: Routledge, pp. 10–14.

2 Becoming a mentor

Karen Vincent

Introduction

The term 'mentor' is used in many different contexts and for different purposes. In primary education, it is used to describe a relationship of support between a teacher who is more experienced as a teaching professional and a teacher who is less experienced. In the context of this book, the less experienced teacher is referred to as the beginning teacher. Both the mentor and the beginning teacher work together in order for knowledge to grow so that the act of teaching is enhanced and learning is maximised. Mentoring also supports the professional growth of teachers undertaking new educational roles as well as new settings.

As a mentor for beginning primary education teachers, your role is particularly important in inducting new teachers into the profession. Beginning primary teachers may have limited experience of primary education as teachers, perhaps based on limited work experience. The education that they themselves had at school will also undoubtedly have influenced their perception of the primary teaching role. Your role as mentor is therefore largely to induct them into the world of primary teaching as a profession. You are required to facilitate an understanding of how and why certain professional teaching decisions are made and how they might be enacted in support of children's learning. So, as a mentor, you are effectively required to make pedagogical decisions about how to teach your mentee about teaching and learning.

The mentoring role requires you to engage in what has been described as 'second-order' practice (Murray, 2002). This means that you are required to reflect on your own practice before relating this to the teaching of others – such as beginning primary teachers. Beginning primary teachers may have a tendency to think that imitating your practice as an experienced and proficient professional is what is required in learning to teach. However, without facilitating a deep understanding of why you make the pedagogical decisions that you make, through conversations, the beginning primary teacher will not be able to learn how to make their own informed pedagogical decisions. As you know, being a teacher is not a case of performing to sets of predetermined rules or rigid planning. As a second-order practitioner who is assisting someone else to understand the teaching role (Murray, 2002), your role is to facilitate conversations that promote a deeper understanding of the teaching strategies that you employ. Doing this will foster learning about teaching for the beginning teacher and thereby promote the learning of the children that they will teach. This means that you will be adopting particular pedagogies of practice in relation to the learning of your student teacher, such as engaging in learning conversations that help them to see into your thinking, promoting their independence in making decisions about teaching strategies and enabling them to try these out and encouraging reflective practice through open-ended questioning, to name a few examples (these examples will be extended in future chapters).

The partners with whom you work to support the education of these new professionals, such as university partnerships, school-based training partnerships and academy partnerships, are therefore vital in supporting your role as a mentor in this endeavour. You may be fortunate to be working with a lead tutor in support of your professional development as a mentor. Being a mentor is challenging, but it can also be rewarding as you develop your own professional learning in support of the teaching profession. This chapter will explore the qualities that appear to be important when mentoring and give you an opportunity to reflect on your own mentoring through reflective questions. It will also consider what mentors claim to be the benefits from mentoring others and seek to understand what supports mentors in continuing in the role in the long term.

Objectives

At the end of this chapter, you should be able to:

- Understand what qualities are important when mentoring and reflect on your own mentoring
- Consider what mentors claim to be the benefits from mentoring others
- Understand what supports mentors in continuing their role in the long term.

Why mentor?

Mentoring others can be a very personally rewarding and interesting experience that develops both your professionalism, increases your job satisfaction and can further your career (Ghosh and Reio, 2013) as you induct new beginning teachers into the profession. However, doing this well requires a significant investment of time and energy, along with relying on the support of others. You will most likely have been mentored yourself as part of your own professional development, and this will undoubtedly influence how you engage in the mentoring of others. Many mentors state that being a mentor gives them a sense of satisfaction, along with the opportunity to 'give back' and to help develop the next generation of the teaching profession. Others express the view that mentoring others develops their own teaching as new, enthusiastic recruits bring fresh, new ideas into the classroom and question received wisdom in relation to practice. Being a mentor will foster your own reflection on the teaching role and can serve to reinvigorate your practice. To begin this process of reflection, complete Task 2.1.

Task 2.1 Your motivation for mentoring

- What motivates you to consider mentoring others?
- How would you describe your own experiences of being mentored?
- Do you identify any of these experiences as influencing the way that you mentor others?
- What do you think the benefits of mentoring are?

The qualities of a good mentor

Rogers, Luksyte and Sitzmueller (2016) emphasise the importance of mentors' motivation to mentor in conjunction with their 'getting along' qualities. Both need to be present in order to achieve a successful mentoring relationship and to maintain positive relationships between colleagues. You need to have the desire to be a mentor, along with an ability to develop your skills in self-monitoring, level of political skill, learning goal orientation and strategic outlook. Complete Task 2.2 before we look more closely at these 'getting along qualities'.

Task 2.2 Mentoring behaviours

Consider the following questions:

- How aware are you of your own mentoring behaviours?
- Are there certain things that you do when inducting beginning primary teachers into your setting?
- When do you have opportunities to review this practice with others? (Perhaps you might work in partnership with a university or with others to support you in your mentoring.)

Rogers, Luksyte and Sitzmueller's (2016) 'getting along qualities' include self-monitoring, political skill, having learning goals and being strategic in your outlook. Their reflective framework has been adapted and presented in more detail for you to consider your own recent social interactions with your mentees and the extent to which your personal 'getting along qualities' facilitated these interactions:

- *Self-monitoring.* This is crucial in forming and maintaining relationships, as mentors engage in counselling, befriending and affirming. To what extent are you aware of, or do you monitor, your own behaviour as you counsel, befriend and make affirmations in support of your mentees' teaching?

- *Political skill.* What levels of political skill do you possess? For example, how do you enhance the goals of the school through attention to understanding and influencing others? Do you prioritise helping behaviours over task performance? How do you know?
- *Learning goals.* Being able to take the initiative, being ambitious, taking risks and attaining status all facilitate movement towards learning goals, and the possession of these qualities mean that mentors will create developmental learning opportunities. In what ways do you model these qualities and encourage your mentee to take the initiative, seek ambition, take risks and seek status, thus acting as a role model for developmental learning?
- *Strategic outlook.* How adept are you at navigating the organisation in order to obtain resources for the mentee? Can you think of some examples where you have been proactive in securing resources for your mentee? (Adapted from Rogers, Luksyte and Sitzmueller, 2016)

What do beginning primary teachers say about the qualities that mentors need?

When nominating their mentors for a recent award, a large group of student teachers at a university in the South-East of England cited the following as important qualities (Burton, 2017). Mentors should:

- be approachable
- be collaborative
- be generous with their time
- be committed
- model good practice
- go above and beyond
- be an expert practitioner
- challenge me to be the best
- be truly inspirational.

Many of these aspirations held by student teachers for their mentors align closely with the 'getting along qualities' highlighted by Rogers, Luksyte and Sitzmueller (2016). However, being approachable, collaborating, finding time, committing to partnership working, going above and beyond, challenging your mentee and being inspirational can be demanding work! What one student teacher might consider being approachable might translate as encouraging neediness for another mentor. Collaboration takes many forms and, while it might be appropriate for one mentor to include their mentee in children's progress and assessment meetings, it might not be so appropriate to include them in a difficult meeting with a set of parents talking about an appeals process. However, another mentor might give their beginning teacher a role in a meeting after having introduced them to the parents and checking that they are happy for them to be present (for example, taking notes in the meeting).

Getting on with your mentee relies as much on the mentee qualities as your mentoring qualities, so knowing yourself as a mentor and being able to articulate this in conversations at the beginning of the mentoring relationship helps when establishing a positive relationship. Next, complete Task 2.3.

Task 2.3 Reflections on your own practice

- How do you induct the beginning teacher into the ways of working in your setting?
- What sorts of meetings do you involve your mentee in?
- What role (if any) do they play?
- Are there any instances where it would not be appropriate to include your mentee?
- What kinds of personal support do you offer to prevent your mentees being overwhelmed by the demands of the job?

The multidimensional mentoring role

This section will help you to consider how you operate as a mentor and to consider the role as multidimensional. Butler and Cuenca (2012) categorise the mentoring role into three aspects, which is helpful in reminding us of this multidimensional role. Their work draws on empirical research and proposes that mentors operate in three modes: as instructional coaches, emotional support systems and socialising agents. These are not mutually exclusive, and the mentoring role incorporates each of these modes to a greater or lesser degree, depending on the situation faced by mentor and mentee as represented in the Venn diagram in Figure 2.1.

Butler and Cuenca (2012) describe mentors as:

- *Instructional coaches*: giving pedagogical, technical and organisational advice. In so doing, you assist rather than prescribe practice and facilitate reflection based on prior learning within a new setting. Mentors could observe and evaluate giving constructive feedback.

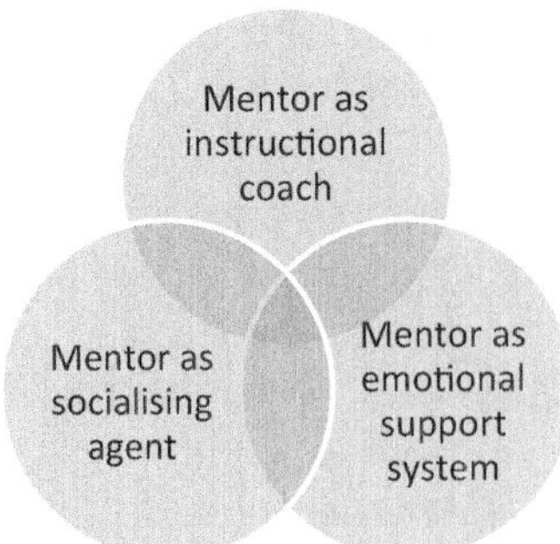

Figure 2.1 Mentoring types
Source: Adapted from Butler and Cuenca (2012).

- *Emotional support systems:* developing trust, collaborating and communicating consistently. They advise offering both support and honesty, and help to address emotions and uncertainties.
- *Socialising agents:* influencing others' perspectives and practices. You can either inspire conformity and penalise innovation or focus on addressing larger purposes for education and help to prepare beginning teachers for the many unknowns that they will face.

Mentors draw on their depth of knowledge and experience to support new teachers in learning to teach in many ways, as you may already have experienced. It is heartening to know that many of your qualities and skills are underpinned by an emotional endeavour that is recognised in much of the research on mentoring.

Being a socialising agent

As beginning teachers become socialised into your setting, there may be a tendency for the practical knowledge of teaching, as enacted in your setting and classroom, to become reified and seen as 'the' way to teach. However, as you will understand, the teaching role is a relationship between a professional and their learners. This requires minute-to-minute decision-making and responding moment to moment. Beginning primary teachers may sometimes struggle to develop a relationship with the children that supports learning. Challenging this thinking can be a source of professional growth for both you and the mentee.

Many mentors view the development of the mentoring relationship and related teaching practices as collaborative self-development (Kemmis et al., 2014). This means that, alongside viewing their role as impacting the professional learning of the beginning primary teacher, they recognise the contribution that the student teacher makes to their own developing mentoring expertise. Many beginning primary mentors aim to promote independence and resilience, proactiveness and initiative for their mentees. However, socialising a new primary teacher into the profession relies on the strength of the relationships developed. As a mentor, you will be relied on to offer emotional support when it is required, but it is also important to recognise that the development of the skills to facilitate this will emerge as your confidence grows.

Placing the mentee's experiences, thoughts, reflections and analysis at the centre of the professional learning dialogue can transform an individual's teaching significantly. However, this relies on a relationship built on 'collaborative self-development' (Kemmis et al., 2014) as mentors seek to make explicit their tacit knowledge of teaching. Seeing mentoring as collaborative self-development for mentor and mentee will develop dispositions towards engagement in a professional community committed to individual and collective self-development (Kemmis et al., 2014). Approaching mentoring in this way is more likely to induce new professionals to act with agency and autonomy.

Being an emotional support system

Personal support is vitally important in order that mentees experience a positive school experience. However, it is important to emphasise that mentors also need support from senior leaders.

Many mentors believe that serving as a mentor has benefits such as improved job performance, career progression and job satisfaction (Ghosh and Reio, 2013), but these positive returns of mentoring rely on the establishment of effective mentoring relationships (Rogers, Luksyte and Spitzmueller, 2016) and support. Being clear about the expectations you have of your mentee and articulating what they can expect from you from the outset is important. It is equally important that you make clear the support that you require to support others effectively.

Being an instructional coach

There is sometimes an assumption that effective classroom teachers can be an effective mentor (Talbot, Denny and Henderson, 2018), but this is not always the case. In the same way that teachers support the children in their classes through the adoption of particular pedagogies of practice, mentors need to give equal consideration to the specific pedagogies that they will employ to support their adult mentees. Knowledge about approaches to teaching teachers about teaching, through critical analysis and finding the space in which to have hard conversations when required, needs careful consideration. Talbot, Denny and Henderson (2018) warn of the dangers of basing professional learning on a narrow set of teaching competencies rather than mapping teaching competencies onto professional learning experiences. Many mentors adopt coaching approaches to support them in drawing out these skills and abilities in others (Vincent, 2018). Taking a coaching approach can also be an effective way of supporting mentees' growing independence and resilience, proactiveness and initiative. This approach, alongside reflecting on your own mentoring practice, is an important aspect of developing a healthy mentor-mentee relationship and will assist you in modelling professional practice. Consider now the scenario-based Task 2.4.

Task 2.4 Modes of mentoring

- Recall one of your recent experiences as a mentor. Given your overall impression of working with that beginning primary teacher, how would you say that you operated over the passage of time in each of the three modes (socialising agent, emotional support system or instructional coach)?
- Would you say that one was more prevalent?
- If one was more prevalent, was there a reason for this? Was this an issue?

Taking a coaching approach

The use of coaching as a technique for fostering potential in others is a potentially helpful approach when working with beginning primary teachers. It is defined by Cox, Bachkirova and Clutterbuck (2014, p. 1) as a 'human development process that involves structured, focused interaction and the use of appropriate strategies, tools and techniques to promote desirable and sustainable change for the benefit of the coachee and potentially for other stakeholders'. Coaching will be covered more extensively in Chapters 7 and 17.

Becoming a teacher is a developmental process. In our earliest days, we needed others to signpost suitable approaches and to regularly interact with us in order to help us to understand the effects of our actions on the children that we are teaching. This requires the will to develop in our teaching and to make changes according to what we believe needs to change. We need a mentor who can help us in our thinking in order to increase our understanding so that we can take confident action (Pemberton, 2006). As a mentor promoting a solutions-focused (Pemberton, 2006) coaching approach, you will assume that the other person has the ability to find solutions, is able to work with what motivates them, sees the partnership as one of equals and is willing to move forwards (Pemberton, 2006). Together, you will be in a better position to be able to address the root of the challenges that you face.

The benefits of mentoring others

How mentors view their role and the benefits that they perceive they will receive in return will influence the interactions they have with their mentee. These early experiences as the relationship develops begin to shape the beginning teacher's identity and in turn the style that they may adopt in years to come when they too become a mentor!

As a mentor, you model the roles that are required of a professional teacher for the beginning teacher. In undertaking this role, significant benefits for your own professional learning can be gained. Many of these benefits will be related to the growth of your own professional development through modelling the critical self-reflection required in order to support the learning of the beginning primary teacher, for the benefit of the children that you will both teach. As you engage in these thinking behaviours and voice them to the beginning teacher, your confidence, self-esteem and mentoring morale will undoubtedly increase as you articulate and justify your teaching decisions and their impact on learning. Attending opportunities for networking and engaging in learning communities will also enable you to feel more competent in making judgements about the teaching abilities of the beginning primary teacher. These opportunities for collaboration can foster a real sense of purpose in the mentoring role and will, in turn, support you in developing strategies for the challenges that you will face as a mentor.

Many mentors state that it is through a focus on their own practice, alongside the opportunities that they are given to talk to others about the mentoring role, that they derive the most benefits. New ideas, perspectives, teaching styles and strategies arise from these activities (Hobson et al., 2009). It is support for these activities, however, that remains important. Releasing mentors to do their work of being a mentor means time away from the demands of the classroom to be able to regularly co-reflect and develop shared understandings (Spooner-Lane, 2016). Tensions can arise when the demands of the role exceed the support system in place. Ways to develop a community of mentoring within a school are discussed in Chapter 18.

Tensions in mentoring

Primary initial teacher education mentors often state that an important part of the mentoring role is inducting new professionals. However, this takes time. Mentors need to have space to be able to acknowledge the unique context in which they work and to be able to consider how best to prepare the beginning teacher to teach primary education anywhere and not just in your setting and your school. These sorts of tensions can work to inspire confidence in one's ability to mentor and prepare new professionals to teach, yet are not without their issues.

One such issue concerns the vocabulary adopted in initial teacher education. This varies, and terms such as 'training teachers', 'inducting new professionals' and 'experiencing being an apprentice' are commonplace, but it is important to consider how this use of language might influence beginning primary teachers' experiences of their new profession. For example, the idea of training has connotations that might lead one to view the professional role as one where there is one 'right' way to approach the teaching of children - that we can 'train' or 'induct' new professionals to think in particular ways about how to teach or that they can learn through imitation. Of course, learning to teach is not so straightforward. As you will understand, professional decisions are made based on a knowledge of children as individuals and not everything always goes to plan.

Many tensions arise from the assessment role that mentors carry. Supporting the development of beginning primary teachers relies on a compliance model where tracking progress against the standards for teaching means that mentors act as gatekeepers to the profession. This role could lead mentors towards adopting a supervisory approach; where mentors act as 'agents of the state' (Kemmis et al., 2014) in enforcing a particular view of teaching and command compliance towards this. This approach could lead away from a more collaborative, self-development approach (Kemmis et al., 2014) and towards that of 'judgementoring' (Hobson and Malderez, 2013), where judgements can compromise the quality of the mentoring relationship and impede potential benefits. As gatekeepers to the profession, judging a beginning teacher through feedback and comments is totally understandable. Mentors are very conscious of this weight of responsibility, and initial teacher education is subject to a rigorous inspection regime; however, the approach that you take in doing this is key. Adopting a developmental approach is a more effective way of supporting adults learning to teach and many university partnerships offer mentor training and development opportunities in support of these approaches. Having the support of fellow mentors at regular intervals during such training and development sessions can go a long way towards enabling mentors to feel supported and that they are part of a network that fosters such an approach.

Developing your skills as a mentor

Walker-Smith's (2017) model (Figure 2.2) has been designed to support mentors as they facilitate learning conversations in the context of professional practice. It is particularly useful in facilitating a collaborative self-development approach. The model aims to diagnose the source of particular pedagogical and professional issues through specific and focused attention on the matter in hand. It aims to foster a co-constructed approach where mentor and mentee work together to move as quickly as possible to set targets for the development of practice. The next section will look at the model in more detail.

Diagnosing issues

Being a mentor involves developing the ability to diagnose issues and get to the source of the issue.

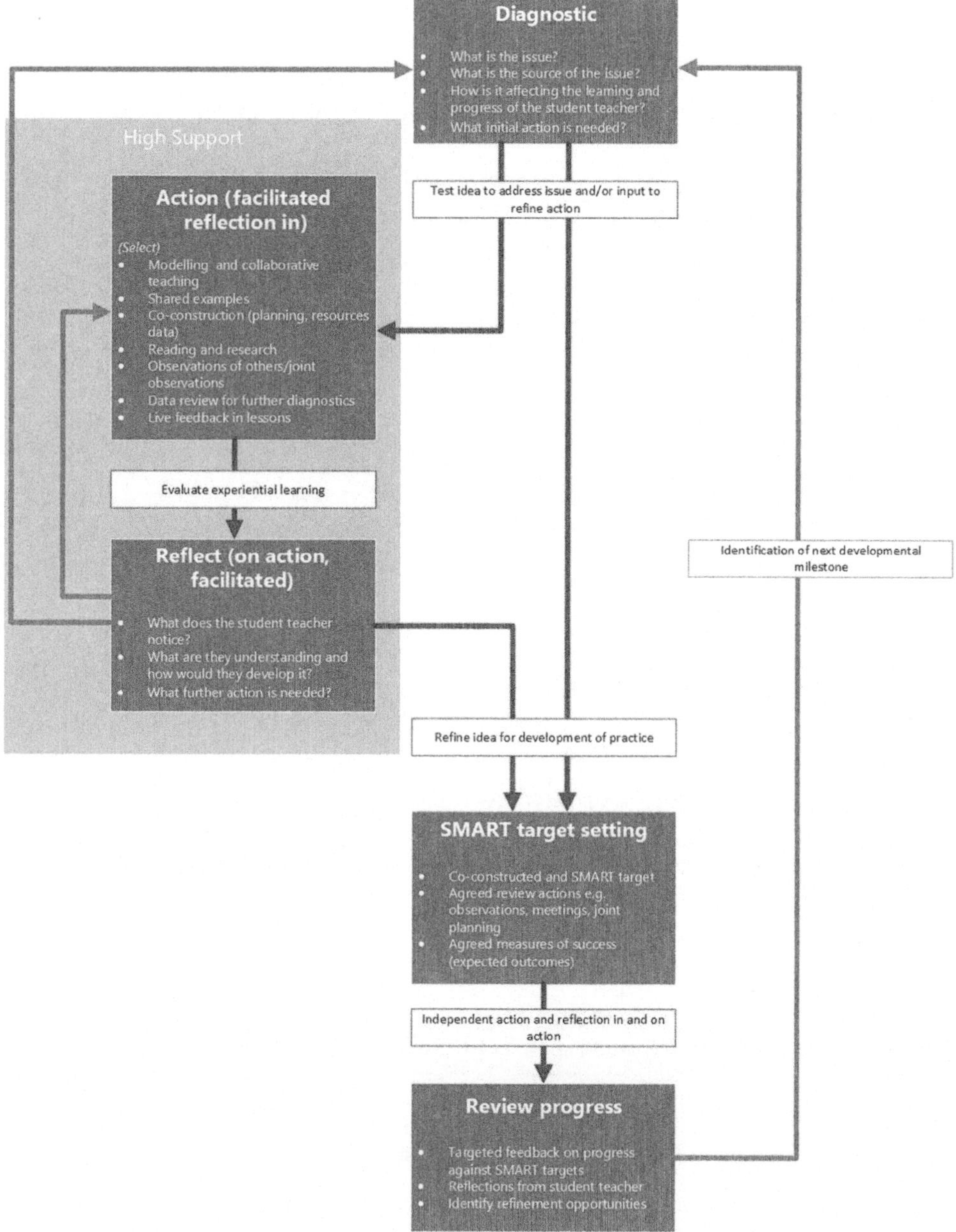

Figure 2.2 Walker-Smith's model of facilitated learning conversations in development of professional practice

Source: Walker-Smith (2017), included with permission.

Diagnosing the specific nature of an issue through questioning and investigation is the starting point, as suggested by Walker-Smith (2017). This can lead to collaborative target setting where co-constructed and realistic targets are regularly reviewed to inform future action. Consider Task 2.5) and reflect on how you might tackle the issue.

Task 2.5 Reflecting on your practice

A child in your class is always moving around the classroom instead of doing their work, failing to follow instructions and leading to the beginning primary teacher becoming distressed and anxious when they are leading the teaching. How might you, as a mentor, tackle the issue with your mentee?

Setting targets

Sometimes setting targets requires a higher level of support (as in the Walker-Smith 2017 model), in which particular and specific types of action are required, such as observing particular teachers in action, co-teaching and live feedback during the mentee's teaching sessions. How might you draw on others to support your mentee? Consider this in Task 2.6.

Task 2.6 Supporting colleagues

'It takes a whole village to raise a child.' (African proverb)
How do you draw on the support of your school colleagues' expertise to support beginning teachers?

Action

What action will you take to scaffold and support the beginning primary teacher? This is a pedagogical decision that will arise from the discussion that you have together (see Task 2.7).

Task 2.7 How can I best support my mentee?

- What will support your student teacher at this point in time?
- Would collaborative planning and teaching be beneficial?
- Would signposting them to a particular chapter, article or resource be a good next step?
- Or would it be helpful to recommend that they observe a colleague through a particular focus for reflection– for example, how they use their voice to command the attention of the children?

Reflection

Reflecting on this action can support the setting of targets or lead to further support. Reflect on how you could use the Walker-Smith (2017) model in Task 2.8.

Task 2.8 Strategies used in mentoring

- Do you select from many of the strategies in support of your mentee? If not, why not?
- How could this model facilitate collaborative self-development for you both?

Your mentoring role, if supported effectively, should enable you to experience a wide variety of benefits for your own professional learning alongside that of the beginning primary teacher. Using models such those discussed above can be a useful tool in this endeavour. There are more suggested models in the further reading section below.

Summary

Investing in the mentoring role will give you an opportunity to develop the next generation of the teaching profession while reinvigorating your own teaching as you model the teaching role and reflect on practice. The qualities, knowledge and skills that you have developed during your professional life so far will support you in getting along with a beginning primary teacher in support of the professional learning of both of you. Your ability to self-monitor and fulfil different roles such as counselling, befriending and affirming the work of your mentee, along with your political skills in understanding and influencing others (Rogers, Luksyte and Sitzmueller, 2016) will make a huge difference to the experience of the beginning primary teacher and to the teachers that they may eventually mentor. Facilitating movement towards your own learning goals and seizing opportunities for your own professional learning are vital in securing a fulfilling mentoring role that will enable you to grow professionally and increase your confidence, self-esteem and morale within the teaching profession.

Further reading

Bassot, B (2013) *The Reflective Journal*. London: Palgrave Macmillan.

CollectivED: The Mentoring and Coaching Hub, www.leedsbeckett.ac.uk/carnegie-school-of-education/research/collectived

Department for Education(2016) National Standards for School-based Initial Teacher Training (ITT) Mentors. Available at: https://assets.publishing.service.gov.uk/government/uploads/system/uploads/attachment_data/file/536891/Mentor_standards_report_Final.pdf. Accessed 6 January 2019.

3 Successful mentoring in action

Victoria Blake

Introduction

At the heart of successful teacher development lies an effective mentoring relationship. Yet in my experience this relationship is often left to chance, a consequence of observations and scheduled meetings. If research tells us that the mentoring relationship is key to effective teacher development (Furlong and Maynard, 1995; Hudson, 2016; Spooner-Lane, 2016), then we must plan for it in the same way that we plan for observations, feedback and continuous professional development (CPD) opportunities. Throughout this chapter, we consider successful mentoring in action through reflecting on what makes a mentoring relationship effective and consider practical steps to build and maintain mentoring relationships with beginning primary teachers.

Objectives

At the end of the chapter, you should be able to:

- Explain the impact of mentor expectations on teacher development
- Consider how to develop trust with a beginning teacher and plan to do so
- Recognise and prepare for possible challenges that may arise within the mentoring relationship and ways to overcome them.

The chapter starts with reflective Task 3.1. It would be helpful to make a note of your responses to enable you to return to them later in the chapter:

Task 3.1 Your experiences of being mentored

- What professional goals were you and your mentor striving towards? Were you both striving towards the same goals?
- What were your expectations for successfully completing your initial teacher training? Did your mentor share the same expectations? Did this have an impact on your professional development?

- Make a list of the challenges you faced as a beginning teacher. What approach did your mentor take in order to support you with these?
- What factors do you believe facilitate the establishment of an effective mentoring relationship?

The mentor

Beginning primary teachers have the vital responsibility of ensuring that pupils have the best possible education without yet possessing all the experience or skills necessary to provide it. They must make continuous and rapid progress to build their experience and skills, while remaining resilient and committed in the face of challenge. They cannot do this alone. They require an experienced and supportive team member to guide them through this early stage of their career. Enter you as the mentor.

A mentor is often selected for their teaching expertise. However, this is not enough. To be truly effective, mentors also need to possess the skills to enable their mentee to feel safe, to explore, to make mistakes, to learn and to grow. You also need the empathy necessary to champion your mentee through challenging times, while also maintaining high expectations so that your mentee continues to drive forward in their development. With trust and high expectations, the professional mentoring relationship can support a beginning teacher to achieve their teaching potential for the pupils in their care.

Trust

As we are all likely to remember, the process of learning to become a teacher can be tense with emotions. This is understandably so: what you say, how you say it, how you stand, where you stand, how you relate to others, what decisions you make, how you balance your priorities, how you inspire, motivate, encourage – all of this and more is called into question and interrogated with one of the most important consequences: the education of children.

In order for a beginning teacher to remain resilient and respond positively to this feedback, they need to be in a safe, reassuring yet challenging environment. Mentees need to trust their mentors not only to guide them in the right direction, but also to truly believe they have their best interests at heart. Trust is the foundation of an effective mentoring relationship, yet it is often something that is left to chance. Approaching trust in a thoughtful and strategic way will enable you to successfully fulfil your role as a mentor while providing the beginning teacher with the platform to flourish.

Bryk and Schneider (2002) identify four key leadership qualities that result in trust. These are explored in Table 3.1.

Table 3.1 Four key leadership qualities that result in trust

Leadership quality	*What this means*	*Impact*	*What this could look like in action*
Respect	Recognising the value of others, listening to their views and using them to inform decisions	Feeling respected, heard and valued as part of the school community will support a beginning teacher to embrace the mentoring relationship in a professional and proactive way.	• Recognising a beginning teacher as a professional; listening to their ideas and solutions and actively seeking and responding to their feedback. This is particularly important during the lesson observation feedback process. • Effectively communicating that you are actively listening through body language and the use of SOLER (Egan, 1975): - Sit squarely/straight forward - Open posture - Lean towards the other - Make eye contact - Relax • Valuing your developmental time together by protecting meeting times so that you can both focus and concentrate on what is being shared • Respecting differences; recognising that we may have different ideas and teaching methods and allowing opportunities for exploration and mutual learning • When disagreeing, explaining how you have taken the beginning teacher's views into account and why you have made the decision you have • Challenging disrespect; ensuring that others in school recognise the beginning teacher as a professional member of the school community
Personal regard	Showing care in both a professional and personal capacity to *all* colleagues	This will allow the beginning teacher to feel confident that they will be effectively supported and can seek help when needed. 'Knowing that others care reduces a teacher's sense of vulnerability, strengthens social affiliation, and invites reciprocal regard' (Robinson et al., 2009, p.184).	• Including discussions about 'wellbeing' as a regular feature of mentor meetings • Supporting the beginning teacher to balance their workload and recovery time; helping them to prioritise tasks and plan for upcoming deadlines • Being mindful of the number of targets a beginning teacher is working towards, ensuring that they are challenged while not being overloaded with differing priorities • Showing an interest and being supportive of the beginning teacher's professional development and longer term career goals • Encouraging the beginning teacher to recognise opportunities to network with their peers and colleagues • Modelling how to show personal regard to colleagues – for example, sharing resources with your phase team and working effectively with Teaching Assistants (TAs)

Integrity	Demonstrating consistency between words and actions. Working in line with values and morality	Trusting in their mentor to keep to their word will allow the beginning teacher to feel safe and confident in their support role. Recognising that decisions made and actions undertaken are driven by values will motivate the beginning teacher to undertake these decisions and actions too.	• Modelling keeping to your word by protecting meeting times, sending written feedback within appropriate timeframes and giving all support agreed upon • Where unable to meet timings or immediately follow up with support, communicating how you will follow through with expectations at another mutually convenient time • Sharing key values and goals so that you are aware of what you are both striving towards and where there are mutual goals • Communicating decisions and feedback in line with how it impacts pupil learning and progress • Professionally challenging attitudes and behaviours that are not in line with values and mutual goals
Competence	Reliably meeting role expectations and being someone others can count on Unfortunately, 'it is often easier to discern incompetence than competence' (Robinson et al., 2009 p188)	The beginning teacher will recognise their mentor as an experienced and valuable support, trusting in the feedback they receive and instructions given.	• Making decisions and sharing feedback based on research and values • Having an open door policy within your classroom so the beginning teacher can observe how you implement teaching and learning strategies • Managing your own time and priorities effectively so that you can meet all role expectations • Mistakes will be made by all; it is accepting and responding to mistakes and feedback that encourages trust in your competence.

Source: Adapted from Bryk and Schneider (2002).

Considering the leadership qualities in Table 3.1, complete reflection Task 3.2.

Task 3.2 Reflecting on your own practice in relation to the four leadership qualities

- Which of the four qualities - respect, personal regard, integrity, competence - would you consider to be your own particular key strength?
- How visibly do you think you demonstrate these qualities to a beginning teacher?
- Are there any qualities that you would you like to focus on for your own development? What actions would you set yourself?
- What motivates you to consider mentoring others?
- How would you describe your own experiences of being mentored?
- Do you identify any of these experiences as influencing the way that you mentor others?
- What do you think the benefits of mentoring are?
- You might ask your mentee or another colleague about how they see you in relation to these.

In working with beginning teachers and supporting their mentors, I have identified three further considerations when developing trust: shared values, vulnerability and honesty.

Establishing shared values

'Common values build trust, and trust is the foundation of cooperative action' (Fairholm, 1994, p. 11). We feel connected to and trusting of others when we recognise a commonality between one another. Teaching is a profession driven by values, so it is useful to recognise what those values are and establish the drives and motivations we share. This can be particularly useful when differing opinions or conflicting priorities arise, as we can acknowledge the differences and challenges while recognising that we are ultimately on the same team, striving towards our mutually shared goals and values.

Vulnerability

'Being trustworthy does not demand that I be rigidly consistent, but that I be dependably real' (Rogers, 1961, p. 50). Being vulnerable in a professional capacity does not mean baring all; instead, it is being an authentic human being, capable of making mistakes and being genuinely open to feedback. Presenting yourself as the perfect teacher and mentor will only create a space within which the beginning teacher feels they cannot make mistakes themselves. Alternatively, recognising when things have gone wrong and responding positively will build a positive and professional learning environment in which you can both grow, with the beginning teacher approaching you with questions and challenges to which, together, you can find solutions.

Honesty

'Honesty includes not only telling the truth, but also leaving the right impression' (Covey and Merrill, 2006, p.64). Sometimes it is difficult to give feedback, especially if you know the beginning teacher is highly self-critical or can respond sensitively. On occasion, as a mentor, you may even be required to engage in difficult conversations about the beginning teacher's professionalism. This aspect will be taken up in Chapter7 specifically in relation to learning conversations.

It is important for both the mentoring relationship and the beginning teacher's professional development that you are transparent and honest in the feedback you give. However, it is also important to demonstrate to the beginning teacher that the reason you are giving the feedback is because you are invested in their success. Understanding your honesty as constructive rather than critical should lead the beginning teacher to be able to accept your feedback and act upon it. That being said, you may not wish to give *every* piece of feedback at once, but instead concentrate on the two or three highest leverage actions so as not to overwhelm. Giving feedback is discussed further in the 'Challenging Relationships' section of the chapter.

Task 3.3 illustrates how you can help your mentor meetings with the beginning teacher to be successful in action through the use of prompts. At an initial meeting with the beginning teacher, where you outline your expectations for your work together, prompts will provide you with a good foundation from which trust can be built. To make this meeting as impactful as possible, it is important that you also allow the beginning teacher to take the time to carefully consider their motivations, expectations and ways of working in preparation for the meeting. If you have already begun your work together, consider arranging a meeting to review your work so far and how you would like to build on the mentoring relationship moving forward.

Task 3.3 Exploring your expectations of mentoring

Share what brought you both to teaching, and in your case mentoring, to establish key values, motivations and shared goals.

- Explore your expectations for the roles of a mentor and beginning teacher: What must happen? What should not happen?
- Consider how you will both respond when mistakes are made.
- Ensure that you both have the necessary administrative information (e.g. contact details, contact times, important deadlines, methods of assessment).
- Share ways of working: When do you work at your best? What do you find can be a trigger for stress? How can you both support each other through more difficult times of the year? Is there anything you should both be aware of?
- Be transparent about confidentiality: What information will be shared with others? Why is this necessary? How this will take place?

Mistakes are a necessary part of learning, but they are also a by-product of being human. A beginning teacher will need to be open to their mentor's guidance and a mentor will need to be equally open to feedback. Consider how you would both respond when 'mistakes' are made and how you would like feedback to be shared.

High expectations

Read the following case study and reflect in Task 3.4 on the different elements that may have led to the outcomes for the beginning teacher.

Case study 3.1 Faye's experience of mentoring

Faye has changed careers in order to become a primary school teacher and pursue her passion for education and child development. She was previously a successful publicist, having graduated from a reputable university. She believed that teaching would be a challenge, but was not expecting to find it quite so difficult, nor was she used to having to learn by making mistakes. Jo, her mentor, gives regular feedback and attends weekly mentor meetings in an attempt to offer support; however, she privately doubts Faye's suitability for primary school teaching. She believes that people either 'have it, or do not'. Faye works very hard to improve, often staying up until after midnight to plan the perfect lessons and resources, but she does not recognise the progress she is making. Over time, Faye also feels that teaching is not for her and, fearing failing her pupils, returns to publishing.

Now imagine that the mentor was Jordan. Jordan had a challenging start to his own teaching career, which led him to question his ability to become an effective teacher. However, he remained resilient and eventually qualified as the teacher he set out to be. He believes that with the right support and attitude, people can achieve the same success he did. Like Jo, he gives regular feedback and attends weekly mentor meetings in order to offer support.

Task 3.4 Case study 3.1

Reflecting on Case study 3.1:

- How may Jo and Jordan's differing expectations for Faye's success have impacted the mentoring relationship?
- Could Jordan's positive expectations have changed the outcome for this beginning teacher? If so, how and why?
- Reflect on your own beliefs about teacher development.
- Is being an effective teacher based on an inherent ability, or can teaching skills be learnt by all? What do you think? What views do you hold on this?
- What impact may this view have on your mentoring?

Studies have shown the impact that expectations can have on performance. One of the most famous studies was from Rosenthal and Jacobson (1968), where teachers were told that certain pupils in their class had the potential to become high achievers. The pupils had, in fact, been selected randomly, yet at the end of the study the average results showed that each of these selected pupils made accelerated progress. This 'Pygmalion effect' demonstrated how teachers' high or low expectations of pupils could either positively or negatively influence their pupils' performance, creating a 'self-fulfilling prophecy'. Although criticisms have been made of the methods used in the study, it did highlight how there can be subconscious ways in which an educator may communicate their expectations of their pupils, which can have positive or detrimental effects on progress made.

Applying this to mentoring, if a mentor truly believes the beginning teacher has the ability to succeed, they are more likely to consciously and unconsciously communicate this through their actions and words. For example, a mentor who believes in the beginning teacher is more likely to allow them to have a go themselves and to take risks. The mentor may even use an idea or strategy that the beginning teacher has identified and implement it in their own classroom. A mentor who expects the beginning teacher to fail is likely to hold them back. In an effort to protect them from making mistakes, they may limit their opportunities to teach and build confidence by taking an overly directive approach, not giving the beginning teacher the room to explore their own teacher persona and classroom ethos.

These ideas are reminiscent of Dweck's (2007) work on the 'growth mindset'. The basic premise is that people may have *fixed mindsets* or *growth mindsets*. Those with *fixed mindsets* attribute successes and failures to an innate ability with which we are born, believing that there are limitations to what we can learn and how we can grow. Those with *growth mindsets*, however, believe that our brain has the capacity to continually develop and that intelligence and skills can be mastered through effort and practice. A beginning teacher with a *fixed mindset* may believe themselves unsuitable to teaching, thinking they just do not have 'it'. A beginning teacher with a *growth mindset* may believe they just have not mastered the skills *yet*, but if they keep trying, then eventually they will.

Both mentors and mentees alike need to recognise learning as a continual process, attributing successes to effort and determination, and viewing failures as a case of having not applied the right skill this time, believing that next time can be different. Trusting in the learning process and maintaining high expectations means beginning teachers are far more likely to remain resilient in testing times. With recruitment of teachers at an all-time low, it is even more vital that we support those who want to take on this challenging yet highly rewarding role. For some, the journey to success may take longer, but with the right attitude and the right support they will get there. Within Task 3.5, consider your own practice and the mindset of your mentee.

Task 3.5 Mindset in mentoring

- Does the beginning teacher with whom you work have a growth or fixed mindset when it comes to their teacher development?

- Do you have a fixed or growth mindset when considering the development of teachers?
- What would be the implications of you both having a fixed mindset, or you both having a growth mindset?

In your relationship as a mentor, you are able to guide your mentee to attribute their successes and failures effectively so that they can truly believe their efforts will result in effective development. Support your mentee to recognise their successes as a result of their efforts by highlighting the positive and consistent impact it has on their pupils. Help them to understand their mistakes or 'failures' as changeable; they have not achieved what they set out to *yet*, but they are on the learning curve to achieving it in the future. For example:

> Beginning teacher: 'I can't get them to listen to me'
> Mentor: '... Yet.'

Dweck's (2007) 'power of yet' helps us to recognise that mistakes are all part of the journey, making the success even more worthwhile when it arrives. When giving feedback, attribute the beginning teacher's next steps to a behaviour that can be changed, rather than their character or a personality trait, which could be viewed as inherent. For example, rather than, 'You are too shy in front of the children', you may wish to say, 'When you fold your arms across your body, it suggests a lack of confidence. In your next lesson, I would like you to work on using more open body language.'

Giving them specific actions tied to a behaviour, rather than a personality trait, will allow them to see that it is changeable. Consider explicitly using the language of *growth* and *fixed* mindset, drawing attention to when mindsets may be fixed and what needs to change in order to enable learning to happen. For example, 'You are telling me you cannot do it; is that a "fixed" or "growth" mindset? What would you say to one of your pupils if they told you they could not do it?'

Be a positive role model. Demonstrate how you respond positively to your own successes and mistakes so that you are empowered rather than defeated. Remain firm in your belief that the beginning teacher will succeed with time and effort. Communicate this to them, especially in times of doubt. Hearing a consistently positive voice may be necessary in order to drown out the internal critical messages beginning teachers often give themselves, especially in challenging times. This does not mean you should avoid giving difficult feedback or messages that could be received negatively, but rather that it is important to deliver feedback while communicating that they can ultimately move past the issue and be successful.

Challenging relationships

Tension can potentially exist in the mentor and beginning teacher relationship before the relationship has even begun. Time is of the essence as the beginning teacher needs to be 'up and running' as soon as possible in order to make the necessary impact on the pupils. As experienced teachers, mentors are already balancing priorities, extra responsibilities and time constraints. Furthermore, the progress of the beginning teacher is impacting young people's lives: the pressure and stakes are high.

You need to remember that we are working with human beings. You will arrive at this relationship with different experiences, personality traits, values, drives and triggers. Schools are often pressurised environments in which emotions can run high. These are sometimes/often repressed for the majority of the day in order to provide the best experience for the pupils. Sometimes there is a clash in personality between people, or perhaps an event takes place that gives rise to new tensions and emotions that are not always easy to navigate, especially in times of challenge.

As part of your role as a mentor, it will be important to maintain a professional relationship in which the beginning teacher can seek support and grow. There may be many differences between you, yet something has brought you to the same place and time, and it is important to hold onto these similarities, recognising and reaffirming your mutual goals and interests: the development of the beginning teacher for the progress of your pupils.

Revisiting the initial meeting

At the end of the 'Trust' section of this chapter, we looked at the benefits of an 'initial meeting'. As useful as an initial meeting is for setting out expectations, mutual goals and establishing trust, it can also be used to resolve conflict. By being clear about your expectations and understanding what the beginning teacher expects from you, you can quickly identify when these expectations are not being met. This can be addressed in a 'revisiting' meeting, where you remind the beginning teacher of the expectations and conversations had. For example, you might say:

> Remember when we first met, we discussed the importance of meeting deadlines. Rather than letting deadlines pass, I hoped you would feel confident to approach me ahead of the deadlines to let me know if you are struggling to meet them. That way, we could problem solve together and ensure you are completing all your important tasks on time. It would be helpful to know what has been a barrier to this happening.

Reminding the mentee of the expectations and asking what have been 'the barriers' to meeting them communicates the need for the expectations to be met, while creating an open space for the beginning teacher to communicate what the difficulty has been. This is more likely to result in a solution moving forward, rather than creating a culture of blame.

Following your initial meeting, factors influencing your professional relationship may change. For instance, halfway through the year your mentee may disclose new information about their health, or your role may change within school, increasing your responsibilities and availability. If new information or changes are likely to impact your professional relationship, you will both need to be confident about what is expected of you moving forward in order to maintain trust. Therefore, you will need to set time aside to make your new ways of working clear in a 'revisiting meeting'.

Other potential challenges

Tensions will inevitably arise, but by overcoming these conflicts successfully you can in fact build trust and strengthen the mentoring relationship. Before looking at Table 3.2, which lists a number of common challenges to the mentoring relationship and suggested steps towards resolving these issues. Complete Task 3.6.

Table 3.2 Potential challenges and suggested steps to resolutions

Potential challenges	*Suggested steps towards resolution*
Personality clash (Ranting Teacher, 2005)	Revisit mutual goals and shared values, reminding each other that you are working towards the same aim, namely their development as a teacher and their pupils' progress. Reframe the 'clash' as an opportunity to develop professionalism and engage in personal growth, recognising that we do not always work with people who are similar to us. Ultimately, you do not need to be close companions, but the relationship must feel safe and productive so that you can both achieve your goals. Organise a meeting where you can agree what you both need in order to work together productively. It may be useful to have a third, unbiased party to support you both with this.
Beginning teacher may conduct teaching in a different way to their mentor (Beutel and Spooner-Lane, 2009)	Identify any hidden truths that lie behind this challenge: Are you feeling that your approach is being questioned? Although different from yours, could the teacher's approach be effective with the right support? Have you seen their approach work anywhere else, or is there evidence to back their approach? Recognise that there are different teaching styles and agree that you will be open to each other's ideas. You may agree that you will try the beginning teacher's approach first (or vice versa) and be open to the outcome; however, also agree a time limit for when it would be reasonable to try a different approach. Where you are both in deep disagreement, seek research or alternative opinions from an unbiased party if you feel unable to move forward.
Beginning teacher resists mentoring, perhaps struggling to receive constructive feedback (Aspfors and Fransson, 2015)	Again, it is important to establish a mutual, shared goal, reminding them that in order to achieve this goal, you will need to be able to give constructive feedback. Ensure feedback is focused on a specific behaviour and pupil impact, rather than personality traits (see chapter section on expectations). Focusing feedback on observed pupil behaviour and pupil impact will support the feedback given to be heard constructively and avoid being received as a personal criticism: For example, instead of, 'You did not engage the pupils in their learning', it would be more helpful to say, 'I noticed the pupils struggled to focus halfway through the lesson. What could have led to this?' Explain how their response to feedback is having an impact on their development, speaking from the 'I' rather than an accusative 'you', and allow them the opportunity to respond with how it feels from their perspective – for example, 'I feel that when I give feedback, it is received as a criticism rather than constructively, as I am intending it. I believe that this is having an impact on your development. What are your thoughts?'

Table 3.2 (Cont.)

Potential challenges	*Suggested steps towards resolution*
Time for mentoring relying on 'goodwill and generosity' of the mentor, who is balancing a number of priorities (Berry, Hopkins-Thompson and Hoke, 2002)	It is important to timetable the time and place for your mentor meeting each week. This should be in the school calendar and recognised by your line manager so that the time is protected. By meeting ad hoc, it is likely that other priorities will take over and meetings will be delayed, shortened or interrupted. The beginning teacher will also need regular feedback, especially at the beginning of their career when they need to make rapid progress. Do you have a free period in the week that allows you time to do this? If not, can this be arranged? Consider who is in school to support you to balance your mentoring tasks with your other school responsibilities. It is important that you proactively prioritise your wellbeing, both for your own health and so that you are in the best place to offer support to others.

Task 3.6 Dealing with challenges in relationships

How would you respond to challenges and what would you wish to include in a revisiting meeting:

- a personality clash with the beginning teacher
- the beginning teacher conducting teaching in a different way to you as their mentor
- resistance to being mentored; perhaps struggling to receive constructive feedback
- time for mentoring relying on 'goodwill and generosity' of the mentor, who is balancing a number of priorities?

Summary

When considering how to develop effective mentoring relationships with beginning primary teachers, it is important to remember the following:

- Building trust is integral to the success of your mentoring relationship. A focused meeting where you share your goals and agree expectations will support you to build an open and trusting relationship.
- Having high expectations of the beginning teacher and supporting them through mistakes will allow them to remain resilient and purposeful during challenging times.
- If and when tensions arise, remember that this too can be an opportunity to build trust. Revisit your initial meeting; reiterating shared goals, values and agreed expectations in order to maintain trust.

Mentoring is a two-way relationship in which you are both reflecting and continuing your professional development, so it is important to be kind to yourself and enjoy engaging in the learning process. If mistakes are made, model to the beginning teacher how you can move forward in a positive and professional way, inspiring them to make the same journey you have.

Further reading

Bryk, A.S. and Schneider, B.L. (2002) *Trust in Schools: A Core Resource for Improvement*, New York: Russell Sage Foundation.

Dweck, C. (2007) *Mindset: The New Psychology of Success*, New York: Ballantine Books.

Hudson, P. (2016) Forming the mentor-mentee relationship, mentoring & tutoring, *Partnership in Learning*, 24(1), 30-43.

4 Managing your role as a mentor

Julia Lawrence

Introduction

Most people acting as a mentor do so because of a desire to support new teachers in the profession. Your role might include supporting trainee teachers, those who are newly or recently qualified and those who are new to the school or roles within the school. While the core role of the mentoring role will not change significantly (see Chapters 2 and 3, which explore the role of the mentor), your challenge as a mentor on many occasions is to successfully manage the role while maintaining the plethora of other activities you must undertake within your teaching day. The aim of this chapter is to consider how this might be achieved successfully. It will encourage you to reflect on your own experiences and strategies adopted, and use tasks and case studies to guide you to consider how you might best manage this role.

Objectives

At the end of the chapter, you should be able to:

- Understand different roles that, as a mentor, you might be required to undertake
- Identify key strategies you could undertake to minimise the impact of mentoring on your other work
- Explain your clear expectations for when you mentor your next mentee.

Your role as a mentor

Before looking at the role of the mentor, let's start by considering some definitions of mentoring. Mentoring can be defined 'as a one to one relationship between a relatively inexperienced teacher (the mentee) and a relatively experienced one (the mentor) which aims to support the mentee's learning and development as a teacher, and their integration into and acceptance by the cultures of the school and profession' (Hobson and Malderez, 2013, p. 90). Lawrence and Woolliscroft (2019, p. 74) suggest that 'effective mentors are able to identify the differing needs of beginning teachers and are able to adapt their approaches to mentoring to reflect these needs'. How you define mentoring will impact on what you see your role to be. Task 4.1 asks you to identify what you feel your role is.

Task 4.1 What is my role as a mentor?

Identify two mentoring relationships in which you have been involved. This could include when you have acted as a mentor or been mentored yourself.

- What were the positives about the experiences?
- What were the negatives about the experiences?
- What strategies did you adopt to make the relationships work?

Being clear about your role

While Chapters 2 and 3 focused on the role of the mentor in more detail, it is important to appreciate that how you define the role will differ from others around you. Your definition will reflect your own experiences, both positive and negative, as well as the values, attitudes and beliefs you hold. Peiser, Duncalf and Mallabun (2019) identify seven core mentoring activities:

1. facilitation of learning opportunities
2. liaison with others (training providers, other staff)
3. teaching (your own expertise)
4. pastoral care
5. acting as a critical friend
6. acting as a role model
7. evaluation and assessment of progress.

While such characteristics are not new - for example, Wang and Odell (2002) identified emotional support, reflective practice and modelling of behaviour as core requirements - all have the potential to provide challenges between yourself and a beginning teacher in relation to expectations and how they may differ, as well as aspects of assessment, socialisation and accountability. Primarily, though, the role of the mentor can be as a guide, role model and monitor of progress.

The evolving role of the mentor

The role of the mentor in school is constantly evolving. Peiser, Duncalf and Mallabun (2019) identify that a move towards a more school-led focus in initial teacher training in England has seen an extension to the role, requiring mentors to have a deeper understanding of the links between theory and practice, a role traditionally undertaken by university-based staff. The publication of mentoring standards in England (DfE, 2016a) clearly identifies an expectation for mentors to take on a more divergent role, including supporting beginning teachers to access and use 'robust educational research to inform their planning', as well as 'developing their own mentoring practice and subject and pedagogical expertise by engaging with robust research (2016a, p.12).

Such suggestions are not new. White (2014, p. 447) argues that to 'expect those with a dual role of teacher and teacher educator to develop an academic identity may be very challenging in terms of time commitment and accessibility to academic studying resources'. Coupled with potential changes to mentoring support for newly qualified teachers, the specific roles and responsibilities of mentors are ever changing. Complete Task 4.2 and reflect on the evolution of your role.

Task 4.2 How has your role evolved?

- Consider the range of beginning teachers you have mentored.
- How has the role changed overtime?
- What are you doing differently now to when you started mentoring?

With the increase in school-based training in England, an emphasis on organisational professional development, whereby the beginning teacher is prepared to work within the specific context in which they train, may be creating short-term development rather than the occupational professionalism evident in other types of training, which focus on more universal skills and strategies that prepare beginning teachers for long-term involvement with the teaching profession. Thus, as a mentor, you need to clearly identify the skills needed by the beginning teacher to teach across a range of schools, rather than only in the context where they are working with you.

Who benefits?

Barrett, Mazerolle and Nottingham (2017, p.153) suggest that mentoring is beneficial because it provides the person being mentored with a chance to feel connected, assimilated and eventually legitimised. But what about the mentors themselves? For some mentors, time will be allocated for this, while for others there may be an expectation that they will undertake the role outside of the school day. But what about the additional activities that might be required - for example, attending training events, completing observations of teaching, keeping up to date with relevant paperwork and research? When we start to list what a mentor might be expected to do, we may well ask ourselves 'Why should I bother?' Task 4.3 encourages you to consider the personal benefits of mentoring.

Task 4.3 What could be the benefits to you of mentoring?

- Can you list the benefits that you feel you get from mentoring?
- What are the positives for you, what do you get out of engaging as a mentor? For example:
  - Does it allow you to reflect on your own teaching?
  - Does it allow you to develop your own subject knowledge?

Setting boundaries

So how do we manage our role as mentors? For me, the key to success within the role is to clearly establish the ground rules (or foundations) on which your mentoring relationship will be based. Doing this as early as possible will allow both you and the beginning teacher to understand expectations and also boundaries. Chapter 5 looks at setting ground rules in more detail. Task 4.4 encourages you to consider what will be the most important ground rules for you.

Task 4.4 What are your personal preferences for mentoring?

- What are the things that are not negotiable?
- What would you say are your ground rules?
- How will you work with the beginning teacher to ensure that these are adhered to?
- How will you manage these should they need amending?

From my own experience, setting core expectations/ground rules ensure that the beginning teacher knows from the start what you expect from them, but equally what they can expect from you. It allows you to establish boundaries, and also have something to fall back on if things start to go wrong. Now read Case study 4.1 and consider how you might deal with the situation in which Joanna finds herself.

Case study 4.1 Examples of mentoring experiences 1

Joanna is a new mentor. She has been asked to mentor Peter, a beginning teacher who is on his first placement.

As well as acting as a mentor, Joanna is also a lead teacher, so regularly gets requests to support other teachers within the school as well as still teaching her own class.

Peter is hard working but lacks confidence in his own ability. As a result, he is regularly seeking out Joanna and asking that she review his lesson planning and also provide detailed feedback after each lesson she works with him.

Joanna is becoming overwhelmed by the pressure he is placing upon her. She wants to be supportive, but what options does she have?

Mentoring as a relationship

When I am working with mentors and beginning teachers, I try to stress that mentoring is a relationship. It is in essence two people working together to achieve a goal. For the beginning teacher, that will be to pass the programme or make improvements. For the mentor, it might be to gain experience. The key is how engaged the individuals are within the relationship.

Barrett, Mazerolle and Nottingham (2017) talk about active engagement, arguing that for mentoring to be successful, it needs to involve two-way communication, a commitment from both parties to teaching and working together, a level of motivation that ensures a willingness to engage and take on responsibility and, finally, commitment to being available when and where it is set up.

When we look at Case study 4.1, we can identify when this has not been the case. This is perhaps one of the main reasons for a failure in the mentoring relationship. However, within the context of teaching we need to be aware that we undertake aspects of monitoring and inherent to this is the provision of a judgement on the progress of the beginning teacher. Hobson (2016, p. 87) calls this 'judgmentoring', and argues strongly for the impact this can have on 'beginning teachers' professional learning development and wellbeing'. While there is little we can do to remove this outcome when working with a beginning teacher, we need to try to understand the impact our word might have on them, as well as how their reaction might impact us. Peiser, Duncalf and Mallabun (2019, p. 4) suggest that one way to achieve this is through 'openly exploring possible courses of action'. Read Case study 4.2 and consider how you might manage the conversation with the beginning teacher.

Case study 4.2 Examples of mentoring experiences 2

Jeff is an experienced mentor. Over the years, he has worked with a range of beginning teachers. Over time he has realised that one challenge he continually faces is being asked by the beginning teacher about what he thought of the lesson. To move away from this approach, Jeff organises with the beginning teacher that feedback will be given at the end of the day of the observation. This means that the beginning teacher has time to self-reflect on the lesson.

At the start of the feedback session, Jeff always asks the same question: 'Please can you tell me what you wanted the pupils to be able to do by the end of the lesson, and what evidence do you have that they achieved this?'

- Why do you think it is important that Jeff gives his beginning teacher time to reflect?
- Why do you think Jeff asks the question he does?
- Reflect on how you start your own mentor learning conversations?

In thinking about the approach Jeff adopts in Case study 4.2, we can start to consider the expectations of the different parties. For example, Jeff is wanting the beginning teacher to reflect on their own teaching, while the beginning teacher may be wanting, in some cases, to be told. Depending on the stage of development of the beginning teacher, it may be that they do need to be told, but over time the emphasis should be on moving towards more of a beginning teacher-led conversation.

Questioning current approaches

Mentoring is unlikely to be your only job. However, you will need to make time to do it. But where will this time come from? For many of us as mentors, we tend to follow the directions we are given from either a training providers or the organisation in which we work. Practice will also reflect that which we ourselves have experienced. We have already identified that establishing clear ground rules/expectations/boundaries is an important first step, as are the mentor conversations with beginning teachers. But have we ever looked at what we are being asked to do and whether there may be a different way of doing it? Do we ever question the purpose, validity, reliability and value of what we do?

In 2017, the Association of School and College Leaders (ASCL) published a series of blogs by Stuart Kime that challenged readers to consider 'The Pillars of Assessment'. Kime (2017) argued that these pillars should be considered when planning any assessment; however, I believe that they are equally applicable when considering how to manage your role as a mentor. Table 4.1 provides an interpretation of these pillars and how they could be considered in relation to the role of the mentor. Having read the table, complete Task 4.5,which asks you to consider the activities you currently undertake in relation to their purpose, validity, reliability and value.

Task 4.5 How can I do things differently?

Review Table 4.1. Reflecting on what you currently do in your role as mentor, identity two things you might do differently in the future.

Having considered how you might look at things differently, read Case study 4.3, which considers how you might use a mentor meeting for more than one purpose.

Table 4.1 Pillars of assessment within a mentoring context

Core pillar	*Question to ask yourself*	*Within a mentoring context*
Purpose	What specifically do I want find out?	• Teaching ability • Ability to plan for differentiation • Ability to assess pupils effectively
	What am I going to do with the information?	• Monitor progress against specific teaching standards • Write progress reviews • Feedback to beginning teacher
	What is the best way of collecting this information?	• Observation of teaching • Review of planning • Mentoring conversations? • Feedback from pupils?
Validity	Does what I am doing provide me with the information I need?	• How does observing a lesson support me to give feedback on planning?
	Should I collect this information in this way?	• What other ways could I use to collect this information?
Reliability	Am I saying the same as others?	• Am I collecting evidence from a range of sources? • Do I ask others to feedback to me?
Value	If I do this what will I not be able to do?	• What are my priorities?
	What impact will what I do have?	• How will I evidence impact?

Case study 4.3 Examples of mentoring experiences 3

Jennie has responsibility for monitoring pupil progress across her small primary school. Recently she has been asked to undertake the role of mentor to Sam, a beginning teacher. Sam has struggled at times to prepare for their mentor meeting and this has led to some frustration for Jennie, who sees her role as mentor 'taking over' and limiting her time to discuss pupil progress.

For the next mentor meeting, Jennie has asked that Sam comes prepared to discuss the progress of the class. In particular, Jennie has asked that Sam provides evidence of his assessments of pupil progress so that Sam can talk through the planning, and how the assessments they have undertaken have supported this.

- What benefits will Jennie get from focusing her mentor meeting around progress?
- How might this focus on progress work to support Sam?

It is interesting to reflect on how as a mentor meetings with a beginning teacher can be used to gain more than just an opportunity to discuss their teaching. In Case study 4.3, Jennie would have been able to gain insight to the progress Sam has seen in the pupils being taught, as well as providing evidence of how Sam has used the assessment to support planning and lesson delivery. In adopting such an approach, the emphasis is placed on Sam to provide the evidence. This means that Sam will provide most of the input into any conversations. Lawrence (2019, p. 216) identifies the review process (see Table 4.2) as a good starting place to support such conversations. Adapted from the work of Lawrence and Mellor (2011), the process provides a structure for supporting effective beginning teacher-led conversations.

The process identified takes time to become established. It requires an understanding of the expectations of those engaging in the conversation and therefore allows a shifting of focus away from just receiving feedback to providing self-reflection.

Summary

This chapter has encouraged you to start to reflect on how you can manage your role as a mentor. What has emerged is that the role of a mentor evolves, and ensuring that you have clear strategies in place to manage these changes is an important consideration to ensure that the role does not take over.

- Your role as a mentor is only part of your wider role as a teacher.
- Establishing clear ground rules will allow you and the beginning teacher to see what you can both expect.
- Take time to consider how you want to structure your mentor conversations to ensure that most of the work is done by the beginning teacher.
- Making time to effectively mentor can be challenging, so question the activities you are undertaking in relation to the purpose and value they add to the mentoring process.

Table 4.2 The review process

Stage	*Focus*	*Characteristics/key questions*
Reassure	The beginning teacher about the lesson	Mentor provides reassurance about the lesson, which may include specific examples of what went well.
Establish	What the beginning teacher wanted pupils to have achieved during the lesson	Mentor asks questions of the beginning teacher about the objectives for the lesson. The beginning teacher explains the extent to which they felt these had been achieved by pupils.
Review	Pupil progress, beginning teacher progress against targets and against specific teaching standards	The mentor poses specific questions that encourage the beginning teacher to reflect on specific aspects of the lesson, paying particular attention to examples of both pupil and their own progress. The beginning teacher is encouraged to provide specific examples from the lesson to expand the depth of their answers.
Input	Your observations	The mentor provides specific feedback based on their observations, bringing in aspects that have not previously been covered. Emphasis is placed on the provision of specific examples from the lesson (this might include the use of video evidence).
Emphasise	Provide a summary of the discussion	The beginning teacher provides a summary of the discussion to draw key aspects out. This is later written up by the beginning teacher and shared with the mentor.
Way forward	Identify targets for the next observation and focus for development	The beginning teacher and mentor identify strengths from the lesson and targets for development based on discussion.

- Finally, you are not alone. Work alongside other mentors to share experiences (both good and bad) and realize that they are probably experiencing the same challenges as you.

Further reading

Lawrence, J. (2018) Reflective practice in primary schools, in A. Hansen, *Primary Professional Studies*, London: Sage, pp. 203–14.

Lawrence, J. (2019) Holding pre- and post-lesson discussions, in S. Capel and J. Lawrence (eds), *Mentoring Physical Education Teachers in the Secondary School*, Abingdon: Routledge, pp. 207–20.

Peiser, P., Duncalf, D. and Mallaburn, A. (2019) The role of the mentor in an increasingly school-led English initial teacher education policy context, *Professional Development in Education*, doi:10.1080/19415257.2019.1694053.

SECTION 2

Mentoring relationships

5 The importance of working with beginning teachers

Sandra Eady

Introduction

This chapter identifies the importance of working with beginning teachers and builds on the 'mentor as relationship builder'. We start by looking at why we should mentor beginning teachers, moving on to consider how you might develop your mentoring role. We consider how models of mentoring might inform the way you conduct professional mentoring conversations.

Objectives

At the end of this chapter, you should be able to:

- Understand why support for beginning teachers is necessary
- Learn more about different mentoring models
- Explain approaches and strategies to help you carry out your role as mentor.

Why is it important to mentor beginning teachers?

Before considering how to work with beginning teachers, it is worth taking a step back to briefly reflect on *why* mentors should work with beginning teachers. There is much evidence to suggest that beginning teachers often find the transition into teaching, be it during their early development or from initial teacher education into a full time job, challenging. Consequently, many experience 'burnout' and leave after three to five years of teaching (Ewing and Smith, 2003). There are, of course, many factors that might contribute to this situation; however, concern about class control and discipline, the heavy workload, lack of administrative support and working in isolation are frequently cited (Krueger, 2000).

A survey published in October 2015 by the National Union of Teachers (NUT) and YouGov found that over half of teachers were thinking of leaving teaching in the next two years, citing 'volume of workload' (61 per cent) and 'seeking better work-life balance' (57 per cent) as the two top issues (NUT/YouGov, 2015). In the twelve months to November 2016 (the most recent year for which statistics are available), Department for Education (DfE) figures show that over 50,000 qualified teachers in England left the state sector, which equates to one in ten teachers leaving the profession. The number of teachers leaving as a proportion of the total number of teachers in service, known as the 'wastage rate', is 10.5 per cent. The same figures reveal that more than 100,000 potential teachers have never taught, despite finishing their training (NUT/YouGov, 2015).

The latest DfE (2018) survey of teacher retention found that workload remained the key reason for leaving teaching. Another factor cited by both primary and secondary teachers was the perceived lack of support from the senior leadership team (SLT) for issues such as managing workload, pupil behaviour and progression. Teachers also claimed that they did not have access to other sources of advice and support. In particular, they reported that adequate time was not provided with mentors, who in turn had limited time to support beginning teachers. Some felt there was a disparity between the expectations of schools of teachers' capabilities from their training (CooperGibson Research, 2018). The report goes on to suggest beginning teachers generally made the decision to leave the profession much more swiftly than more experienced teachers, typically within three months (CooperGibson Research, 2018). Their reasons for leaving focused predominantly on pupil behaviour management, not knowing how to deal with special educational needs (SEN) and a general lack of support.

In England, Recommendation 4 of the National Standards for School Based ITT mentors (Teaching Schools Council, 2016, p.9) states that

> in light of the proposals set out about teacher accreditation in the White Paper, *Educational Excellence Everywhere*, the role of the mentor should extend beyond the initial training period to teacher accreditation and early career. Mentoring support is crucial in a system where we will move to a stronger and more challenging teacher accreditation.

In order to address issues around teacher retention, one of the recommendations from the CooperGibson Research report (2018) was to invite early career teachers (ECTs) to 'opt in' to an offer of a support package in their first five years of teaching. This could include support from a mentor and continuing professional development (CPD) in the early years of their teaching career, something many primary ECTs would like (DfE, 2018).

The Teacher Induction Scheme introduced in Scotland in August 2002 guarantees beginning teachers a year's structured support from a more experienced colleague, a reduced timetable and opportunities for professional development (O'Brien, Christie and Draper, 2007). However, just putting a support system in place doesn't solve the problem. It is the quality of support and mentoring that makes the difference. From this evidence, it would appear that providing strong, effective mentoring support, particularly for beginning teachers, could result in fewer teachers leaving the profession so early in their careers. However, it is also clear from the evidence that mentors need support to carry out this role effectively. In some schools, the senior leadership team (SLT) may have a formalised system for supporting both mentors and beginning teachers while in others a mentoring system may be in place but mentors are not provided with the skills to carry out the role effectively and are often unaware of the kinds of support and professional development opportunities available in their school. Before looking in more depth at how to establish mentoring relationships with beginning teachers, it is worth considering what CPD opportunities and barriers are available to support your development as a mentor and to your mentee. Task 5.1 will support you to do this.

Table 5.1 CPD opportunities and barriers

What kinds of CPD opportunities are available in your school? (e.g. inquiry/action research, mentoring, coaching, project work, working groups
What is the general attitude to CPD in your school?
What is the SLT's attitude to CPD? (If this is you, what is your view?)
What is the role of middle managers in CPD?
What is the school's policy on CPD? Is it suitable?
How is CPD evaluated? Is it a suitable method of evaluation?
How useful have you found the appraisal process in your school?
Has it had an impact on your practice?
How are in-service days used?
How does CPD in the school fit in with the improvement plan? Does one complement the other?
Is CPD given priority within your school?
Is learning encouraged beyond minimum standards or competence and accountability? If so, how?

Task 5.1 Auditing available support and CPD opportunities

Based on your responses to the questions in Table 5.1, what opportunities are there within your school for you to:

- develop professionally as a mentor?
- provide mentoring support to beginning teachers?

A beginning teacher's perspective

Having provided a rationale for why beginning teachers need support, and undertaken a review of professional development opportunities for both mentor and mentee, consideration is now given to what the mentor should consider before entering into a mentoring relationship with a beginning teacher.

As the DfE (2018) report suggests, beginning teachers face considerable challenges as they develop their professional identities as teachers. Having successfully completed their initial teaching qualification, they now face the prospect of developing professional knowledge and skills as they embark on their first teaching post. On a day-to-day basis, this often results in reacting and responding to particular situations as they arise rather than reflecting at length on how they might tackle a particular situation, or which teaching strategy might be more effective to motivate, inspire or progress pupil understanding. Dealing with workload issues, challenging behaviour and increasing accountability can lead to beginning teachers feeling isolated and exhausted. A regular link with a mentor can help alleviate some of the day-to-day stresses. The extract from a blog posted on the General Teaching Council for Scotland (GTCs) illustrates the difference a mentor can make.

Case study 5.1 Example of blog support

Me and my mentor blogspot GTCs

When we were introduced, someone (and it may have been me) made a rather weak pun: 'Ah, you must be the tormentor'... Oh how we laughed.

Three months on and I am afraid the only torment I feel is the rather panicky feeling I get when I know she is not in school and I have to do something without asking her what she thinks - like, 'Is it time for my dinner now, Jane?'

I fear I have come to rely on her rather too much and I have been undeservedly lucky in getting her. Not just because she is a fab teacher and a master at controlling unruly second years, but she and I are about the same age; we both have three kids; are both refugees from England and both teach English. I have been slightly alarmed to hear from other probationers that they are not as smitten as I am with their mentors. Poor things.

Constant support

Aside from offering brilliant advice in my own subject and frequent criticism of my lessons, she displays an almost German efficiency in sorting out all the bits of paper and forms and things I have to fill in.

She oversees my bulging CPD diary and tells me off when my first years leave her classroom untidy. And, when she is not teaching her own full timetable or acting as my 'playground buddy', stopping big hairy fourth years from scaring me when I walk down the corridors, she somehow finds time to mentor two other probationers in our school.

But I'm not jealous because I know I am her favourite. Which leaves me with a bit of a problem come June and the possibility that I will register and lose her to another probationer.

I am not sure it is healthy to become so reliant, but it shows that the system seems to work in providing a constant support and point of contact for new teachers.

Moving on?

I am going to have to be weaned off her, and I fear periods of enforced separation are planned towards the end of the year. But we'll still have our weekly meetings because I need to be tormented for a little bit longer.

However, for a mentor to find time to work with a beginning teacher can be a challenge, as schools are busy places and there is little time for teachers at any stage of their career to reflect and engage in professional mentoring discussion. If it is to be effective, mentors also need support and an opportunity to become aware of possible issues and develop the necessary skills.

The ethics of mentoring

In order to consider the most effective way to work with beginning teachers, it is important to be aware of the common problems and pitfalls that can result when a mentor is new to this role. Often ethical issues and tensions concerning the imbalance of power can be overlooked and this can be more problematic if there is a limited number of mentors in schools and/or a large number of beginning teachers.

Eby et al. (2000), cited in Moberg and Velasquez (2004), warn that a dysfunctional mentoring relationship will become a barrier to any productive professional development and may even contribute to beginning teachers deciding to leave the profession. In their study, they report on key areas where mentees felt that the mentoring relationship had not worked. These can be broadly organised into four main areas:

1. mismatches in mentee/mentor personality, values and workstyle
2. mentor neglect
3. manipulative behaviour
4. mentor incompetence.

Moberg and Velasquez (2004) suggest that the 'ethics of mentoring' can easily be overlooked when entering into a mentoring relationship, with many of the tensions stemming from the power difference between mentor and mentee. For example, they suggest that the role of manager and mentor are morally contradictory as a mentor needs to be loyal, partial and have concern for the professional development of the mentee, while a manager has to be fair to all those they line manage. The greater power difference between mentor and mentee means that the mentor has more ethical obligations. They suggest that, right from the outset, mentors need to be aware of the ethical obligations of these roles. Task 5.2 encourages you to consider relationships in more detail.

Task 5.2 Your relationship with your beginning teacher

- How might the power difference influence your relationship with the beginning teacher?
- Use the seven 'mentor obligations' provided below from Moberg and Velasquez (2004) to structure your thoughts regarding particular moral and ethical issues that might arise.

The seven 'mentor obligations'

1. *Beneficence* - have you been able to participate in appropriate mentor training and do you feel you have the necessary skills and knowledge to take on the role of mentor?
2. *Nonmaleficence* - are you aware that your position might influence, or be perceived as manipulating or persuading, the mentee to adopt particular actions - for example, actions that fit better with school priorities rather than supporting the development of the beginning teacher?
3. *Autonomy* - to what extent do you feel comfortable about allowing your mentee to use self-judgement even if it is different from what you would do? How easy will it be for you to avoid making decisions for your mentee or stop them talking to particular people?
4. *Confidentiality* - how easy will it be for you to maintain any confidences explicitly requested by the mentee, whether professional or personal? This is the key to trust and it is core to the mentoring relationship.

5. *Loyalty* - how does your status within the school enable you to avoid conflicts of interests but also protect the actions and needs of the mentee?
6. *Fairness* - how will you ensure that the mentoring relationship does not put the mentee in a more favourable position than other teachers excluded from the mentoring process?
7. *Concern* - does your position in school enable you to have a deeper duty of care to the mentee without simultaneously being unfair towards others?

Depending on the beginning teacher, it is easy for mentoring conversations to end up as a cosy chat over coffee. Alternatively, they can become a platform for the mentor, eager to share their experiences, to dominate the conversation and recount what they did or would do in a similar situation. While this might be comforting and reassuring, it is not always the most productive way of supporting the beginning teacher. Equally, the beginning teacher may like to offload everything they are experiencing and conversations tail off in lots of directions without any clear focus or outcome. In order to avoid this, it is important for both of you to be clear about the purpose of the mentoring relationship and how to engage in productive conversations with clear outcomes and actions.

Establishing a clear understanding of roles and responsibilities

Before you start mentoring a beginning teacher, it is important to come to a mutual agreement with them about the purpose of the mentoring relationship, what the mentoring process will entail and how you will both benefit. It is important for both mentor and mentee to reflect upon and be clear about their roles and responsibilities right from the beginning of the mentoring relationship. Establishing a working agreement in this way could form the basis of the first discussion, allowing your mentee to have an equal say regarding how the mentoring relationship will play out. As a mentor, it is important to facilitate rather than lead this process. Now complete Task 5.3.

Task 5.3 Establishing ground rules

Bearing in mind the ethical obligations outlined above and using the list below, draft a mentoring agreement or 'ground rules' (Gravells 2017), which could form the basis of an initial conversation with your mentee. It should include:

- confidentiality
- boundaries
- expectations
- mutual responsibilities
- evaluating progress
- giving and receiving feedback
- how and when to meet
- note-taking and records.

Is there anything else you would add?

Having considered some of the possible tensions that can arise in a mentoring relationship due to the power balance, the next section provides a brief overview of four ways to conceptualise the mentoring relationship and the roles played by the mentor and mentee.

Models of mentoring

Daloz's (1986, cited in Cameron-Jones and O'Hara, 1997) original model of mentoring relationships suggests that for optimal learning to take place, a mentor should provide both challenge and support. The challenge aspect refers to your ability as a mentor to question a beginning teacher to enable them to reflect critically on their own beliefs, behaviours and attitudes. The support aspect relies on you being able to offer an empathetic ear, actively listen and encouraging the beginning teacher to find solutions in order to continue to develop and progress.

The skill of the mentor is in evaluating how much support and challenge are needed, and this will depend on a variety of factors such as the confidence and experience of the beginning teacher as well as the context in which they work. Low levels of both challenge and support are likely to result in little change in practice, or 'stasis', while high levels of challenge with low levels of support will lead to retreat or withdrawal from the mentoring relationship. Although high levels of mentor support and low levels of challenge produce confirmation of the beginning teacher's practice, it is when the mentor is skilled in providing high levels of both challenge and support that real professional growth will occur. These situations are summarised below:

- High challenge high support: mentoring leads to professional growth.
- High challenge low support: retreat from mentoring relationship.
- Low challenge low support: mentoring leads to little change, or stasis.
- Low challenge high support: confirmation of practice rather than professional growth.

Maynard and Furlong's (1997) model focuses more on how the mentor perceives their role. They propose three categories of mentoring:

1. *The apprenticeship model*: the skills of being a teacher are best learned by supervised practice, with guidance from imitation of experienced practitioners.
2. *The competence model:* learning to teach requires learning a predefined list of competences (the current Teachers Standards in England (DFE, 2011) could be described as a competence model). In this model, the mentor becomes a systematic trainer supporting a beginning teacher to meet the competences.
3. *The reflective model:* requires the beginning teacher to have some mastery of the skills of teaching to be able to reflect upon their own practice and for the mentor to be a co-inquirer and facilitator rather than instructor. The promotion of reflective practice through mentoring is key.

The categories suggested by Maynard and Furlong (1995) enable us to consider the mentor's role in more depth, and to think about whether the mentor might take different approaches. In any given mentoring relationship, a mentor may need to adopt a different

Table 5.2 Four styles of learning

Traditional Coach	Guardian
Nurturing	Counselling

Source: Clutterbuck, 2014).

style and/or approach to challenge and support a beginning teacher at various stages of their development.

Clutterbuck's (2014, p. 10) model of developmental mentoring suggests that an effective mentor draws on two dimensions of learning – directive/non directive, and stretching/nurturing – and four styles of learning (Table 5.2):

1. guiding
2. coaching
3. counselling
4. networking.

You may wish to refer back to Figure 1.1, which provides more detail on the four styles of learning.

In developmental mentoring, it is the mentee who sets the agenda based on their own development needs and the mentor provides insight and guidance to support the mentee to achieve the desired goals. As a mentor, it is important to select the right 'helping to learn' style for the beginning teacher's needs.

Van Ginkel et al.'s (2016) 'adaptive mentoring' notes the skill of the mentor to adopt a flexible and versatile mentoring approach when working with the beginning teacher. Their study found that mentors adapted by:

1. aligning mutual expectations of mentoring
2. attuning to mentees emotional wellbeing
3. adapting to mentees' capacities for reflecting
4. building tasks to match mentees' levels of development (2016, p. 212).

Now complete Task 5.4.

Task 5.4 Reflecting on models of mentoring 1

By referring to the models of mentoring above, in what ways has the Deputy Head Teacher in Case study 5.2 managed the mentoring relationship?

Case study 5.2 Mentoring newly qualified teachers (NQTs)

St Vincent's Primary School was inspected as part of a national sample of primary education.

The Deputy Head Teacher provided exemplary support in her role as mentor for NQTs. In particular, she:

- maximised opportunities for the NQT to be exposed to good practice within the school and to learn from other schools
- made clear what was expected of the NQT in meeting the needs of the pupils in her class and shared school policies and programmes
- developed effective working relationships with all staff, parents and pupils
- shared her skills as a classroom practitioner very effectively through modelling very good up-to-date learning and teaching practices for the NQT
- encouraged the NQT to be reflective and self-critical in her own practice
- managed and used time very effectively to provide evaluative feedback and challenge on how the NQT could improve her teaching and impact upon pupils' learning
- gave appropriate emphasis to support and challenge, including how to engage effectively with parents, and in wider aspects of the work of the school, such as effective liaison with the parish priest
- supported the NQT effectively to develop confidence in the sharing and celebration of pupils' achievements with parents and the wider community.

Structuring mentoring conversations

As we have seen, there are a number of ways of conceptualising your role as a mentor. The flexibility in the way you might work with the beginning teacher will vary depending on the context in which you are working, the confidence of the beginning teacher and whether the beginning teacher is in their first, second or third year of teaching. Equally, your own beliefs about mentoring, along with your confidence and experience as a mentor, will also influence how you approach this role and how you might structure a mentoring conversation. Timperley (2009) refers to a productive mentoring conversation as one that is a 'learning conversation' for both mentee and mentor. It can be argued that for communication to be effective, a learning conversation should be:

- two-way
- built on trust and respect
- given enough time,
- planned
- only as good as the people who operate it.

However, Gravells (2017) offers some good straightforward advice for the mentor:

- Ask don't tell.
- Listen don't speak.
- Understand don't solve.

A popular way of structuring a mentoring conversation is the GROW model of mentoring and coaching (Whitmore, 1998) (see also Chapter 8).

GROW stands for:

- **G**oal.
- Current **R**eality.
- **O**ptions (or Obstacles).
- **W**ill (or Way Forward).

Mentors often use the analogy of thinking about how you would plan for a journey, first deciding where you are going - the goal, then deciding where you actually are - your current reality. The next step would be to explore possible routes for your journey - your options - and finally establishing how much you want to go on the journey and overcome any obstacles - the motivation or will to find a way forward.

Another model not dissimilar to the GROW model is the CLEAR model. It was established in the early 1980s by Peter Hawkins (1985), and is frequently used by coaches and mentors. CLEAR stands for:

- **C**ontracting
- **L**istening
- **E**xploring
- **A**ction
- **R**eview.

Now complete Task 5.5, which asks you to look at the GROW and CLEAR models in more detail and consider your own practice.

Task 5.5 Reflecting on models of mentoring 2

Visit the websites for the GROW and CLEAR models of mentoring using the links below. Evaluate the strengths and weaknesses of each model and their suitability for mentoring a beginning teacher. How will a model support you in structuring your conversations?

GROW model: www.mindtools.com/pages/article/newLDR_89.htm
CLEAR model: www.personal-coaching-information.com/clear-coaching-model.html

Egan's skilled helper model

This model is used a lot in counselling or coaching situations, but it can also be an effective way to support a beginning teacher and to facilitate reflection and action. The aim is to empower the beginning teacher to manage their own problems more effectively and to develop unused opportunities more fully. The following is a short summary of the skilled helper model, adapted from Egan (2002, 2006).

Stage 1: Exploration

Initially it is important to get the beginning teacher to explain what is happening in their own words and then for you to reflect it back to them, without judgement. This involves:

- *attention giving* - positive body language, eye contact, etc.
- *active listening* - learning forward, nodding, focusing on what is being said not what you plan to say in response
- *acceptance and empathy* - it is vital to detach from your judgement about what you are being told. Keep your views to yourself if you want to find out what is really going on. Nobody opens up in a situation where they feel judged.
- *paraphrasing and summarising* - to check your own understanding of what has been said, focusing on which of the issues discussed seems the most important to the mentee
- *reflecting feelings* - helps mentees to uncover blind spots or gaps in their perceptions and assessment of the situation
- *questioning* - useful questions are:How did you feel about that? What were you thinking? What was that like? What else is there about that?

You may find that just getting the beginning teacher to reflect and clarify the issue or situation helps to make the way forward obvious. However, when upset or confronted, it is often difficult to see things clearly and this is where the 'skilled helper' can support in identifying the blind spots or misperceptions.

Stage 2: Challenging

This stage involves you challenging existing views - one issue at a time. Encourage the beginning teacher to think about whether there is another way of looking at the issue. Some useful questions to do this are:

- What might this look like from another person's point of view?
- What in particular about this is a problem for you?
- If you were describing someone else in this situation, how would you describe them?
- What does the mentee think/feel?
- Goal setting - this is where you seek to move the mentee forward from being stuck, by identifying an area in which progress can be made.

Stage 3: Action planning

Your goal is to turn good intentions into actions, so it is important to help your mentee to set realistic, practical and achievable targets. Useful questions here include:

- What are possible ways forward in this situation?
- Which of these feel best for you?
- What will you achieve if you do this?
- What will you do first and by when?

Make sure the targets are specific and measurable so that the beginning teacher can know what has been achieved. Agree a time period. Always follow up at the next meeting: did the

Table 5.3 Mentoring SWOT analysis

Strengths What do I do well?	**Weaknesses** What areas do I need to improve?
Opportunities Who or what can I use to support me?	**Threats** What can I not control? What might stop me being successful?

mentee do what they said they were going to? Do not judge if they haven't achieved the goal, but remind them why they committed themselves to it when you spoke before. Now complete Task 5.6.

Task 5.6 SWOT analysis

- Considering what you have read in this chapter, complete the SWOT analysis (Table 5.3) for yourself as a mentor working with a beginning teacher (some guiding questions have been included).
- From your SWOT analysis, set yourself an action plan for your professional learning as a mentor.

Summary

This chapter has outlined why mentors should work with beginning teachers and the importance of being aware of possible pitfalls. It has outlined four well-known models of mentoring to support reflections on the mentoring role and how this might be different depending on the beginning teacher and educational context. Finally, it has provided some guidance on ways to structure mentoring conversations.

Further reading

Cordingley, P., Higgins, S., Greany, T., Buckler, N., Coles-Jordan, D., Crisp, B., Saunders, L. and Coe, R. (2015) *Developing Great Teaching: Lessons from the International Reviews into Effective Professional Development*, London: Teacher Development Trust.

Timperley, H. (2009) *Professional Learning and Development in Schools and Higher Education*, Toronto: Springer.

Timperley, H. (2020) Enablers for effective professional conversations, www.aitsl.edu.au/docs/default-source/default-document-library/professional-conversations-a3.pdf?sfvrsn=b0c1ec3c_2

6 Working with a beginning teacher to negotiate the setting

Victoria Blake

Introduction

When done right, mentoring can stabilise the shifting ground on which beginning teachers try to stand, according to Kardos and Johnson (2010). As a mentor, the focus is often on what is happening in the classroom. However, to truly be successful, beginning teachers need to be effective across the school and wider community. The school has many faces: the face presented to inspectors, governing bodies, parents; the face we know as the teaching staff; the face experienced by the pupils. As a mentor, how do you guide beginning teachers to recognise and navigate the different faces; to criss-cross through the minefield of school politics; to overcome the external pressures arising from the changeable educational climate? Throughout this chapter, consideration is given to the school culture in which beginning teachers must immerse themselves and thrive, and to the possible risks and opportunities that may support them to negotiate their new school.

Objectives

At the end of the chapter, you should be able to:

- Explore different school culture types and their implications for beginning teachers
- Analyse your school culture, reflecting on what the beginning teacher will need to be aware of
- Consider critically your role in supporting the beginning teacher to be effective within their new school community.

Before reading the chapter, complete Task 6.1, which asks you to consider a specific scenario.

Task 6.1 Supporting beginning teachers to understand the culture of the school

School A regularly communicates how it goes the extra mile for its pupils, teaching the best of lessons, offering 'out of class' support and providing extra-curricular opportunities. This requires a lot of hard work. A beginning teacher in their second term does not want to let their new school down, so finds that they are often behind closed classroom doors, trying desperately to get all their tasks done and not fall behind.

However, the school culture within which they work upholds the value of being social, celebrating those who often visit the staffroom and pop into each other's classrooms to share a laugh, problem or resource. Teachers who remain in their classrooms are considered recluses who do not want to be part of the school community. The beginning teacher may not be aware of this and, despite doing their best to maintain their reputation, is regarded poorly by the team.

In your role as a mentor, consider the following questions:

- How could you have supported the beginning teacher to learn about their school culture?
- What steps could have been put into place to prevent the teacher from becoming isolated and regarded negatively?
- How might you have supported the beginning teacher to successfully become part of their new school community?

School culture

Although schools may have a vision statement or core values to which the pupils work every term, there often exists a deeper level of assumptions and beliefs that are shared by the school staff, almost 'unconsciously' (Schein, 1985). It is these shared beliefs, assumptions and values that result in the school culture, and determine 'the way we do things around here' (Bower 1966). The quandary is that if the values and beliefs underpinning school culture are 'unconscious' or invisible to the eye, how is a beginning teacher supposed to learn this important information; to know what is right and wrong; to know what should be strived for and what should be avoided? Yes, their induction will include an explanation of the school's shared vision and the formal ways of working, but this is just one of the many faces of the school. As a mentor, you are in the position to make the invisible, visible; to share those unwritten rules, and support the beginning teacher in their transition to becoming a fully-fledged member of the school community. In order to do so, it is important that you first take the time to understand and analyse your school culture and what is important for the beginning teacher to know.

When analysing school culture, it is useful to consider the six school culture 'typologies' described by Gruenert and Whitaker (2015): collaborative, comfortable-collaborative, contrived-collegial, balkanised, fragmented and toxic. The first five were originally proposed by Fullan and Hargreaves (1996), and the sixth by Deal and Peterson (1999) (these are summarised in Table 6.1). Complete Task 6.2, which asks you to consider your current practice in relation to school culture.

Table 6.1 School cultural types: A summary

School culture type	*What this looks like in practice*
Collaborative	Staff share strong educational values and prioritise achieving the very best for their pupils. Meetings are focused on pupil achievement and collective reflection. Collaboration and supporting one another are key; teaching staff can often be found observing one another and sharing research or approaches. Members of this culture are 'aggressively curious', willing to ask questions and to critically analyse teaching methods, ensuring every step forward and every new idea will directly benefit the pupils. Even if people do not get on, this will be put aside and support will always be given for the benefit of the pupils.
Comfortable-collaborative	The most important thing is that everyone gets along. Meetings allow people to get together and share successes or support one another in achieving job satisfaction and a work-life balance. People support one another, and share jokes, advice and resources. Teachers have a general awareness of what others are doing in the classroom and may observe one another, but always to celebrate, never to expose weakness. To question or give feedback may be avoided in case of offence, even if it risks pupil progress. Reflecting on how to improve or asking important questions is only for less busy times, so as to maintain the comfort levels that have been achieved and to prevent disturbing the peace.
Contrived-collegial	Leadership is looking to improve the school with quick fixes and quick results. They require teachers to work together because they know this is looked upon positively by external institutions, rather than because they value collaboration. This seemingly artificial notion of collaboration means that teachers are not invested in the approach. Teacher autonomy diminishes as more strategies and improvements are brought in and staff are not given the opportunity to reflect, embed and feel ownership over what is happening in their school and classrooms.
Balkanised	Teachers are not solitary, nor do they work together as a school. Instead, they form smaller collaborative groups with their immediate peers. Members of these 'subcultures' or 'cliques' may laugh, whisper and share lunch together, demonstrating their bond. They may possibly invite new members to join their group. Often, they are competitive against other cliques, competing for power and resources, with stronger groups intimidating the less confident ones. Long-standing teachers often dominate meetings.
Fragmented	Teachers simply wish to survive, fearing micromanagement, welcoming autonomy and staying within their classrooms with doors closed. Accountability and performance-related pay results in a competitive air, with teachers choosing to work independently and keeping resources to themselves. Although staff may appear to engage with one another, perhaps sharing lunch or a joke, they do not engage in professional dialogue, nor do they feel invested in the school as a whole. Meetings are full of people checking the time, eagerly waiting to get back to their islands where they can look after their own needs.
Toxic	Within this culture, there is an underlying belief that staff are battling against the pupils and parents/carers. In this tough environment, anything goes to survive, even hostility to pupils. Expectations for pupil performance are low and any celebration of pupil success feels artificial. Sarcasm and pessimism are rife, and seem to be the main way staff bond. Considering themselves victims of poor policy and lack of support, the majority of staff are comfortable with their low expectations and may even be content with their work. They may not have always been this way; accountability and pressurised working environments may have led to cynicism as a means of surviving. Unfortunately, good teachers with high expectations for pupils will often leave, looking for more positive and values-driven schools in which to work.

Task 6.2 Identifying your school culture

Re-read through the school culture types in Table 6.1.

- Consider whether you recognise aspects of your own school culture in the descriptions?
- Which description best describes the prevalent culture in your school?
- Reflect on the risks and opportunities that may exist for a beginning teacher learning within this environment.

It is possible that, as you read through the typologies, you identified with more than one of the school culture types. This is unsurprising as cultures are complex. Subcultures may exist within your school, each one linking to a different culture type. In considering the culture in your school and completing task 6.2, the aim of the exercise is not to label your school culture, but rather to support you to analyse and consider how you may guide a beginning teacher to be successful within it. The task can also be used as a whole-school staff exercise to identify the best description that fits your school, the culture you are aiming for and what whole-school CPD could be used to enhance your school culture or make a start at moving culture forwards.

Having considered the culture of the environment in which you work, the next section explores what risks and opportunities may exist for a beginning teacher learning within these different cultures. As you read through, think about what other risks and opportunities may exist. Task 6.3 asks you to do this in more detail at the end of the section.

Collaborative culture

Risks

Considering the 'theoretical nirvana' of school cultures (Gruenert and Whitaker, 2015), it is hard to imagine that there are many risks here. However, as a beginning teacher this environment may be overwhelming. Although there is a great opportunity to learn from a variety of effective teachers and to collaborate with research-informed practitioners, the beginning teacher's first steps are to come to grips with the teaching basics. 'Aggressive curiosity' in the beginning teacher will inspire continuous growth, but they need to be given a solid foundation of ideas and strategies on which to base their curiosity. Contrasting research may lead to confusion, or the beginning teacher may not have time to engage in lots of different research. This could leave your mentee feeling unable to take part in conversations or know what questions to ask.

Opportunities

Aspiring to great teaching and collaboration is important, yet beginning teachers, like other colleagues, must recognise that the journey towards that is long. They must be supported to build up to this in manageable steps and understand that making mistakes is part of the learning journey. You will need to manage the expectations of the beginning teacher who is surrounded by high-performing staff. Furthermore, you will need to ensure that the colleagues supporting and line managing the beginning teacher also have appropriate expectations. Share with the beginning teacher the main research on which the school's practice is founded so they understand the key teaching and learning strategies they are expected to embed. Once they have embedded these, it will be important to model how to interact with research critically. Share any interesting blogs or theorists you follow and support the beginning teacher to make research part of their daily life without it becoming too onerous. The key way the beginning teacher will be successful within this culture is if they hold pupil impact at the heart of everything they do. Much like with 'comfortable-collaboration', if pupil impact is the focus of your discussion and feedback, you can model how every decision is made in light of pupils' learning, needs and achievements. Encouraging your mentee to present a positive, solutions-focused attitude to teaching will support others to look upon them favourably too.

Comfortable-collaborative culture

Risks

The beginning teacher will benefit from developing within a welcoming, friendly culture and be encouraged to find a comfortable work-life balance. The risk is that they may become too comfortable and not seek out opportunities to continually develop their practice in a research-informed way. They may not feel confident to ask questions, critique practice or take part in the deep reflection necessary to achieve their full teaching potential. If they do, they may be feared for disrupting the peace and forcing others to reconsider their own comfortable approach.

Opportunities

Focus your feedback and discussions on pupil impact, demonstrating how this is both yours and the beginning teacher's top priority. Encourage them to see that feedback is an opportunity to grow. Reflect on when feedback has enabled both you and the beginning teacher to develop practice and increase pupil impact. It will be important to encourage curiosity, to model asking questions and being actively interested in questions posed to you. Model how to approach research critically, exploring how well informed the research is and what the practical implications of the research may be. As they build in confidence, skill and hold a 'safer' position within the school, you may wish to support the beginning teacher to consider how they share their findings with others in order to influence the wider school community for the benefit of the pupils.

Contrived-collegial culture

Risks

So many of our schools are under tremendous pressure, working hard to be 'seen' to be improving by engaging 'in work that is visible and measurable' (McDermott et al., 2007). Not recognising that 'schools are far from homogenous' (Howes, Davies and Fox, 2009), we work in an educational system that believes what has transformed one school will automatically transform another. Schools feel that they are expected to adhere to the strategies and policies celebrated by inspectors, rather than working from the values and needs that exist within their school community. This can be demoralising. Not being able to exercise creativity or autonomy in favour of a superficial, controlled approach can steer beginning (and experienced) teachers away from the reason they chose to be a teacher in the first place. The pressure put on teachers in a culture of performativity means we are potentially stifling the 'passionate teacher' (Day, 2004); alongside an excessive workload, this is contributing to the crisis in teacher recruitment and retention.

Opportunities

As a mentor, it is possible to problem-solve with the beginning teacher, supporting them to be creative in how they can balance the schools' priorities, while also maintaining ownership over their classroom and the decisions they make for their pupils. Connecting with the beginning teacher over their 'why', their moral imperative for teaching, and supporting them to recognise the steps they are taking towards that will help to sustain their passion and job satisfaction. It will also be important to protect the beginning teacher from unnecessary workload. Supporting the beginning teacher to recognise when to say no, and how to do so professionally, will be extremely useful throughout their career. When it is not appropriate to say no, and when you cannot steer the beginning teacher away from performative tasks, it will be important to talk to them about the educational climate within which we work and the challenges facing teachers. Although a beginning teacher, they have a role in supporting the school to meet expectations and the accountable measures that exist. In order to stay resilient in these circumstances, they must recognise that they are not alone, but instead part of a wider team that faces these challenges together and whose members are willing to support one another.

Balkanised culture

Risks

Risks for the beginning teacher may include getting caught up in office politics, gossip and bullying. Perhaps they will be admonished by one clique for joining another. Perhaps they may feel lost, not knowing which clique to join and so therefore find themselves isolated. Being isolated or confined to one collaborative group will also limit their opportunities to share in best practice across the school more widely and, in turn, inhibit their growth.

Opportunities

First, it is important to recognise if you, as their mentor, are in a clique yourself. Having allies is essential to resilience and will enable the beginning teacher to be welcomed into a group straight away. However, it is important that you allow the beginning teacher opportunities to work with other collaborative groups and make connections across the school more widely so that they may expand their network and learn from a variety of practices. If the beginning teacher is on the receiving end of negativity from a particular clique, or perhaps encouraged to criticise or intimidate another, reframe this as a development opportunity, encouraging them to reflect on their experiences and problem-solve how they can practise professionalism and diplomacy skills. Modelling professionalism and diplomacy will be key to supporting the beginning teacher to embody the inner confidence and resilience they need to maintain strength in a politically charged environment.

Fragmented culture

Risks

A big risk here is the lack of opportunities for sharing best practice and resources. The beginning teacher will need to observe a variety of good practice in order to improve. When they first start teaching, planning and resourcing lessons takes a long time, so the more planning and resources they can share, the better. Teachers isolating themselves will reduce opportunities for the beginning teacher to make connections with others and engage in the professional dialogue that will keep them striving forwards.

Opportunities

Consider how you may create opportunities for the beginning teacher to observe and work with other teachers within the school and, where appropriate, at other well-performing schools. If your co-teachers feel safer keeping themselves to themselves, consider how you can support them to feel satisfaction in supporting others and not consider the beginning teacher as a threat. Highlight to the staff the specific strengths you are hoping the beginning teacher may learn from them so that they feel confident they are being recognised. Encourage the beginning teacher to thank the co-teachers after, demonstrating that they are acknowledging the efforts and work of others, and are not looking to claim resources or strategies as their own. Furthermore, share with the supporting staff the impact they are having on the beginning teacher and their pupils. Demonstrate to your co-teachers how this will not unduly add to their workload, but rather is an investment: as the beginning teacher grows in confidence, they will be able to share their resources and return the support in the future. Change will take time, so it is important to support the beginning teacher to recognise that any closed doors are not a personal affront, but rather a temporary obstacle that you can overcome together.

Toxic culture

Risks

The risks of working in a toxic environment are plentiful. If the beginning teacher arrives with a positive attitude and exciting new ideas, they may be considered a threat and quickly quashed by others. Over time, they may consider the pessimistic attitude to pupil achievement as normal, assuming a similar attitude. Or perhaps they will choose to leave, either in search of more positive pastures or because the profession was not what they hoped it would be. If good teachers and role models are scarce within the school, there may not be many opportunities to observe great teaching. Allies with whom they build connections may come and go, making it difficult for the beginning teacher to feel connected to the school.

Opportunities

In your role as mentor, it will be important to support the beginning teacher to connect with the pupils and recognise the impact they can have as a teacher. Knowing the beginning teacher's key values and reasons for becoming a teacher will be essential in helping them recognise their steps towards their goals and achieving job satisfaction. Identifying the negativity will be important in supporting the beginning teacher to avoid taking on a similar attitude. Modelling to them how you do not engage with this and helping the beginning teacher to make connections with like-minded staff will help them to avoid isolation. Support them to try their new ideas and where appropriate, try them yourself in your own classroom so that you can engage in professional dialogue together. Encourage the beginning teacher to recognise that the school is on a journey and help them to see the part they can play to make the school a brighter, less toxic place. Perhaps together, you can begin to break the cycle of cynicism. Now complete Task 6.3, focusing on risks and opportunities.

Task 6.3 Risks and opportunities

- How do the risks and opportunities that exist in your school influence your role as a mentor?
- How could you proactively seek out and utilise the opportunities and strengths that exist for the beginning teacher in your school?
- What practical steps do you need to take in order to support the beginning teacher to overcome the risks and barriers they face?

Further analysing your school culture

Having looked at the different cultures that exist and ways in which you may support the beginning teacher to be effective within them, now analyse your school culture further and consider what the beginning teacher needs to know. Culture is a complex concept that is difficult to unravel. In order to analyse your school culture further, the culture needs to be broken down into its component parts. Although not an educational theorist, I have found Hofstede's (1980) 'cultural onion' a useful model for analysing the key elements of culture, as shown in Figure 6.1 and explained below.

Hofstede's cultural onion model

Values

As previously discussed, at the core of culture lie values shared by members of the community. These are not necessarily the values taught to pupils during assembly or the vision statement displayed on the school website. They are the essence of what unites the people who work there. This may be comfortable-collaborative culture's value of kindness and support or a collaborative culture's value of 'aggressive curiosity'. If a culture is to have true integrity, then these values should be evident in the practices that run through each of the following three outer layers.

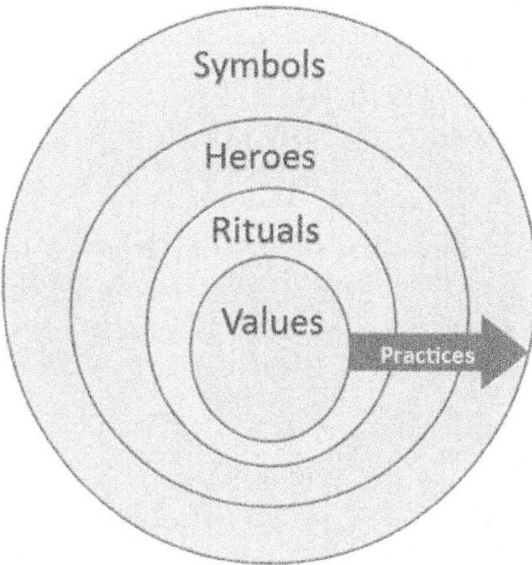

Figure 6.1 Hofstede's onion culture model
Source: Adapted from Hofstede (1980).

Rituals

The first layer surrounding values is described as 'rituals'. These are the traditional practices or behaviours that occur regularly and can be distinctly recognisable as belonging to the culture. In a school setting, these could be prioritising having lunch in the staffroom, actively sharing resources or research via staff emails, a particular way of thanking support staff, or bringing a cake to school on your birthday.

Heroes

The second layer is described as 'heroes'. These are the key players and role models within the community. They are celebrated for the characteristics they possess, which often embody the core values. Perhaps the SENCO is admired for prioritising the wellbeing of pupils, or the head teacher for advocating a work-life balance. It may even be a particular researcher or theorist that is revered throughout the school.

Symbols

The third layer is the most changeable layer as it depends on current trends. They may be pictures, phrases or gestures that communicate a particular meaning for the culture members. They could be jargon used by members of staff, clothing, particular resources that are favoured and should be used regularly, or a specific way in which classroom displays are presented. Next complete Task 6.4.

Task 6.4 Applying Hofstede's model to your current practice

Using the onion culture model, apply this to your own school culture. Use Table 6.2 to help you.

Table 6.2 Onion culture model applied to own school context

	Questions to consider	*Responses*
Values	What key values draw members of staff together? What guides decisions as being right or wrong? What do people strive towards and what do they avoid in school?	
Rituals	What key rituals take place within school and how should one behave at these rituals? As well as thinking about how the beginning teacher may conduct themselves at key events such as staff meetings, consider what else they may need to know. Do teachers give their TAs gifts for special holidays? Should they attend particular social gatherings? How do staff use social media?	
Heroes	Who are the heroes within school? What are these heroes' personal ways of working - for example, do they prefer emails or to speak in person? How can you support the beginning teacher to make positive connections with these heroes? Are there opportunities to watch any 'hero teachers' in action to see what the school recognises as effective practice?	
Symbols	Is there any popular research being shared or jargon being used in school? Do teachers favour a resource or brand? Are there any artefacts in school which carry special meaning?	

Having thought through these questions, consider what you may need to share with the beginning teacher, as well as how and when you might do this. To give all the information in one go may be overwhelming, so you may need to decide how to stagger this information appropriately. Perhaps after their first term, the beginning teacher may complete Table 6.2 for themselves, allowing you to compare your answers and gain greater insight. From here, you could decide on targets that will help them further their success within the school culture.

Additional roles of the mentor: A 'whisper in the ear'

As well as following unwritten rules, beginning teachers need to learn how to 'read between the lines'. For example, in a staff meeting you may be told that visitors are coming to tour the school but that no one should go to extra effort - it is 'business as usual'. As a longstanding member of staff, you know that the explicit statement 'business as usual' in fact implicitly means that displays need to be up, books need to marked and lessons should be flawless. However, a beginning teacher may take what is said at face value, then be surprised to find themselves in trouble because they have fallen below expectations. As a mentor, you can help the beginning teacher by being the 'whisper in their ear' at staff meetings, helping them to be clear about what is expected of them. You can support them by highlighting which directives hold weight, and which can be quickly crossed off the to-do list in order to maintain a balanced workload.

Negotiating workload and prioritising

The National Education Union (NEU, 2018) survey on teachers' workload, which questioned over 8000 teachers in the United Kingdom, found that an astonishing 81per cent of teachers considered leaving teaching in 2018 due to workload pressures. As a beginning teacher, often the day-to-day tasks of planning, resourcing and marking take more time, let alone the additional asks of the school. As a mentor, it is vital that you support the beginning teacher to manage their workload effectively and reduce risks to their wellbeing and retention. This will be challenging, especially as you are likely to be struggling with workload issues too. Try to keep a clear overview of the workload and obligations of the beginning teacher in order to ensure that this remains appropriate. As an established member of your school, you will hold more influence and authority with line managers and phase leaders, so are likely to be more successful in negotiating and canvassing on the beginning teacher's behalf: is it necessary for them to be doing a lunchtime duty or could this time be protected for other work and recovery time? Should they be planning from scratch or are there other teachers and resources available to support them?

Covey (2015) references the 'Time Management Matrix' also known as the Eisenhower Matrix (Table 6.3). This is a useful tool that can help your mentee recognise which school tasks need to be prioritised and which can be considered less urgent. Completing this with the beginning teacher will help make you aware of their current workload and provide you with an opportunity to model how you effectively prioritise activities in light of the school culture and expectations.

You may not agree with the below examples, as they will be determined by your personal teaching values alongside the school culture you work within. Nevertheless, Task 6.5 encourages you and the beginning teacher to have a go at completing the time management matrix, either using your own workload or that of the beginning teacher.

Table 6.3 Time management matrix applied to beginning teacher's workload

Urgent and important	**Not urgent and important**
The tasks that MUST be completed, and quickly. Not doing so would be detrimental to success and reputation. • feedback marking • lesson planning • parent/carer meeting • responding to an emergency **Prioritise these tasks first.**	These tasks often support longer term goals. They are important for success therefore worth investing in, but do not need to be completed immediately. • building relationships with wider team • self- reflection tasks and assignments • classroom environment and displays • recovery time for wellbeing **These tasks need to be scheduled effectively.**
Urgent but not important These may be tasks required of the beginning teacher, which do not directly benefit them. Or they may be something they think is urgent but actually is not. • responding to emails • responding to an interruption • the 'over and above' tasks of a perfectionist. **These need to be streamlined or delegated.**	**Not urgent and not important** These tasks often lead to procrastination and are not an effective use of time. • browsing the internet in search of resources (often aimlessly) • engaging with social media • school gossip **Avoid these during work time.**

Source: Adapted from Covey (2015).

Task 6.5 Apply Covey's time management matrix to your own practice

- How would your school culture inform what you place in each of these boxes?
- Consider asking the beginning teacher to complete the matrix separately and compare your responses.
- It may be helpful as a mentor to understand how the beginning teacher views the school and their priorities. Ask for your mentee to-do lists, timetables and calendars so that you can support them with effective scheduling of tasks.

Building their reputation

As a mentor, you will be influential in how the beginning teacher is viewed by others in school. It will be important to share their successes and celebrate their progress, while being discreet about particular challenges or struggles. Although you must ensure an accurate account of their progress is shared with the appropriate people in the team, it is also essential that they are not viewed poorly by other teaching staff, as this often leads to them becoming isolated or openly criticised. Another way to encourage the beginning teacher's positive reputation is to be mindful of the times of the day when they must present themselves publicly as a teacher. Task 6.6 asks you to identify such moments and how you might model good practice.

Task 6.6 Expected behaviour in schools

- Consider the examples below and discuss with the beginning teacher how they are expected to:
  - walk around the school with their class
  - establish effective behaviour management during assembly
  - collect the pupils from the playground
  - return the pupils to their parents/carers at the end of the day (and avoid complaints by parents and carers for being late)
  - keep on top of the learning environment ahead of learning walks (For clarification a learning walk here refers to visits carried out normally by a member of senior leadership and normally unannounced. They usually visit every classroom in a school to take a 'snapshot' of teaching and learning. Often it is to assess one specific aspect.)
  - anticipate and respond well to an 'open door' school policy
- What other opportunities are available within your school to support the beginning teacher to be viewed positively by others?

As they build in confidence and skill, the beginning teacher may be ready to show their investment in the school and its pupils by running an extra-curricular activity, taking the lead on a class trip or becoming more actively involved in staff and CPD meetings.

Summary

As a mentor, you play a vital role in determining how effectively beginning teachers are able to negotiate their school setting. By taking the time to analyse and understand your school culture, you are enabling yourself to pre-empt and respond to potential risks within the community and to utilise opportunities that may further the beginning teacher's success. Take the time to explicitly discuss school culture with the beginning teacher, acknowledging the challenges that exist, while holding onto the schools' potential to achieve their moral purpose. Recognising their place within the community and the part they have to play in achieving their school's vision will support the beginning teacher's resilience and how connected they feel to the school. Furthermore, investing in them as a member of your school community could lead to new ideas, new alliances and ongoing positive change.

Further reading

Covey, S. (2015) *The 7 Habits of Highly Effective People:Powerful Lessons in Personal Change*, New York: FranklinCovey.

Day, C. (2004) *A Passion for Teaching*, London: Routledge Falmer.

Gruenert, S. and Whitaker, T. (2015) *School Culture Rewired: How to Define, Assess, and Transform It*, Alexandria VA: ASCD.

7 Developing a relationship with mentees

Gill Rowland and Penny Webb

Introduction

This chapter addresses the importance of building early trusting and collaborative relationships between mentors and beginning teachers. It explores how mentors develop relationships with beginning teachers.

Objectives

At the end of this chapter, you should be able to:

- Recognise the importance of building the mentoring relationship in a conscious and planned way
- Reflect on your own early experiences as a teacher and how these can inform your practice as a mentor
- Consider how to overcome the perception of experiential distance between a beginning teacher and an experienced mentor
- Consider how mentor disposition can impact on the relationship between mentor and beginning teacher.

Effective mentoring

Effective mentoring is highly important for beginning teachers to help them on their journey to greater understanding, independence and autonomy, both in their classroom practice and their wider professional life. This should never be underestimated. Indeed, there has been renewed focus on the role of the mentor in recent years as teaching has sought to address the reasons for high numbers leaving the teaching profession at an early stage. Attention has turned to understanding better the qualities and attributes that make for effective mentoring and how these in turn contribute to the wellbeing and resilience that enable teachers to flourish and embrace teaching as a career.

The skills needed by a mentor are many, and while some relate to efficiency and organisation in managing the requirements of the initial teacher education programme or development stage of the beginning teacher, it is harder to learn how to develop a positive and reciprocal mentoring relationship. However, we need to be clear that the nature of the relationship between the mentor and the beginning teacher is at the heart of the best mentoring and the building of this relationship should be a conscious process, even if this isn't always easy.

Like any relationship, that between the mentor and beginning teacher will have several phases and any number of peaks and troughs. It will require the investment of time, energy and emotion. Each relationship will be as unique as the professionals within it and for that reason this chapter will not give a definitive checklist of things to do and not to do in order to create the perfect relationship between mentor and beginning teacher. Instead, you will be given the opportunity to explore ideas and possibilities that will support and guide you towards what can be the most rewarding professional relationship for you, the mentor, and the most affirming and empowering relationship for the beginning teacher. Complete Task 7.1 to consider what experience you already have.

Task 7.1 Reflecting on your own experiences

Think back to when you were starting out in your career, or to a time when you were starting a new school. Note down:

- the things you needed to know in order to feel confident about your first days - for example, practical things such as timings of the day and the code for the photocopier
- how you felt as you entered the school for the first time: what worried you and what you were looking forward to
- who helped you settle into your new role and how they did this.

First things first

In recent years, there has been a focus on developing professional standards for mentoring. In England, the National Standards for School Based Initial Teacher Training (ITT) Mentors (Department for Education, 2016a) identified four key standards that could easily be applied to the mentoring of teachers at all stages. The first relates to the 'personal qualities' of mentors, and states that key to these is the ability to, 'Establish trusting relationships, modelling high standards of practice, and empathising with the challenges a trainee faces'. While this tells us the 'what', we now need to consider the 'how'.

Imagine that you have just been given the details of, or been introduced to, your new mentee. A starting point for your first conversation would surely be to consider some of the points you identified in Task 7.1. Showing you have some understanding of what might be in your mentee's mind and allowing them to articulate worries and concerns will lay a sound foundation for your mentoring relationship.

A tour of the school, or of the key places the beginning teacher will need to know, is a great opportunity for an informal conversation about how the school runs and who works in which rooms. You will probably also bump into people to whom you can introduce your mentee and help them begin to put faces to names. This may sound obvious, but it is attention to the small things that helps to break down the bigger things.

It is also important that you begin to understand a little of the broader picture of your mentee so that you have a context and an understanding of any challenges they face in their lives that might impact their work at school. This is not to say that you should carry out an inquisition, but rather that your conversation should be invitational, giving space for information to be offered.

Establishing trust takes time, but another seed may be sown by being clear from the start about the expectations you have of the beginning teacher and what they can expect from you as their mentor. The beginning teacher may already have had experience of what mentoring is like from either previous placement or work experiences. It is important you each understand what the parameters are and what is offered within your school. Task 7.2 encourages you to consider your role and expectations, which form the basis for any effective mentoring relationship.

Task 7.2 Work-life balance

- How will you respect each other's work-life balance (think about evening/weekend emails, etc.)?
- When will you meet and for how long?
- What will you expect the beginning teacher to bring to the meetings?
- What level of support are you prepared to offer as they seek to develop their skills and expertise?
- How will you move your mentee towards independence?

At a time when teacher retention is an increasing concern, your role as a mentor in helping to manage work-life balance is important and making time for a conversation around this would be a useful place to start. All teachers juggle their time differently according to their circumstances. For example, teacher A might have a young family and may not get to school-related work until after a bedtime story has been read, whereas teacher B, whose family is older, might choose to work as soon as they get home from school and then have 'down' time for the rest of the evening. If teachers A and B happen to be in a mentoring relationship, this might have implications for how and when emails between them are sent and received outside of school hours. Acknowledging this and having a conversation in which email protocols are agreed would help to build a sense of mutual professionalism and support.

Times of transition

Managing transition and change can be tricky for anyone in any context. Such changes might occur during the beginning teacher's training period as well as when they take on their first teaching post. An informal exit survey of PGCE Secondary teachers indicated that the two greatest worries held by the cohort were

- increased workload
- loss of mentoring support.

Starting a new school is always a time of change. It is therefore important to discuss what the changes might be and to explore how you will navigate them together. You could do this by looking at any information the beginning teacher has brought with them as they start with you, which might indicate areas of strength and areas for development. This linking of the 'old' and 'new' will ease the transition. If such information is not available, then a discussion around these areas might be a good starting place.

Figure 7.1 illustrates four areas that have been identified as involving uncertainty or lack of confidence. The mentor can use a simple bar chart at regular intervals to 'take the temperature' of how the beginning teacher is feeling and gauge whether things are improving or if further support is needed. It can be a useful way to prioritise conversations and interventions. We can see, for example, that by Week 5 this beginning teacher feels their wellbeing has almost stalled, while everything else is moving forward. This would flag to the mentor that steps need to be taken here.

Task 7.3 Using a teacher temperature chart

- Reflect on Figure 7.1 and consider the temperature axis as the y axis. Analyse what the chart tells you.
- How could using such a temperature chart help to support the beginning teacher?

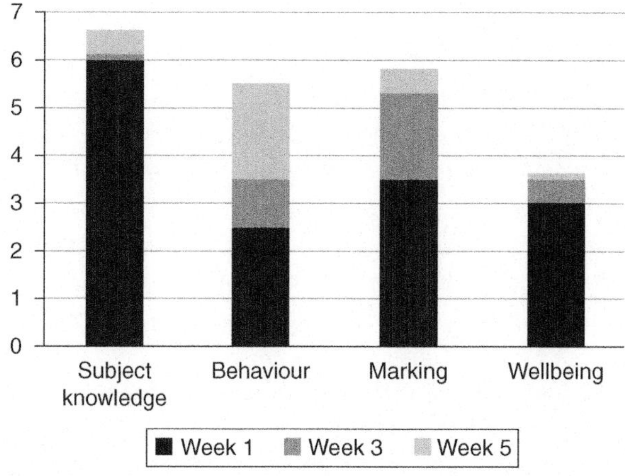

Figure 7.1 Beginning teacher temperature chart

Collaboration

This chapter is based on the premise that mentoring is relational, and a skilled mentor will know how and when to change approach in that mentoring relationship. Sometimes, if a mentor is not mindful - and especially when time is limited - it might be tempting to tell their mentee how to do something or to issue an instruction when what is needed might be a more collaborative approach. While there is a place for 'telling' or 'instructing', if it is done too often it can create a dependency whereas the aim of mentoring is to grow and develop a beginning teacher, moving them towards greater independence and autonomy. Where there is a strong relationship, mentoring is a 'done with' rather than a 'done to' enterprise. Task 7.4 encourages you to consider your own experience of being mentored and how this might influence your current practice.

Task 7.4 Reflecting on your own experience of being mentored

Think back to a time when you were mentored.

- How did your mentor approach the role and how effective did you feel they were?
- When might 'telling' be the best option when working with a beginning teacher?
- How do you think a collaborative approach to mentoring might (or in what ways might it) improve both the progress of the beginning teacher and the mentor-mentee relationship?

Deconstructing practice

So much of what teachers do as classroom practitioners becomes instinctive or automatic over time. When planning a learning sequence, the mentor has a wealth of experience to bring to the task that the beginning teacher does not yet have: knowledge of particular children, activities that have been successful previously, tried and tested techniques for managing the class smoothly. Working collaboratively means that the mentor needs to be able to deconstruct their own practice and make explicit the thinking and knowledge that have gone into their choices and decisions. Given the task of planning a learning sequence, a beginning teacher may have only limited experience of how this is done and might be overwhelmed by the task. A mentoring conversation that talks through the process will go some way towards alleviating anxiety. Similarly, if a beginning teacher is given a target following an observation, say to improve their assessment for learning, they need to know how. A mentoring conversation that explores this, without being prescriptive, will help develop that sense of trust and common purpose.

Outside the classroom, the mentor also needs to model the behaviours expected of the beginning teacher to enable them to navigate the unique culture, ethos and expectations of the school. A good approach here might be to look together, during a mentoring session, at what the coming week will hold and talk through any milestones. For example, a first parents' evening can be a very worrying prospect, raising myriad questions: 'Where do I meet and greet them?', 'Do we shake hands?', 'What happens if there is a question I cannot answer?', 'What if a parent is late and they've missed their slot?' By giving an opportunity for the beginning teacher to articulate their concerns and rehearse possible responses, the mentor displays empathy, which will strengthen and empower the beginning teacher.

Being reflective

An important skill for all teachers is that of being a reflective practitioner, and there are several facets of this skill for the mentor to bear in mind. It seems to be part of many teachers' psyches that, when reflecting on a lesson or an incident during the day, they focus primarily on what has gone badly. Of course, it is important to reflect on things that have not gone well in order to grow and improve, but for the same reasons it is also important to reflect on what has gone well. So a skilled mentor will ensure that the positives are explored as fully as the negatives, and thus enable the beginning teacher to be confident of balance and fairness in professional conversations with their mentor. Reflecting on mistakes and errors can be painful, so the mentor should help their mentee to leave the past in the past and take from it only that which informs the future.

Knowing how to reflect can be an issue for some beginning teachers; if this is the case, offering a simple model to be used in the mentor-mentee conversation may be helpful. Consider starting with Rolfe, Freshwater and Jasper (2001) 'What?', 'So what?', 'Now what?' model. An example of its application is given below.

- *'What?'*: When I led a starter activity last week I found it hard to get the class quiet and listen to me even when I raised my voice.
- *'So what?'*: I observed several different teachers and noted the strategies they used:
    - waiting with arms crossed
    - raising a hand as a signal for quiet
    - ringing a bell
    - counting down from 5.
- *'Now what?'*: I will try raising my hand as this seems to be used quite widely and the pupils will recognise it. I will then have a further discussion with my mentor.

As a mentor, you should also consider articulating your reflections on your own practice so that the mentee understands this is the norm and all teachers learn and grow through the reflective process.

A sense of belonging

From reading the work so far in this book, a sense of the complexity of the role of mentor and the relationship between mentor and beginning teacher should be beginning to emerge. It is a relationship that is defined by aspects of coaching, supervising and a supportive critical friend. At the World Education Conference in 2010, Neacşu (2010) introduced the idea of mentoring in its most simplistic form: the idea of transmitting the abilities and competencies of the experienced teacher to the novice teacher. Adding to this 'copier code' notion of mentoring beginning teachers, Wasconga, Wanzare and Dawo (2015) consider teacher education programmes internationally as being formed from the following elements: subject knowledge, philosophy of education and school experiences. They argue, however, that programmes adopting these components are disjointed, maintaining that beginning teachers find there is a disconnect between the pre-service training and the in-service reality. The central argument of Wasconga, Wanzare and Dawo (2015) is that the disconnect is addressed by effective mentoring relationships that are 'androgenous', consisting of joint planning, self-diagnosis, joint formulation of learning objectives, and collaborative teaching and learning. When evaluation of success occurs, the beginning teacher is involved. However, these (and other) aspects will not develop without the mentor-mentee relationship having secure foundations. Fairbanks, Freedman and Kahn (2000) argue that the relationships must have foundations based on dialogue and reflection, being able to define teaching styles and to provide the basis of the creation of professional partnerships.

The next section considers in more depth how those early relationships are essential to fostering a sense of belonging. When the beginning teacher walks through the door of the school setting, regardless of their previous experience, they are likely to be feeling a sense of disorientation. The professional partnerships that enable the development of reflection and dialogue can only begin to develop once the beginning teacher *feels* part of that school community. On entry into a school for the first time, a beginning teacher may view the mentor in a traditional mentor role, notably that of a relationship between a novice and an expert practitioner. Eriksson (2017), referring to the work of Sundli (2007), argues for the importance of shifting that relationship to one of collaboration, collegiality and interaction as they start on the new stage of their professional career. Eriksson (2017) posits that a key component of enabling this shift in mindset of the beginning teacher is the creation of mentor groups, whereby beginning teachers can meet with the mentor together and thereby break down the expert mentor and novice mentee hierarchy through a more widely collaborative approach. Based on research conducted with beginning teachers across a number of mentor groups, Eriksson (2017) observes that the importance of being in a group enables a democratic approach where the group directs the reflections and goals. Task 7.5 asks you to consider how beginning teachers are inducted into your setting at the moment.

Task 7.5 Induction processes

- What induction procedures for beginning teachers exist in your school setting?
- How are beginning teachers introduced to the documentation and personnel?
- List the induction activities that you have in your setting and reflect on how these activities support the beginning teacher during their induction.

When the beginning teacher arrives, the scope of the mentor role can appear extensive. The beginning teacher needs inducting into the school setting, from familiarising themselves with day-to-day logistics such as playground duties and assembly times to introducing key personnel. These members of staff may, for example, hold safeguarding roles or have responsibilities for coordinating provision for children with special educational needs and disability

(SEND). The 'school improvement plan' of the school might well be an essential document that will need sharing early on in the placement or first teaching year. The beginning teacher may bring knowledge of certain areas, which may benefit whole-school development. Best practice mentoring would ensure that the school development plan is not simply shared, but analysed together. The professional expectations for the beginning teacher, grounded in policy and practice, need clear identification. This forms the basis for continuing professional development (CPD) and goals identified through the process of observation, feedback and target setting, developing subject knowledge and pedagogical understanding. To become part of the community, the beginning teacher needs both the confidence to know where to find the stationery cupboard and who to turn to for a safeguarding concern, and also know that their success is integral to the development of the school. In this way, the beginning teacher will develop a sense of belonging to the school community.

Once the beginning teacher has been inducted into the day-to-day running of the school, an approach that can be adopted for the further professional development of the beginning teacher is co-teaching. Murphy (2016) explains how co-teaching is a pedagogical approach that has developed internationally to address a number of common challenges, including:

- beginning teacher anxiety
- gaps between theory and practice
- ineffective pupil learning
- pupil dissatisfaction
- developing reflective practitioners
- mainstreaming children with special educational needs (SEN).

The last of these points refers to a practice used in the United States, where specialist teachers in SEN co-teach alongside teachers in mainstream school, supporting the inclusion agenda in mainstream schools. In the case of SEN, there would be a particular focus on supporting the needs of individual children rather than the personal development of the teachers themselves, although this aspect will have a parallel influence. However, Murphy (2016) argues that when considering the other challenges outlined above, the fundamental strength of the co-teaching approach is that it is less hierarchical than, for example, an experienced teacher observing a lesson from a beginning teacher, feeding back and setting targets. By adopting a collaborative rationale for the practice, the anxiety levels and inadequate performance of beginning teachers can be counteracted. The three key elements of co-teaching are co-planning, co-teaching and co-reflection. Case study 7.1 explores how these three aspects positively develop the beginning teacher's teaching practice. When reading Case study 7.1, consider how the beginning teacher is valued in a non-hierarchical way.

Case study 7.1 Paired planning and teaching

Julie is an experienced teacher who has been teaching for ten years and has been a mentor for three. Kathy is a beginning teacher in her first year of a three-year degree in primary education in England, which if completed successfully will give her Qualified

Teacher Status (QTS). Kathy did biology at 'A' level and comes to her course with a detailed knowledge of biological sciences.

Whereas the experienced teacher may typically give the beginning teacher the learning objective for the beginning teacher to take away and plan, Julie and Kathy sit down together and co-plan the lesson. They discuss together what they hope the children will achieve. The lesson is about plants, and Kathy shows Julie how her knowledge of plant anatomy can be translated into an interactive lesson for the children. Julie prompts Kathy to think about how the children will transition from activity to activity and how to plan ways to grab their attention. They both carefully consider how to enable participation for a child in the class who has autism and who needs support with group work. Julie and Kathy then teach the lesson together. Julie starts the lesson, Kathy leads the activities, Julie prompts Kathy halfway through to stop the children for a mini plenary to enable assessment for learning, and Julie concludes. Both Julie and Kathy make observations about each other's practice when they are not teaching. Sometimes they teach as a pair from the start. Finally, both Julie and Kathy reflect on the lesson together.

In England, the mentor standards (DfE, 2016a) include a standard related to the building of trusting relationships, stipulating that mentors must be approachable and challenge the beginning teacher to develop their practice. When analysing what this standard is describing, however, there are layers of complexity within these trusting relationships. Kemmis et al. (2014) identify three elements that mentors adopt within their mentoring relationships. They argue that mentoring is essentially a social practice based on relationships. Those relationships are conceptualised into 'doings, sayings and relatings' (Kemmis et al., 2014). 'Doings' refer to *what is done* – for example, completing paperwork, attending meetings, organising pupils into different year groups. 'Sayings' identifies *what is said*, the language used and the cognitive understanding of the mentoring role. The 'sayings' are evident in the actual communication, and in the outcome of the act of communication the mentor is cognitively recognising their role as identifying targets and gaps. Lastly, 'relatings' refers to the affective element of the relationships, the intersubjective power differences, social interaction and sense of solidarity.

Each of those 'doings, sayings and relatings' in turn is influenced by dispositions of mentoring, whether these take on a role of supervision (checking paperwork), support (a sounding board to bounce off ideas) or collaborative development (working together to develop practice). For example, the sayings of a mentor who predominantly views their role as supervisory will be very different from those who see it supportive. However, these three dispositions will interconnect, with certain aspects predominating within certain circumstances. Vincent, King and Webb (2018) applied the dispositions of Kemmis et al. (2014) to research carried out into the impact on mentors of changes in their Higher Education Institute (HEI) teacher training partnerships. Data collected through nine individual mentor interviews and responses from termly mentor meetings were analysed, adopting an interpretative approach (Strauss and Corbin, 1990). The data were then re-analysed as doings, saying and relatings, and the three dispositions of Kemmis et al. (2014) applied to the three elements. The disposition most commonly identified within the data was that of the supportive mentor. However, this finding posed a question for the partnership about whether the disposition of collaborative self-development should be the overall aim of the approach to mentoring. The partnership also considered how the three dispositions of mentoring were interchangeable and often adapted to the needs of the beginning teacher. Beginning teachers may well predominantly need supportive mentoring at the beginning and, once the supportive element of the relationship is established, develop collaborative self-development. A beginning teacher who is struggling in an element of their practice may need the mentor as supervisor and support before collaborative self-development can occur. Task 7.6 asks you to consider how your current approach to mentoring reflects the elements of mentoring established by Kemmis et al. (2014).

Task 7.6 Your role as a mentor

Using Table 7.1 to record your thinking, identify aspects of your role in which you *do* (activities you carry out), *say* (what you say about your role and how you conceptualise your role) and *relate* (how you interact with the beginning teacher and your colleagues).

- For each role, identify whether you would label these as supervisory, supportive or collaborative self-development.
- Consider which disposition appears to dominate (if, indeed, only one does - you may find more than one).
- Consider which disposition you adopt for beginning teachers and as their practice develops. Does your disposition (over time) change and if so how?

Table 7.1 Doing, saying and relating template

	Doings	*Sayings*	*Relatings*
Supervisory			
Supportive			
Collaborative self-development			

Summary

This chapter has explored how effective developmental mentoring for beginning teachers is grounded in relationships. It is essential that mentors avoid assumptions and consciously develop the skills necessary to make the implicit explicit for the beginning teacher, with regard to policies, procedures, protocols and expectations. When considering initiating a relationship with a beginning teacher, the importance of developing a democratic approach is crucial, such as adopting group mentee meetings or collaborative co-teaching. Understanding the importance of mentor dispositions and how they can impact the relationship has been highlighted as significant in successful mentoring. Equally important for the mentor is recognising how to adapt and change according to the needs of the beginning teacher. You need to identify these aspects of their mentoring but recognise that mentoring is not static. Mentoring needs responsiveness to ensure the success of the future teaching profession. To conclude, it is important to remember that the mentoring relationship between mentor and beginning teacher is an organic process that needs to be worked on consciously. An empathetic approach will help to build a firm foundation for the mentoring relationship. A democratic approach is instrumental in enabling collaborative self-development, giving the beginning teacher a voice and confidence in their development. You should remain aware of the evolving mentoring disposition and how to adapt and adjust this according to the needs of the beginning teacher. Remember that every mentor-mentee relationship is unique and special, and should be celebrated.

Further reading

Eriksson, A. (2017) Pre-service teachers' questions about the profession during mentoring group conversations, *European Journal of Teacher Education* , 40(1), pp. 76-90.

Kemmis, S., Heikkinen, H.L.T., Fransson, G., Aspfors, J. and Edwards-Groves, C. (2014) Mentoring of new teachers as contested practice: Supervision, support and collaborative self-development, *Teaching and Teacher Education* 43, pp.154-164.

Murphy, C. (2016) *Coteaching in Teacher Education: Innovative Pedagogy for Excellence.* St Albans: Critical Publishing.

8 Learning conversations

Sarah St. John

Introduction

The role that mentors take in supporting beginning teachers is immeasurable, particularly given the current climate in terms of teacher recruitment figures showing that the recruitment of initial teacher trainees has been below target since 2012, while pupil numbers are on the increase (Foster, 2018). There is increasing pressure on schools, and specifically mentors, to help shape the next generation to become reflective, autonomous teachers who are able to respond with resilience in what is an increasingly challenging profession. In line with this, in England mentoring has now gained increased recognition with the publication of the Mentor Standards (DfE, 2016a). Highlighted within these is the importance of mentors taking ownership of their own professional mentoring practice in order to support beginning teachers in their journey towards autonomy.

Beginning teachers look to their mentor for guidance and direction, but this can turn into an over-reliance on a mentor to the extent that beginning teachers have been heard to claim 'My mentor won't tell me what to do!' As professionals, there is an awareness that there needs to be a shift in this perspective to a position where there is an understanding of the mentor as one who empowers rather than tells in order for beginning teachers to take ownership of their own practice. The issue is how mentors can encourage beginning teachers to become reflective. The answer is not in what mentors do, but more in how the role is carried out. This is outlined by Hennissen et al. (2008, p. 174), who explore two opposing approaches to mentoring by making a distinction between 'directive' and 'non-directive' styles of mentoring. It is this shift from a more directive style of mentoring to a non-directive style that enables beginning teachers to explore the impact their practice has on their understanding of pedagogy and that ultimately leads to the desired goal: a positive impact on pupil and teacher learning. One strategy that can be employed effectively to support this 'non-directive' approach (Hennissen et al., 2008, p.174) is the use of a learning conversation that takes the place of the traditional feedback meeting following a lesson observation.

Objectives

At the end of this chapter, you should be able to:

- Reflect on the role of the mentor following a lesson observation

- Consider the value of a learning conversation that enables beginning teachers to learn to reflect on their practice
- Understand the range of coaching skills that can be used to support beginning teachers to take ownership of their practice.

Skills and qualities of a mentor

Before we look at the objectives, it is important to consider your skill and your qualities as a mentor. To do this, complete Task 8.1.

Task 8.1 Skills and qualities of a mentor

Write a list of all the skills and qualities you need as a mentor to help you carry out your role effectively.

You may have considered some of the following skills and qualities:

- guide
- adviser
- assessor or judge
- supporter
- co-teacher
- role model
- leader
- trusted colleague
- friend
- honesty
- committed
- resilient.

Looking at this list, there appear to be some contradictions. For example, how can those who make judgements, in which you are in effect 'gatekeepers to the teaching profession' (Jones and Straker, 2006, p.166) also be co-teachers and trusted colleagues at the same time? A consideration of the role of mentors and coaches, and the skills they employ when supporting beginning teachers, could help us find a way forward.

Mentoring and coaching

Roberts (2000, p. 162) believes that mentoring 'should allow for positive growth, development and self-actualisation'. Added to this, Rippon and Martin (2003) perceive the mentoring process to be on a continuum that ranges from a systematic - almost formulaic - approach to one that puts the learner at the heart of the process (Harrison, Lawson and Wortley, 2005). Available and varied approaches to mentoring are also explored by Hennissen et al. (2008,

p. 174), who make the distinction between 'directive' and 'non-directive' styles of mentoring. They suggest that a mentor who adopts a directive style is more likely to take on the role of an instructor who 'tells the prospective teacher what to do, assesses, corrects, recites and informs'. Conversely, a mentor operating within a non-directive style presents as a facilitator, someone who encourages reflection and guides beginning teachers to draw conclusions about their own practice (Hennissen at al., 2008). This notion of the mentor as a guide is also highlighted by Parsloe and Wray (2005), where the aim of the mentoring process is to facilitate the learning process.

A non-directive approach to supporting learners is also placed at the heart of a coaching approach. This is highlighted by Pemberton (2006), who states the aim of the coach is to encourage reflection by 'helping someone see their situation clearly and calmly in order that they can make better decisions about what they do'. This is similar to Parsloe and Wray (2005), who also consider coaching to be a process that enables learning and development to occur and thus performance to improve. Underpinning both is the implication that the onus is on the one being coached to take responsibility for their next steps as a result of a conversation with the coach. Pemberton (2006) goes on to state that coaches do not direct practice, which reinforces a point made by Gallwey (1974), who perceives a coach as someone who can release the self-knowledge and potential that everyone possesses (Parsloe and Wray, 2005). This idea of unlocking potential is also at the heart of the description of coaching as discussed by the National College for Teaching and Leadership (NCTL, 2016). Now complete Task 8.2, which encourages you to consider why mentors might adopt different mentoring or coaching approaches.

Task 8.2 Which style to adopt?

- Consider why some mentors might adopt a directive rather than a non-directive style of mentoring or a coaching approach.
- List your reasons and then categorise them as shown below.
- How closely do your responses correspond with those shown below?

Some of your answers may have focused on the following:

1. the beginning teacher's level of confidence
2. the beginning teacher's ability to reflect honestly about levels of achievement - the word 'honestly' is used here deliberately for the following reasons:
   - Some beginning teachers tend to err on the side of caution and say what they think their mentor wants to hear.
   - Some are very hard on themselves and will not openly recognise the strengths in their practice. This can ultimately lead to issues around wellbeing.
   - Some may worry about the mentor being the one who carries out the grading process and so try to 'hide' aspects of practice that they perceive to be not very strong.

- Some struggle with the notion of reflection.

3. the beginning teacher's previous experience in terms of teaching opportunities
4. the beginning teacher's prior experience, or lack of it, in terms of a particular age range
5. the mentor's understanding of the mentoring process
6. time, or lack of it.

It thus seems that there may be a whole host of reasons why mentors may adopt a more directive style of mentoring. However, it would appear from the work cited by Hennissen et al. (2008), Pemberton (2006), Parsloe and Wray (2005) and the NCTL (2016) that a non-directive approach utilising coaching skills is preferable when supporting the development of a reflective practitioner. So how can beginning teachers be supported to become reflective and thus helped to take ownership of their practice? In order to develop this understanding, a consideration of what it means to be reflective and the characteristics of a reflective practitioner are needed.

Being reflective: Reflection-in-action, reflection-on-action

Schön (1983) identifies two distinct types of reflection: reflection-in-action and reflection-on-action. Reflection-in-action refers to the 'in the moment' response when teaching, while reflection-on-action is instrumental in bringing about a change in practice by affording teachers the opportunity to evaluate their practice once a lesson has been completed. Reflection-on-action thus provides an opportunity for beginning teachers to consider implications for future learning. Opportunities for reflection can also be found through the utilisation of various models of experiential learning, where there is a focus on the process of sense-making once an experience has been completed. Such models include Gibbs' (1988) reflective cycle and Kolb's (1984) learning cycle. In interpreting Kolb's model, Hewlett (2013) explains that all deep learning is experiential, and that opportunities for active, 'hands on' learning are necessary, as is the reflection and the consolidation and implementation of new learning. Task 8.3 asks you to consider what a reflective practitioner might look like.

Task 8.3 Behaviours of a reflective practitioner

Identify and list some of the key behaviours you would expect to see in a reflective practitioner.

In completing Task 8.3, you might have identified some of the characteristics of a reflective practitioner as listed below:

- describing events
- revisiting and reviewing practice
- thinking aloud
- displaying misconceptions

- questioning
- seeking clarification
- sense making
- hypothesising
- analysing
- evaluating
- concluding
- setting targets.

How we define reflection and the characteristics we identify in a reflective practitioner impact our engagement in the mentoring process. Complete Task 8.4 to identify your own definitions.

Task 8.4 Creating your own definitions

- How might you define 'a reflection' and 'a reflective practitioner'?
- Write down your definitions before proceeding.
- Ask your mentee to do this task.
- Compare ideas. Do you agree?

Your thoughts may have included the following ideas:

- Reflection is 'a purposeful, deliberate act of inquiry into one's thoughts and actions' (Loughran, 1996, in Harrison et al., 2005, p. 422).
- A reflective practitioner is an individual who is able to adopt a critical stance when reviewing their teaching (Baker and McNicoll, 2006).
- A reflective practitioner is someone who is thinking aloud and so trying to make sense of a particular situation (Harrison et al., 2005).

The rest of this chapter explores one specific aspect of mentoring: the use of a learning conversation, in which beginning teachers can be encouraged to be reflective and so take ownership of their practice. The role of a mentor utilising coaching skills is significant here: if beginning teachers are not helped to make this move towards autonomy, they will struggle when the support of their mentor is not available. Use Task 8.5 to consider your current practice.

Task 8.5 Reflecting on your current practice

- In what ways do you feel you currently support beginning teachers through your mentoring?
- Can you list the ways?

In completing Task 8.5 your list may have included:

- lesson observations followed by feedback
- setting clear targets
- regular mentor meetings
- file checks
- three way discussions that include the class teachers
- at grading points
- co-teaching.

In Task 8.6, consider how the ways you have identified by which you currently support beginning teachers can provide reflection opportunities during mentor meetings.

Task 8.6 Building opportunities for reflection

Go back to your list in Task 8.3;

- Annotate it to demonstrate the ways in which you build opportunities for reflection into your mentor meetings.
- Reflect also on your mentoring style – is it directive or non-directive, or a combination of both?
- Consider why and when there may be a shift from one approach to another?

In order to consider how you can adopt a mentoring style that empowers beginning teachers to be more reflective, and thus develop into confident autonomous practitioners, we now look at one aspect of the mentoring role: how we provide feedback on lesson observations. Use Task 8.7 to reflect on your current practice in managing feedback.

Task 8.7 Managing feedback

- How do you manage the feedback session after a lesson observation?
- Take this opportunity to pause and reflect on your approach.

Beginning teachers' experiences of feedback following lesson observations

While much of the research into mentoring styles may seem a little outdated, it is clear from anecdotal conversations with beginning teachers across programmes that a variety of approaches is still evident. These range from a didactic approach where the mentor gave a judgement on the lesson, to a learning conversation that afforded the beginning teacher an opportunity to reflect on practice and set their own targets. There were also many varying experiences sitting somewhere in the middle of the two. When asked, the beginning teachers who experienced the more traditional style of feedback felt that there were fewer opportunities for them to take ownership of their practice. In contrast, those who were party to a learning conversation felt empowered and confident to engage in a process of reflection.

This variation in approaches is supported by research into the types of dialogue taking place between mentors and beginning teachers. The data indicate that dialogue can vary from five minutes to an hour (Borko and Mayfield, 1995, and Edwards and Collison, 1996, both cited in Hennissen et al., 2008). There are undoubtedly reasons behind this, such as time constraints placed on mentors who carry out this role along with the many other hats they wear in school. However, studies have also shown that while mentors focus on the ways children learn, in some situations less emphasis is placed on the process of learning from a beginning teacher's perspective (Edwards and Collison, 1996, Edwards and Protheroe, 2004, both cited in Hennissen et al., 2008). There is also an awareness that, in the long term, using directive skills are more time consuming than using non-directive skills (Crasborn et al., 2005, cited in Hennissen et al., 2008). So how can we ensure that beginning teachers and mentors can come together in meaningful dialogue that takes into consideration the level of experience that the beginning teacher brings to the table and the added tensions of the mentoring role? We will now go on to explore learning conversations.

Learning conversations

The term 'learning conversation' in a formal sense has been defined by CUREE (2007) as a 'structured professional dialogue'. A learning conversation is a coaching technique that enables professionals, with support, to shine a light on their practice in order to review, reflect and move their learning forward (General Teaching Council (GTC), 2004). The desired outcomes are improved skills, knowledge and understanding. While learning conversations can be used in both mentoring and coaching scenarios (GTC, 2004), in terms of the coaching process, they are a vehicle that enables the coach to 'wipe the steam off the mirror, so that the other person can see themselves and the situation more clearly' (Pemberton, 2006, p. 90). Categorised by Pemberton (2006, p. 26) as a 'helping conversation', each one is a balanced approach that provides an element of support and challenge which, when utilised effectively, can provide an opportunity for the beginning teacher to identify and reflect on an issue from their own perspective. The role of the coach is to challenge the beginning teacher's thinking and, as a result, the beginning teacher is able to come up with a solution (Pemberton, 2006). From this, it is clear that for a learning conversation to be successful, both parties must be honest and worthy of trust, and show commitment and resilience (Rogers, 2004).

Vygotsky (1978) explains that learning is the result of social interaction and relationships. It is this collaborative, social constructivist nature of learning that lends itself to the success of a learning conversation, with dialogue being used as a vehicle to support the ways in which attitudes and behaviours can be developed and performance improved (Garvey et al., 2014). However given that learning conversations are primarily a coaching technique, it is important to consider how a learning conversation works and can subsequently be adopted as part of the mentoring process.

How learning conversations work

In terms of a learning conversation within a coaching scenario, it is the person being coached (the coachee) who must set the agenda, with the coach taking on the role of a listener. According to Pemberton (2006), there are two types of listening skills: type A and type B. At the start of the learning conversation, the coachee is encouraged to voice their own perspective. By adopting type A listening skills, which include 'encouraging, clarifying, summarising, reflecting, empathising' (Pemberton, 2006, p. 76), the coach is able to help the coachee move on from the problem or dilemma they have set as the agenda. Type B listening skills come into play as the conversation progresses. They enable the coach to delve deeper by listening for signs that will give them some insight into the coachee's perspective in order to help them unpack the issue or dilemma as presented. This notion of active listening is also advocated by Kline (2009), who sets out the importance of a thinking environment that allows mentees the space to think for themselves with the mentor demonstrating active listening skills. Here the role of the mentor is to interject with a prompting question only when the mentee remains silent for a period of time.

Models for learning conversations

Pemberton (2006) provides a useful model that is often used in current practice, from which a learning conversation can be structured that incorporates both types of listening skills. Entitled FAST, it enables the coachee to move away from the problem as they see it towards a solution. The model is outlined in Table 8.1.

What is clear from the acronym FAST is that the learning conversation should not be a lengthy process. After the initial focus for the conversation is set out and briefly explained, the aim is not to dwell on the problem but rather to move the coachee on to the next phase - that of action - as soon as possible. It is at this action-orientated stage that the coachee could then begin to consider possible solutions for the issue or problem they have identified. The coachee then has an opportunity to move towards a timely solution.

Another model that could be adopted in a mentoring situation is the GROW model (see also Chapter 5). The framework (Whitmore, 2002) is outlined in Table 8.2 and provides opportunities for reflection. When used in conjunction with a coaching, questioning approach, it enables the coachee to identify a goal and then reflect on current status, and consider

Table 8.1 FAST model for learning conversations

F	Is the conversation **f**ocused?
A	Is the conversation **a**ction orientated?
S	Is the conversation **s**olution-focused?
T	Is the conversation **t**imely?

Source: Pemberton (2006).

Table 8.2 The GROW model

G	**G**oal - what do you want?
R	**R**eality - where are you now?
O	**O**ptions - what could you do?
W	**W**ill - what will you do?

Source: Whitmore (2002).

the options available before deciding on a way in which they will move forward in order to achieve the intended goal.

Take some time to complete Task 8.8 to reflect on how you might adopt either the FAST or GROW approach during your mentoring.

Task 8.8 FAST or GROW?

Return to Task 8.7 and reflect on how you facilitate the feedback in light of either the FAST or GROW Model.

- Are there opportunities for beginning teachers to provide a focus for the conversation?
- Do you use active listening skills?
- Is there thinking time?
- Are there opportunities for the beginning teachers to consider possible actions and solutions?
- Who sets the targets at the end of the session?
- How do you induct the beginning primary teacher into the ways of working in your setting?
- In what sorts of meetings do you involve your mentee?
- What role (if any) do they play? Are there any instances where it would not be appropriate to include your mentee?
- What kinds of personal support do you offer to prevent your mentees being overwhelmed by the demands of the job?

Utilising learning conversations to follow up on a lesson observation

Joint examination of how a lesson observation is planned, organised and facilitated is useful for embedding a learning conversation into a mentor's practice and a beginning teacher's professional development. There needs to be an understanding from both parties of what the expectations are. This can be discussed through an initial conversation that takes the following into consideration:

1. *A focus for the learning conversation.* This agenda should be set by the beginning teacher. It outlines the teaching target they intend to address during the lesson. This can then be followed up in a learning conversation.

2. *Timings for the observation, agreed in advance.* It may be that the mentor only observes the lesson for a limited time to observe the focus in action. For example, if the focus is mini-plenaries, then the observer need not observe the start of the lesson. Similarly, if the focus is on how the beginning teacher facilitates engagement at the start of the lesson, then observing the whole lesson is not necessary. When planning the timings, it is worth being aware that shorter observations allow for a more in-depth analysis of one aspect of pedagogy that the beginning teacher sets as the agenda and thus has the motivation to address.
3. *A time for the follow up learning conversation.* This needs to be planned in advance to allow the beginning teacher some thinking time before the meeting so they can begin to reflect.

The learning conversation itself

The value of the learning conversation is that it provides the beginning teacher with an opportunity to reflect on a specific aspect of practice. As such, the approach taken by the mentor is significant in that it needs to allow the beginning teacher to take the lead and explore what progress has been made in line with the teaching target. In order for this to be facilitated, the mentor needs to come to the meeting prepared with specific questions that will unlock the beginning teacher's understanding of aspects of pedagogy. Questions will need to be open and structured to allow the beginning teacher opportunities for reflection. Using the GROW model (Whitmore, 2002), the questions in Table 8.3 provide examples that could be asked in relation to a teaching target of how to facilitate engagement at the start of a lesson.

Now complete Task 8.9, which encourages you to consider how using the FAST or GROW model might change how you frame your questions.

Task 8.9 Applying FAST or GROW

Think back to a lesson you recently observed being taught by the beginning teacher. Can you frame questions for use in a learning conversation using either the FAST or GROW model?

Table 8.3 GROW model applied to teaching targets

G	Goal - what do you want?	Why did you want to have engagement as a focus? How would the lesson look if this engagement was in place?
R	Reality - where are you now?	What do you feel the issues are at the moment? What strategies did you incorporate into your lesson today? Were they effective and how? If not, why not?
O	Options - what could you do?	Given your reflections on the strategies you employed today what other strategies have you observed?
W	Will - what will you do?	Which of those strategies will you now try? What targets are you setting yourself?

Moving along the continuum from being directive to non-directive

It is important to be aware that, depending on the experience and levels of confidence of some beginning teachers, additional support might initially be needed to support their engagement with the learning conversation. An awareness of the continuum in mentoring approaches from a directive to a non-directive style would enable the mentor to facilitate the required level of support in order to bring about learning. This would provide the beginning teacher with the required level of support and challenge, but with an acknowledgement that there may sometimes be a need for more direction (Hennissen et al., 2008). However, such a shift would be a conscious action/employed as a direct response to the way in which the beginning teacher responds to the questioning approach. Once the conversation develops and the beginning teacher becomes more confident, the mentor can then move back to assume a more non-directive style. For many, though - and particularly as a beginning teacher becomes more experienced in this way of working - the opportunities for reflection through the learning conversation will help them take ownership of their practice.

Summary

It is clear from research and observation that learning conversations can be a powerful way to enable others to take control of their own learning (Parsloe and Wray, 2005). Learning conversations provide opportunities for beginning teachers to identify aspects of practice they would like to explore in more depth while also enabling the process of reflection to develop, thus allowing them to take ownership of their learning. They also provide a framework for mentors that moves them from operating in a directive style to adopting a more non-directive approach that can be adapted, depending on the needs of the mentee.

To summarise, for a learning conversation to be effective, it is important that the following elements are in place:

- a relationship between the mentor and beginning teacher that is built on trust
- ground rules for how the lesson observation and learning conversation will be managed.

It is also important that the beginning teacher:

- is given a voice and feels confident to voice an opinion about practice.
- understands the importance of reflection as a way to take ownership of practice and so move learning forward.

The mentor needs to:

- understand the role they play as facilitator and guide
- understand the importance of shaping a learning conversation that unlocks potential
- know when and how to support and challenge
- know when and whether an intervention is needed.

Further reading

Hennissen, P., Crasborn, F., Brouwer, N., Korthagen, F. and Bergen, T. (2008) Mapping mentor teachers' roles in mentoring dialogues, *Educational Research Review*, 3, pp. 168-86.

Pemberton, C. (2006) *Coaching to Solutions: A Manager's Tool Kit for Performance Delivery*, Oxford: Butterworth Heinemann.

Whitmore, J. (2002) *Coaching for Performance: GROWing People, Performance and Purpose*, London: Nicholas Brealey.

9 Making accurate assessments

Lorele Mackie

Introduction

Learning to teach takes place within the realms of relationships with others (Harrison, Lawson and Wortley, 2005), so having a mentor who is part of the teaching community is necessary (Hargreaves and Fullan, 2000). In the current knowledge society, with its life-long learning agenda, achievement is directly connected with quality teaching and learning (Forde et al. 2006). This context has implications for the attributes required in teachers and how these are developed through mentoring. Effective mentors understand the complexities of mentoring (Ambrosetti, 2010), including assessment of teaching competence (Yeomans and Sampson, 1994; Scottish Government, 2011). This is particularly important, as mentors are increasingly positioned in a dual, potentially conflicting, role of both mentor and assessor (Fransson, 2010). This can create tensions within the mentor-mentee relationship, as discussed in Chapter 2.

Objectives

At the end of this chapter, you should be able to:

- Reflect on the importance of formative and summative assessment as a key part of the mentoring process
- Recognise key components for consideration in the use of formative assessment within the mentoring process
- Reflect on how formative and summative assessment may interact to support the professional learning of beginning teachers.

Before continuing, complete Task 9.1, which asks you to reflect on your experiences of assessment.

Task 9.1 Your experiences of being assessed as a beginning teacher

- Which experiences stand out most?
- Why?
- What is it you remember about them specifically?

Identify assessment practices you currently use as a mentor:

- What are the key ones?
- Why do you use these in particular?
- What kinds of personal support do you offer to prevent a beginning teacher being overwhelmed by the demands of the job?

Summative assessment

Teachers work to attain certain summative competency standards within Europe and worldwide - for example, in Scotland the Standard for Provisional/Full Education (QAA, 2006); in England, Teacher's Standards (DFE, 2013a); and in Australia, the Competency Framework for Teachers (DET, 2004). Competency frameworks stem from a global focus on standards, the quality of teachers, attitudes and choice (Christie, 2008). Definitions of competence have implications for learning, teaching and assessment - for example, transmissive versus reflective, achievement as opposed to learning for understanding (Whitty and Willmott, 1991). At the core of the debate around competency models is whether teachers are trained merely to act or educated to reason their actions: managerialism versus pedagogic excellence (Patrick, Forde and McPhee, 2003, p. 245). These are important issues for teacher education and the teaching profession in general.

Task 9.2 encourages you to reflect on your current practice using competency models.

Task 9.2 Using competency models

- As a mentor teacher, do you use competency models as part of the mentoring process?
- In what way(s)?
- Do you find them helpful?
- Why or why not?

A variety of issues with competency models are identified within the literature. Criticisms include fostering teachers who are technicians, in that this type of model makes it difficult to describe the complexities of teaching where teachers are risk-takers or those who try out different methods (Menter, Brisard and Smith, 2006). The complex nature of teaching or valuing different forms of knowledge is not recognised (Furlong, 2005), resulting in conceptions of teaching as lacking reflection, insight and creativity (Hegarty, 2000). These conceptions assume compliant practice and are more about 'how', not 'why', so they lack attention to broader educational concerns (Kirk, 2000). Technical elements of teaching (products), as opposed to process and reasoning, are more likely to be emphasised because it is easier to develop criteria to assess these more tangible facets of teaching (Whitty and Willmott, 1991). Therefore, teaching becomes a prescriptive set of certain ways to teach - for example, if beginning teachers adhere to particular instructions (competences), they will be successful teachers (Moore, 1996, cited in Smyth and Shacklock, 1998).

However, such issues are now being addressed. For example, the Scottish Teacher Education Competency Framework has evolved to reflect the complexity of teaching in their inclusion of personal and professional dimensions (GTCS, 2012), where the expected elements are indicative of the need for flexibility to allow teachers scope in the evolution of roles and responsibilities reflective of the demands of a knowledge society (Christie, 2008). These documents espouse notions of teacher professionalism underpinned by a concept of the 'extended' (Hoyle and John, 1995) or 'activist' (Sachs, 2003) professional. They profess a wider view of the teaching profession as encompassing knowledge, understanding, skills, critical engagement, attitudes and values (Christie, 2008), and are suggested as an attempt to reconcile the government view of competences with the perspectives of others to include reflective practice (Menter, Brisard and Smith, 2006).

Competences may be viewed as serving a professional purpose in terms of accountability on the part of teacher education institutions, identifying common goals for university and school mentors, fostering focused criteria for beginning teachers and initial teacher education programmes, providing a basis for assessment and dialogue for university and school mentors, and developing competent teachers (Kirk, 2000). In addition, they can foster clarity regarding assessment and thus lend themselves well to the profiling procedures used in teacher education, and to both formative and summative assessment (Whitty and Willmott, 1991). However, it may be suggested that they foster standardisation rather than quality through the use of specific criteria (Sachs, 2001). Compliance therefore becomes a central factor, with views of learning constrained by misalignment of mentee requirements and competency frameworks (Hargreaves, 1992) in opposition to more democratic views where mentee needs are key, with competences employed as a foundation for critical reflection (Bleach, 1997).

Formative assessment

Assessment should be an integral part of the education process, continually providing both 'feedback and feedforward', and therefore needs to be incorporated systematically into teaching strategies and practices (DES, 1988); however, it can become disconnected from the learning process (LTSc, 2008). Effective learning occurs where it is connected to assessment that focuses on the gap between where a learner is in their learning and where they need to be (Black and Wiliam, 1998). In this respect, it helps to provide an emerging picture of achievement such as that espoused by summative competency frameworks in the case of teachers (QAA, 2006).

Formative assessment is a dialogic process that focuses on improving the process of learning as opposed to merely measuring progress (Black and Wiliam, 1998; Hargreaves, 2007). Teachers, learners and peers are involved in obtaining, interpreting and employing assessment information to inform their decisions about appropriate next steps in learning (Black and Wiliam, 1998). Its principles are fourfold: learners learn best when they understand clearly what they are trying to learn, and what is expected of them; they are given feedback about the quality of their work and what they can do to make it better; they are given advice about how to go about making improvements; they are involved in deciding what needs to be done next; and they know who can give them help if they need it. Associated practices are, for example, sharing learning intentions and success criteria, self- and peer-assessment, improved questioning and feedback (Black and Wiliam, 1998).

Given the prevalence of formative assessment in school assessment policies and practices, such as those of: Scotland, England, Australia, Canada, Ireland, Israel, New Zealand, Norway and the United States (Birenbaum et al., 2015), and the reported positive outcomes for pupil learning (e.g. Black and Wiliam, 2001; Harlen, 2005; OECD, 2008), it may be suggested that this could be reflected in the ways in which beginning teachers are supported in their professional learning. Complete Task 9.3 and reflect on how you use formative assessment in school and the implications of this for your role as a mentor.

Task 9.3 Reflecting on experiences of using formative assessment with school pupils

- What practices have you used?
- Are there any practices you would consider useful within the mentoring process?
- Which practices and why?

Case study 9.1 is from a project that was a small-scale empirical research study from Scotland (Mackie, 2020), aimed at investigating mentors' and mentees' perceptions of the use of formative assessment principles and practices to support professional learning within the mentoring process. A selection of class teacher mentor and student teacher views are presented (Mackie, 2020). Findings suggest that formative assessment was part of the mentoring process but not explicitly used, as it is with school pupils. Some key elements were constructive dialogue, self-evaluation and quality questioning. These are reflective of key practices in seminal formative assessment research (Black and Wiliam, 1998). In this respect, mentors and mentees may be engaging more with formative assessment within the mentoring process than they are explicitly able to articulate.

Case study 9.1 Constructive dialogue between Abigail (beginning teacher), and Anna and Diane (mentors)

Anna

I think I used formative assessment not as formally as I would with the children ... I think quality feedback would be a mixture ... Probably more heavy on the positive comments and maybe just one or two areas to develop. I think too many developmental points would not be good for ... confidence.

Abigail

She would tell me things that I have done well, as well as things that she felt that I need to improve on. It is always good to start on a positive, either that or end on a positive to make you feel a bit better.

Identifying next steps for mentee learning was also part of the discussion.

Diane

We didn't call it two stars and wish but I think ... these are your strengths and here are your things that maybe next time, look at building on ... your areas for development ... I think that's just a very natural way of how things work in schools now.

Constructive dialogue

Constructive dialogue was apparent in that mentors and mentees consistently discussed how lessons had gone in terms of mentee strengths and development points. The dialogue in Case study 9.1 may be interpreted as constructive in that discussions were concerned with both successful elements of mentees' lessons, areas for development and consideration of next steps in learning (Crasborn et al., 2011). This accords with other studies where both praise and criticism were elements of mentor feedback in order to progress learning (Hennison et al., 2008; Hoffman, et al., 2015). Identification of next steps for beginning teacher learning is important as learners are more likely to be motivated to engage in future learning opportunities (Black, 2007) when they have clear goals to pursue and know who can help them in pursuit of these (Black and Wiliam, 1998). These elements accord with the principles of formative assessment, namely that learners learn more effectively when they are given feedback about the quality of their work, what they can do to make it better and advice about how to make such improvements (Black and Wiliam, 1998). Now complete Task 9.4, which requires you to reflect on the feedback you currently provide for beginning teachers.

Table 9.1 Examples of feedback offered to beginning teachers

Relevant competency standard(s)	*Mentee strengths*	*Mentee areas for development*	*Mentee next steps*	*Mentor reflections*

Task 9.4 How are you currently feeding back?

- Using Table 9.1, write down in each column of the table examples of feedback you have offered beginning teachers.
- Consider the ways in which they are constructive and any amendments based on reflections about the knowledge, understanding and skills required of an effective mentor.

Self-evaluation

Mentees reported that self-evaluation independently and in dialogue with mentors was helpful in making them think constructively about their practice. Mentors also talked about their role in encouraging mentees to engage in self-evaluation, as illustrated in Case study 9.2.

Case study 9.2 Self-evaluation between Abigail (beginning teacher), and Anna and Diane (mentors)

Anna

> We talked about ... what did we think went well, what did you think went well, what did I think went well? ... and what one thing or two things we could maybe improve in the next lesson ... And just trying to help her evaluate well so that she could then self-evaluate and work out herself where to move on to ... Once she kind of identified things we would talk about whether that would be a good strategy to use or not or how things might develop.

Both mentors and mentees viewed mentees as taking responsibility for their own learning through factors such as making decisions about how to improve their practice by thinking for themselves as well as observing and having discussions with their mentor.

Diane

> Deciding what the next steps were ... I think it gave her ownership ... it made her think about, she was reflecting critically on what she had done. It's what we expect

children to do ... as we are learning ... I think she needed to understand ... where the slight issues were so that she could then build on them.

Abigail

We are always encouraging pupils to take responsibility for their own learning and managing their next steps. I think it is important to have that input from somebody else but you need to identify where you want to go next, there is no point in someone just telling you, 'This is where I think you should be going' if you don't agree. I think it is important that a lot of it comes from yourself because it is where you want to be as a teacher, where you want to progress to.

Teacher self-evaluation is reflective of the formative assessment practice of pupil self-assessment and related principles that learners learn best if they understand clearly what they are trying to learn and what is expected of them, and they are involved in deciding the next steps in their learning. The ability to assess work in relation to learning goals is essential to learning with respect to making meaning from tasks and developing metacognitive capacities (Wiliam, 2014).

The importance of taking responsibility for learning in respect of promoting engagement and independent thinking is facilitated by mentors adopting roles such as quality questioning and encouraging self-evaluation. These are indicative of more interactive, non-directive methods where the focus is on facilitating beginning teachers' understanding using a variety of educative strategies (Young et al., 2005). This can be more or less challenging for teachers, depending on their philosophies of teaching (Hoffman et al., 2015). Teachers who are more constructivist in approach are more likely to use such methods in order to encourage the mentee to construct and co-construct learning. This construction can assist in learners taking responsibility for their own learning through the development of self-regulatory capacity (Carnell, MacDonald and Askew, 2006). In this context, formative assessment is significant through its advocacy of learner involvement (OECD, 2008) within a collaborative environment (Nicol and Macfarlane-Dick, 2006) and the promotion of self-determined motivation, which relies on understanding why success has been achieved and knowing about capacity to learn (HMIe, 2008, 2011). Having a mentor is therefore essential where self-regulation develops through processes such as quality feedback (Higgins, Hartley and Skelton, 2001), which includes the use of self-evaluation and effective questioning, as apparent in this study.

Quality questioning

Beginning teachers talked about the importance of questioning - both being asked questions and asking questions themselves - as part of constructive dialogue, as illustrated in Case study 9.3.

Case study 9.3 Quality questioning between Abigail and Evelyn (beginning teachers) and Anne (mentor)

Abigail

She questioned ... how she thought my lesson went ... You know, is there anything I could improve on. I suppose she questioned me so that I would think about my practice.

Both the mentor's and the beginning teacher's descriptions of the questions posed to the beginning teacher were mainly literal 'what' and 'how' questions.

Anne

I'd ask her how do you think that went? What do you think you did well? What do you think the children enjoyed and is there anything that you feel you could improve for your next lesson? These are the main questions I would ask.

Evelyn

So there was an awful lot of 'Hmmm, it was okay ... but how would you have made that better ... What could you have done? What could you have left out? You know, what other tools were available?'

Quality questioning is a key component of interactive formative assessment practices (Black and Wiliam, 2009). Its aim is to foster dialogue in order to encourage learners to think for themselves and in order that teachers can elicit the required information (Black, 2003) using different kinds of open questions, ranging from simple literal questions based on fact-finding to more complex inferential questions such as those concerned with more complicated ideas and reasoning (Brown and Wragg, 1993).

The prevalence of literal questions evident in this case study may be a barrier to the use of formative assessment. It could be suggested that they are reflective of form-focused understandings, where formative assessment is described through classroom practices, thereby understanding may be viewed as based on pedagogical experience ('form') compared with the specific principles articulated in key research focusing on cognitive, situative and metacognitive elements of promoting learning (Black and Wiliam, 1998, 2009). These form-focused understandings are documented (Cowan, 2009; Hayward and Spencer, 2010; Marshall and Drummond, 2006) and interpreted as teachers' lack of depth of understanding of key principles, resulting in surface level enactment. This is indicative of an uncritical, technicist (Orland-Barack and Yinon, 2007) approach to learning and teaching (Hobson, 2003). This technicist perspective may be elucidated by acknowledging the current education context with its many accountability-focused demands and external influences (Peters and Pearce, 2012). It may be suggested that these demands, pervasive managerial agendas and inherent technicist views of teaching, focused on the most efficient way to meet narrow product-driven goals, are not conducive to the time required to engage with more understanding-oriented approaches to teaching. However, it may also be argued that this kind of engagement with formative assessment is challenging for teachers, as it involves adopting new strategies (Black and Wiliam, 2009) that do not always align with their existing beliefs about teaching and learning (Carnell, MacDonald and Askew, 2006).

Having read the section on questioning, complete Task 9.5, which asks you to consider how you are currently using questioning in your mentoring.

Task 9.5 Use of questioning

- Why is the use of questioning important?
- What types of questions could you use to develop understanding?
- What types of questions could you use that would encourage a beginning teacher to think independently about their practice and find answers to their questions?

Formative and summative assessment as a connected process

Within the context of teaching competency frameworks, the data suggest that participants viewed formative and summative assessment as connected processes. Mentors viewed them as linked, in that the end-of-placement summative assessment report was seen as an accumulation of formative assessment dialogue. In this respect, the formative dialogue undertaken informed the summative report, as illustrated in Case study 9.4.

Case study 9.4 Formative and summative assessment as a connected process

Claire

> There's not gonna be anything in the summative assessment that she doesn't already know about ... because we've talked about things on a daily basis ... you've discussed things and you've given them feedback already. So they probably have ... a good idea of whether it's gonna be good or bad already.

Mentees further specified that this meant they were not worried about the contents of the summative report because discussions about their teaching practice had been ongoing.

Evelyn

> I would have been shocked if I'd failed due to the conversations I have with her ... If I'd got to the end and she said there's something drastically wrong with my practice I'd have been devastated because I wouldn't have seen it coming ... It [the formative dialogue] gave me reassurance.

This was not the case for one mentee, Chloe, who maintained that she felt she received little feedback. This made her concerned about the final summative report.

Chloe

I just got no feedback whatsoever on ... anything ... I got my report at the end which I was terrified to get because ... from the feedback that you're getting throughout your placement, how you're doing, I had no idea whatsoever.

Participants' views of formative and summative assessment as connected processes are in opposition to traditional perceptions, where they are placed in a duality with summative assessment based in positivist conceptions of knowledge and thereby aligned with the quantitative measurement of defined criteria, which are used as a comparative measure against wider attainment expectations (Sach, 2015). In contrast, formative assessment with its basis in constructivism (HMIe, 2011) is an integral, dialogic part of daily learning and teaching focusing on knowledge constructed by individuals and in collaboration with others (Serafini, 2001) to foster appropriate decisions about progression in learning (Black and Wiliam, 2009). In this respect, it may be viewed as valid in its provision of substantive evidence across more variety of areas than is typically encompassed in summative assessment (Harlen, 2005); however, it can also be less reliable due to its interpretative nature (Yorke, 2003) and the influence of different contexts on perceptions of learner capabilities (Harlen, 2005).

It may be argued that formative and summative assessment can be used effectively in tandem, but the roles played by each and how they are related must be accorded due attention (Black and Wiliam, 2009). If used simultaneously, learners may not attend to the formative advice and may focus on product, which for beginning teachers refers to their concern with being 'satisfactory' on the summative assessment form rather than thinking about what they are learning. This was not the case in this study, in that the formative dialogue undertaken informed the competency standards-based summative report, so was confirmation for mentees and alleviated anxiety around the report. Harlen (2005) suggests that the use of feedback to communicate about progress in learning as well as teaching learners to self-assess in relation to assessment criteria is particularly useful in this regard. It can be argued that the combination of placement dialogue and competency standards serves the functions of both formative and summative assessment (Cheng and Tang, 2008). In addition, these formative practices have the potential to make a contribution to summative reports in that a substantial amount of information is gathered about learning and used to inform progressive next steps (Black, 2003) which helps in determining whether summative criteria have been met (Harlen, 2005). In this sense, their relationship is a complementary one rather than a duality, with their different purposes remaining distinct.

Summary

This chapter has discussed formative and summative assessment within the context of mentoring beginning teachers. It is suggested that, given the prevalence of formative assessment in school assessment policies and practices and the reported positive outcomes of it for pupil learning, this could be reflected in the ways in which student teachers are supported in their professional learning. Further, in opposition to the traditional duality, summative and formative assessment may be viewed as working together within the process of mentoring to promote mentee professional learning in an open, collaborative manner. After working through this chapter, you should be able to:

- recognise the need to understand formative and summative assessment, and the ways in which they might be relevant within the mentoring of beginning teachers
- identify key aspects of formative assessment practices that may be useful within the mentoring process
- be aware that the traditional formative/summative assessment duality may be framed as a more dynamic interaction within the mentoring process.

Further reading

Fletcher, S.J. and Mullen, C.A. (eds) (2012) *The Sage Handbook of Mentoring and Coaching in Education*, London: Sage.

Tang, S.Y.F. (2008) Issues in field experience assessment in teacher education in a standards-based context, *Journal of Education for Teaching: International research and pedagogy*, 34(1), pp. 17-32.

Tillema, H.H. & Smith, K. (2009) Assessment orientation in formative assessment of learning to teach, *Teachers and Teaching*, 15(3), pp. 391-405.

10 Supporting the wellbeing and additional needs of your mentees

Wendy E. Cobb, Bea Stevenson, Lindsay Joyce and Cornelia Lucey

Introduction

Working with beginning teachers is immensely rewarding and a real privilege. As we were writing this chapter, we reflected on the beginning teachers with whom we work who have joined the profession excited about their future role in shaping the lives of young people through their education, yet anxious about the huge challenge ahead of them. Beginning teachers who are passionate about promoting the wellbeing of children may be understandably daunted by the increasing reports from schools of the complexity of wellbeing and mental health issues among children, young people and staff (Stirling and Emery, 2015). In defining student wellbeing, the Organisation for Economic Co-operation and Development (OECD) refers to 'the psychological, cognitive, social and physical functioning and capabilities that students need to live a happy and fulfilling life' (OECD, 2017 p. 8). Findings from the 2015 international wellbeing survey highlight a clear link between the environment in which students learn and their development and life satisfaction.

> Every school has its own distinct climate and there is no universal recipe for creating a 'happy' school. But schools, together with other social institutions, can attend to children's fundamental psychological and social needs, and help students develop a sense of control over their life and resilience in the face of unfavourable situations. (OECD, 2017 p. 8)

Beginning teachers themselves may be particularly vulnerable to anxiety, stress and burnout, with estimates of 40 to 50 per cent of early career teachers in many countries leaving the profession in the first five years of teaching (Gallant and Riley, 2014). As a mentor of beginning teachers, you have an equally daunting, yet also exciting task of supporting and promoting the wellbeing of both staff and children and acting as a role model for positive emotional health. This chapter will offer thoughts and strategies for supporting both your own and your mentee's mental health and wellbeing.

Objectives

At the end of this chapter, you should be able to:

- Present a clear rationale for putting a focus on positive mental health at the heart of teaching and learning

- Understand the boundaries of your role and the importance of prioritising your own positive wellbeing
- Adopt a range of approaches to supporting and promoting the wellbeing of beginning teachers and apply these to practical mentoring tasks.

Definitions of wellbeing

Wellbeing is a complex term that has multiple different perspectives (Diener, Helliwell and Kahneman, 2010; Huppert and So, 2013; Seligman 2002, 2011). With the development of Positive Psychology, wellbeing varies from an understanding of the hedonic (perceptions of happiness in terms of pleasant/unpleasant feelings), to an understanding of the eudemonic (human flourishing) to a combination of both. All contemporary perspectives note a range of factors that enhance a person's sense of subjective and psychological wellbeing. A key factor in all models is relationships or social connectedness. An important part of your role as a mentor, then, is to enable a beginning teacher to feel connected on a social and emotional level to a trusting figure, and to the school.

The connection between individual and organisational wellbeing

The impact of an emotionally healthy school on learning and behaviour cannot be overestimated. Non-cognitive skills are associated with a range of positive outcomes for young people, including improved academic attainment (Durlak et al., 2011) and improved resilience (Luthar, 2006). Promoting emotional health in schools for staff, students, parents and the wider community has three key benefits:

1. improving wellbeing of individuals in the school community
2. preventing poor mental health
3. developing key social and emotional competencies for learning, achievement and ultimately employability.

The connection between good emotional health and strong social and emotional competencies is well researched. Goodman et al.'s (2015) review for the Early Intervention Foundation concluded that emotional health (including self-esteem, self-regulation and locus of control) at age 16 is a stronger predictor of mental health and life chances at age 30 than either demographic or socio-economic factors.

Gilbert's (2009) explanation of the emotional regulation system draws out why the 'contentment' system (which is stimulated by safe, supportive and attuned social relationships) is so key to wellbeing. Critically, this system needs to be nurtured for optimum learning at all stages of development. We can link this to Bowlby's (1969) work on attachment theory, which explains why nurturing attachment relationships continues to have significance in adulthood (Mikulincer and Shaver, 2007). Ultimately, the mentor-mentee relationship has the potential to profoundly impact the mentee's capacity to replicate nurturing supportive relationships with colleagues and students.

Human beings are most effectively supported when in an emotionally healthy culture, one in which trusting relationships are built, challenges are openly and honestly worked through in partnership and individuals feel valued and supported to develop in their roles. It is therefore important to consider the wider context within which you and your and mentee work together.

Research shows that school culture influences the resilience of teachers in their early careers. Cultures characterised by isolation and threats to self-esteem and self-efficacy result in feelings of disempowerment, whereas those characterised by an ethos of trust and respect, supportive leadership, teacher autonomy and ongoing support lead to increased self-worth and empowerment (Johnson et al., 2014). Resilience, as Day et al. (2011, p. 3) point out, 'is more than an individual trait. It is a capacity which arises through interactions between people within organisational contexts.'

School senior leadership teams should therefore explicitly plan for a whole-school approach to emotional health and wellbeing, one that genuinely holds the wellbeing of the entire school community at its forefront. This school culture and ethos impact teacher wellbeing, teaching practice (including classroom management strategies), the teacher-pupil relationship and the culture within individual classrooms, all of which mediate a range of pupil wellbeing and academic outcomes (Jennings and Greenberg, 2009). Public Health England (2015, p. 2) states that the 'physical, social and emotional environment in which staff and students spend a high proportion of every week day has been shown to affect their physical, emotional and mental health and wellbeing, as well as impacting on attainment'.

In 2017, the British Prime Minister commissioned a review into mental health at work in the United Kingdom. The report authors, Stevenson and Farmer (2017, p.6), set out a key goal for the next ten years that, 'Every one of us will have the knowledge, tools and confidence, to understand and look after our own mental health and the mental health of those around us.' The working environment plays a key role in developing these tools, for both the individual and the organisation or school. Cultivating good emotional health is achieved through both targeted skill development at an individual level and embedding supportive practices throughout the culture and daily operations of a workplace (Tanner, Yeo and McManus, 2018). Factors to consider include the ability to maintain a healthy work-life balance, relationships with colleagues, workplace culture and organisational leadership. Therefore, before we consider opportunities for promoting the wellbeing of both yourself and your mentee, we look first at some practical examples of the working conditions and context in which your mentoring relationship is built. Now complete Task 10.1 and reflect on the current approaches to emotional health and wellbeing in your context.

Task 10.1 Emotional health and wellbeing

- Review the context in which your school's professional development programme operates compared with the practical recommendations in Table 10.1 for a whole-school approach to emotional health and wellbeing.
- Try to include your school's leadership team in this task, or alternatively report your findings to them.

Table 10.1 Template for whole-school approach to emotional health and wellbeing

Key questions	*Useful links*	*Reflections/ actions to take*
Aspect 1: Leadership commitment		
Are those on the senior leadership team committed to a whole-school approach to supporting positive mental health? *Note: Public Health England (2015) identifies seven key principles of adopting a whole-school approach, all of which are underpinned by the eighth principle - effective leadership and management.*	www.gov.uk > government > publications > promoting children and young people's emotional health and wellbeing (Public Health England, 2015)	
Are all members of the school community involved in modelling and supporting emotional wellbeing? Do *all staff*, including senior leadership, receive training and CPD in supporting their own and pupils' emotional health? Is there a culture of ongoing monitoring and reflection for emotional health? Are regular opportunities planned to draw on staff, parent and pupil voice to consider the thoughts and feelings of the wider community? *Note: Governing bodies and trustees also play a significant role in supporting the emotional health of a school.*	youngminds.org.uk > 360° Schools' Community (Young Minds, 2018) place2be.org.uk the-people-project.com familylinks.org.uk > Emotional Health at School (Family Links, 2018) thriveapproach.com mentallyhealthyschools. org.uk/whole-school-approach/leadership-and-improvement/governors/	
Aspect 2: Creating an emotionally healthy environment		
Do school-wide policies and practices support emotional health? Do behaviour policies, anti-bullying policies, teaching and learning approaches, etc. promote emotional health and support the development of social and emotional competencies? Are policies and practices regularly monitored and reviewed to ensure they are conducive to positive wellbeing, for both pupils and staff?	National Children's Bureau, 'A whole school framework for emotional wellbeing and mental health' (Stirling and Emery, 2015)	
Does the school have a named set of values in place to support an emotionally healthy culture? Are staff (including leadership) clear about the roles they play in creating an emotionally healthy culture and working as part of an emotionally healthy team?	valuesbasededucation.com	
Are there opportunities for all members of the school community to express their feelings and opinions and contribute to decision-making processes?	nasuwt.org.uk > student voice (NASUWT, 2018)	
Are emotionally healthy practices embedded within the culture and values of the organisation? Do day-to-day interactions support healthy self-beliefs and empower others? Are interactions founded on building positive relationships?	See CPD organisations suggested above	

(continued)

Table 10.1 (Cont.)

Key questions	*Useful links*	*Reflections/ actions to take*
Aspect 3: Skill development of staff, parents and pupils		
Explicit training and skill development: Is provision in place for all staff including leadership to develop each of the emotional health assets and cultivate their intra and interpersonal skills? *Note: This could be through explicit training or through reflection during supervision and target setting during performance reviews.*	See CPD organisations suggested above	
Ensuring meaningful work: • Do all staff have work which is meaningful and allows opportunities for • learning and development; • fostering positive self-beliefs; • choice and autonomy; • encouraging self-agency? *Note: All staff should have 'good work' (Stevenson and Farmer, 2017 p. 6) that supports the development of emotional health.*	See more info on self-determination theory	
Work effectively with parents: Does the school work in partnership with parents to promote emotional health? *Note: The National Institute for Health and Care Excellence (NICE, 2018) advocates working in partnership with parents to promote emotional health, including running parenting programmes within schools. This has the additional benefit of increasing parental engagement.*	peeple.org.uk familylinks.org.uk	
Use an explicit social and emotional curriculum, alongside embedding skill development across the curriculum: Do pupils receive explicit support to develop their social and emotional skills through discrete lessons using a relevant curriculum? Is social and emotional skill development embedded within *all lessons* across the curriculum, particularly those with applicable lesson content or delivery methods - that is, group-based tasks?	coramlifeeducation.org.uk/scarf/ circle-time.co.uk familylinks.org.uk > circle time pshe-association.org.uk jigsawpshe.com	

'Put on your own oxygen mask first': Looking after your own wellbeing

Beginning teachers usually care passionately about the wellbeing of their pupils and will often put the needs of children above their own. As a mentor, you are also a wellbeing role model, and you may feel daunted in your ability to embody the skills of an effective and supportive mentor. Sometimes we talk to school staff, who are worried that they need specialist 'mental health' training to support the emotional wellbeing of mentees. It is worth noting here we can provide a foundational level of wellbeing support through our skills of attunement and compassion. As a mentor, you can use skills like rapport-building, deep listening and wider empathy skills to enhance your mentee's wellbeing. You are also able to model your own methods and time-built strategies that you have developed to support your own wellbeing.

It is important to recognise your own ongoing needs and wellbeing. As educational professionals and mentors it can be all too easy to seek to support somebody else's needs without first recognising your own. Therefore, it is critical to recognise what is within your capacity and what is not, and to be aware of and comfortable in reaching out for wider support mechanisms if the need arises. In calmly and proactively seeking additional support when you need it, you are again modelling an adaptive strategy for protecting wellbeing to your mentee. Use Task 10.2 to consider how you maintain your own emotional health.

Task 10.2 Supporting your own emotional health

Using the prompts in Table 10.2, reflect on what you do on a day-to-day level to support your own emotional health. You may find this useful to share with colleagues or others who may also be mentoring in your school.

Having reflected on your own approaches, use the prompts with your mentees, recording their responses.

The categories within Table 10.2 are connected to promoting better psychological wellbeing. The questions are as important as the discussion around them. Engaging with these questions can help the mentor and mentee understand each other better, and also consider personal and bespoke ways to support each other.

Table 10.2 Template for prompts to promote better psychological wellbeing

Managing your emotions
• Do you have a strategy for calming down if you feel stressed or panicky (e.g. a breathing exercise)? • Are there ways that you can lift your spirits if you are feeling unhappy or low (e.g. listening to a certain song or reading a particular poem)? • How do you handle situations that make you feel angry? • How easy do you find it to think clearly and make decisions? **Something to try** • Take time out to reflect on your successes, however small.
Your relationships • Do you consider yourself to be open and honest with your friends and colleagues? • Do you think you express yourself well? If not, why not? • Do you make time to listen to those you are close to? • How do you give or receive feedback that is constructive or supportive? • How do you show compassion for others? • How often do you experience or recognise a quality connection with a friend, family member or colleague?

(*continued*)

Table 10.2 (Cont.)

Managing your emotions
Something to try • Show gratitude by giving thanks to someone for a helpful act.
Your boundaries • Do you think you manage your time well? • Do you let others know when you think you may be saying 'yes' when you should be saying 'no'? • How successfully do you balance work and leisure? • If you feel exhausted, do you give yourself permission to stop? • Do you feel that you can let a colleague know if you are feeling overwhelmed?
Something to try Self-compassion involves 'treating yourself the way you would treat a friend who is having a hard time' (Neff and Germer, 2018 p. 9). • Notice when you are being critical of yourself or suffering. • Say or do something to be kind to yourself. Do any of the following expressions work for you? - I am having a hard time right now - Let me be strong - May I be kind to myself in this moment - I allow myself to take a break and do something I enjoy
Living your values • Do you ever reflect on your personal values? • If so, how do they connect to your work?
Something to try Personal values reflection activity (personal values card sort resources are freely available on the web, see Table 10.1). • Pick your top 5 most important values and explain why they are your top 5. • How do these values relate to your work?
Positive emotions • How often do you experience/savour: - gratitude - humour - joy - curiosity?
Something to try • Think about opportunities to experience these emotions more often. • Schedule a time to intentionally experience these emotions by yourself, with a colleague or with a friend.

Practical approaches to supporting beginning teachers' wellbeing

Beginning teachers or those in the early stage of their career lack professional confidence and operate in a 'survival' mode. They may feel that teaching is overwhelming, classroom management too challenging and organisational skills difficult to develop (Bressman, Winter and Efron, 2018). However, research undertaken by Teach First in the United Kingdom (Fletcher-Wood, 2015) found that teachers who had thrived in particularly challenging schools emphasised the importance of emotional support. Case study 10.1 provides a brief example.

Case study 10.1 The importance of emotional support

'We had a relationship that wasn't just meeting once a week,' Liza said of her mentor. 'We spoke every day. I think the relationship we formed was both professional and friendly and I've been able to talk to her both about school and how school is affecting my life, and that was really big for me.'

Having read Case study 10.1, complete Task 10.3, which asks you to consider the mentoring relationships you form.

Task 10.3 What type of relationship?

How would you describe the relationships you form with your mentees?

Socratic questioning method and emotional health

Active listening approaches, such as coaching with Socratic questions, can support mentees to become more self-aware, encourage reflection and improve problem-solving thinking (Neenan, 2009). Lawrence (2014) argues that the Socratic method, which dates back to the era of the Greek Philosopher Socrates, is the 'key to effective mentoring'. The method involves asking and answering questions aimed at stimulating critical thinking, illuminating ideas and uncover underlying presumptions. Table 10.3 provides some examples of Socratic questions that mentors might use for different purposes.

Case study 10.2 is an example of a role-play dialogue used as a discussion point during primary mentor development training. Maya is a beginning teacher who is usually enthusiastic about teaching but has recently had a difficult time with her class and is feeling quite

Table 10.3 Socratic questions

1. Clarification	'What do you mean by ...?' 'Can you give an example?'
2. Challenging assumptions	'Is this always the case?' 'Why do you think that assumption applies here?
3. Probing reasons/evidence	'How do you know that?' 'Why do you say that?'
4. Alternative viewpoints/perspectives	'Are there alternative ways of looking at this?' 'Did anyone see this another way?'
5. Implications/consequences	'What would happen if...?' 'How would...affect...?'
6. Questioning the question	'Why do you think that I asked that question?' 'Which question was the most important for you?'

negative. She has a good relationship with her mentor, who has arranged a meeting with her. The mentor uses Socratic questions to help Maya unpick and reframe what has been happening.

Case study 10.2 Role-play dialogue

Mentor: So how are things going, Maya?

Maya: I'm a complete failure. I don't have what it takes to be a teacher.

Mentor: You look really fed up when you say that. Do you feel fed up?

Maya: Yes. I'm just rubbish and exhausted.

Mentor: What do you mean when you say, 'I'm just rubbish'?

Maya: I've completely messed up in the classroom. I haven't done anything right.

Mentor: Has something happened to lead you to this conclusion or have you felt this way for a long time?

Maya: I think I see myself more clearly now.

Mentor: So this is a change in your thinking?

Maya: Yes. Erin and I went to that NQT [Newly Qualified Teacher] conference last week and got chatting. She looked so happy and had great stories about her class. And all I could think about was the chaos in my classroom in the afternoons and how much Erin's children seem to like her. And it's all my fault because I'm just rubbish at teaching. If the children were in Erin's class they'd be better off.

Mentor: And so, because you care about your children, you then decided that you've let them down.

Maya: That's right.

Mentor: You also indicated this was a change in your thinking. How did you think about yourself as a teacher in the past?

Maya: I guess I used to think I was okay because I try to really listen to the children and be the best teacher that I can be. But I see now that trying isn't enough.

Mentor: I'm not sure I understand. Why is trying not enough?

Maya: Because no matter how hard I try, they still are not doing as well, or seem to be as happy as they would be with another teacher.

Mentor: Is that what they say to you?

Maya: No. But I can see how well children are learning in other classes and how happy they seem to be.

Mentor: And you'd like your class to be happier and to achieve more?

Maya: Yes.

Mentor: What things would you do differently if you weren't feeling so miserable and felt more confident about your abilities as a teacher?

Maya: I think I'd be a lot calmer and would smile a lot more and be much more positive with the children - give them praise for the things they do well more often, like Erin does.

Mentor: Are these things you could do even when you're tired and frustrated?

Maya: Well, yes, I think I could try.

Mentor: Would that feel better to you - trying some new positive approaches rather than feeling cross and upset with the class?

Maya: Yes. I think it would. But I'm not sure it would be enough if I'm still as tired and exhausted as I feel now. I'm just not sure that I have got what it takes.

Mentor: How could you find that out?

Maya: I guess I could try it for a week or so.

Mentor: And how will you evaluate whether these changes are making your children feel happier and learning more?

Maya: I could try using that emotions chart we discussed in the staff meeting last month and Erin mentioned a rewards scheme she uses with her class. Perhaps if they were earning rewards for doing well I would know things were going better in class.

Mentor: Are you feeling any better now that we have talked this through?

Maya: Well, I guess yes, a bit ... at least I've got something I can try and just talking has made me think more clearly about things.

Mentor: Okay, so shall we make a time to check in next week to see how things are going?

Having read the role-play dialogue, Task 10.4 asks you to consider the use of Socratic questioning in practice.

Task 10.4 Applying Socratic questioning

- Do any of the mentor's questions from Case study 10.2 fit the six categories of Socratic questioning in the table above?
- Think of a mentee you know who has presented negative thoughts. Could coaching with Socratic questions have helped the mentee to see things more positively?
- What questions might you ask the mentee?

How relationships between mentors and mentees can be built on a foundation of emotional health through the Family Links four constructs

The skills of emotional health, as shown in the foundational block in Figure 10.1, including self-agency, beliefs about others, self-awareness, social awareness, self-regulation and relationship skills, can be supported and developed for both the mentor and mentee through four key areas:

- self-awareness
- appropriate expectations

- empathy
- positive discipline.

For example, listening and Socratic questioning draw on the ability to be truly *empathic*. An empathic response contributes to positive self-belief and makes our relationships stronger.

Equally, as a mentor you may draw frequently on concepts of appropriate expectations with a beginning teacher, checking that your expectations of the beginning teacher are appropriate (see Sofia's experience of high expectations in Case study 10.3) and that the beginning teacher has appropriate self-expectations. If you expect too much, it can lead to frustration and feelings of inadequacy; if you expect too little, it can lead to a feeling of disempowerment and a tendency to give up.

Earlier in the chapter, the importance of being aware and taking care of your own needs - having a good level of self-awareness - was emphasised. This supports us to be more nurturing to others and contributes to our social awareness - being conscious of the effect of our behaviour on others. Finally, Family Links supports individuals - staff, parents and children - to find the balance of responding positively to positive behaviour while ensuring clear boundaries. This applies as much to colleague interactions as it does to working with children and young people. We can also be aware of the personal power we have to make choices and guide our own decision-making.

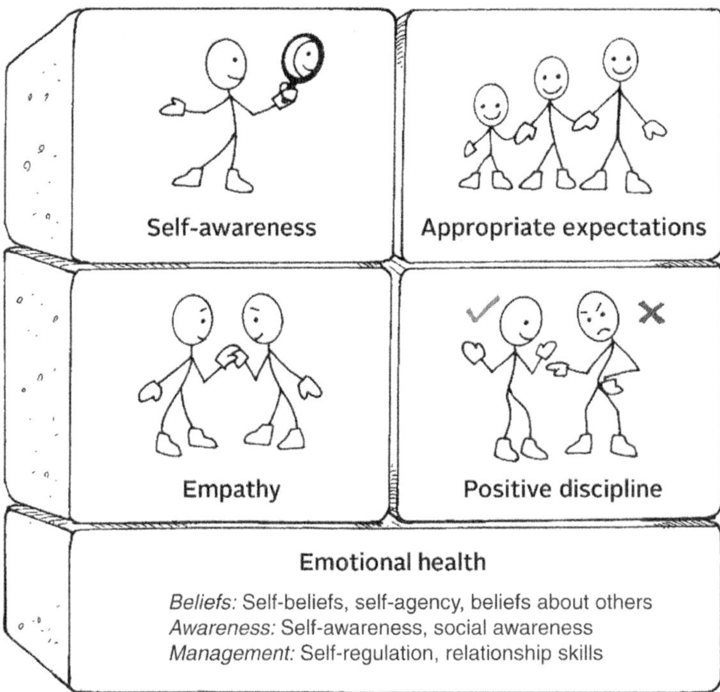

Figure 10.1 Emotional health and the four constructs
Source: © Family Links: The Centre for Emotional Health (2018), reproduced with permission.

Case studies 10.3 and 10.4 provide examples of what beginning teachers in diverse contexts have shared with us about helpful and unhelpful mentoring. We have fictionalised the case studies, although the content of each is drawn from real-life examples taken from our various experiences. In our work in schools, we observe that the mentoring relationship is often one of the critical protective factors for trainee teacher wellbeing. Where that relationship has broken down, or the mentor does not apply compassion and attunement to their role, it is often one of the most significant predictors of the participant withdrawing from the training programme. As you read through the case studies, complete Task 10.5, which encourages you to reflect on the beginning teacher's wellbeing.

Task 10.5 Analysing relationships

- How would you describe the relationship between the mentor and mentee in each case study?
- To what extent are the mentee's needs recognised and supported?
- In what way is the mentee empowered/disempowered in each school setting?
- Are there any implications for your own practice from developing positive relationships with your mentees to support both the mentees' wellbeing and your own?

Case study 10.3 Sofia's story

Sofia studied on a year-long postgraduate teacher training course, which included three placements at two different English primary schools. She describes her experience of being mentored at each school in these terms.

> My mentor at my main school, where I carried out my first and last placement, was really helpful and supportive. I was very anxious at the beginning, but the induction was brilliant. I was introduced to parents early on, so I felt like the children's teacher, not a TA, which was a bit scary, but I felt very much part of the team. My mentor and class teacher eased me into the role gradually. They helped me to focus on one thing at a time and we had brilliant debriefing sessions, where we unpicked why things went well or why children had behaved in certain ways.
>
> My second school was entirely different. I felt that so much was expected of me from day one, which was really hard as I didn't know the children or the school policies, even though I had done my best to prepare fully before I arrived. My mentor always seemed stressed and put so much pressure on me to perform. The school was expecting an Ofsted [Office for Standards in Education, Children's Services and Skills] inspection; everyone was so busy and very few teachers went into the staffroom at lunchtime. It was even harder because during the placement we had a flood in our flat and I had to move out and live with friends for a while so travelling

> to school was a real challenge. My mentor knew that, but she never eased up the pressure. I made so many mistakes and began to think I was a rubbish teacher. I was close to failing the placement and I think I would have quit the course if I hadn't had such a great initial experience at the other school. I went home and cried most evenings. It was a horrible time.

Case study 10.4 Kieran's story

Kieran trained on an undergraduate course over three years. He had placements in three schools, each with a different mentor.

> My first placement was in a fairly small primary school. I really enjoyed that school. I got to know the children, parents and staff really well. My mentor found out that I was keen on sports and encouraged me to get involved in lunchtime and after-school clubs. That gave me a lot of confidence. I was struggling initially to get to grips with subject knowledge in maths and felt like giving up. I'd had some bad experiences of maths at school and my link tutor knew that I had been missing some of the university sessions through anxiety. My mentor organised support with the maths coordinator and he encouraged me to build on my strengths. Together, we set up and ran an intervention group combining maths and football. My link tutor organised for me to share what we had been doing with my peers at the university. That placement was transformational. I don't think I would have completed my course without the support of that first school.

Summary

Wellbeing is a complex term with multiple perspectives. A key factor of all models is relationships or social connectedness. Your role as a mentor includes enabling a beginning teacher to feel connected on a social and emotional level to a trusting figure and to the school. Research shows that school culture influences the resilience of teachers in their early career. It is important to consider the wider context within which you and your mentee work together. Factors to consider include the ability to maintain a healthy work–life balance, relationships with colleagues, workplace culture and organisational leadership. Remember to 'put on your own oxygen mask first': it is important to prioritise looking after your own wellbeing. Active listening approaches, such as coaching with Socratic questions, can support mentees to become more self-aware, encourage reflection and improve problem-solving thinking. Positive relationships between mentors and mentees are built on a foundation of emotional health through the development of skills, which include self-agency, beliefs about others, self-awareness, social awareness, self-regulation and relationship skills. Empathic responses contribute to positive self-belief and make our relationships stronger. The mentor-mentee relationship is one of the critical protective factors for beginning teacher wellbeing.

Further reading

Boing, Boing (2018) *Resilience Framework (Adults)*, www.boingboing.org.uk

Family Links (2015) *The Teaching Puzzle: Your Guide to Social and Emotional Learning*, Oxford: Family Links.

Headspace (2018) Headspace app, www.headspace.com

11 Supporting resilience in practice: Mentoring to enable others to 'thrive' in teaching

d'Reen Struthers

> My mentor really helped me understand my own resilience and this helped sustain my commitment to the profession. Without his encouragement to see things from a different perspective and to understand there were things I could control about the job, I wouldn't still be here. He also gave me permission to find pleasure again in asking questions and exploring research. (Beginning Teacher, 2017, SW London)

Introduction

The preamble to the National Standards for School-based initial teacher training (ITT) mentors (Teaching Schools Council, 2016, p. 11) in England states:

> An effective mentor sets high expectations for pupil achievement, models high-quality teaching, and acts as an ambassador for the profession. ITT providers that have invested in effective mentoring will support trainees to become high-quality teachers and build their resilience so that they are more likely to remain in teaching once their initial training is complete.

This statement suggests that besides supporting beginning teachers in the classroom, your role as a mentor is linked to supporting a developing professional to be resilient and more likely to remain in teaching. This might seem like a tall order, but help is at hand. This chapter introduces the concept of resilience and looks at how you as a mentor can assist a beginning teacher to develop strong attitudes about themselves. This will enable them to feel sufficiently robust within themselves, and to tackle challenging events and behaviours encountered in the teaching profession. Coincidentally, the chapter also introduces ideas that will support you as a teacher in a school setting, with responsibilities as a mentor/coach for beginning teachers. Implicit in the chapter is the belief that what makes a mentor significant to a beginning teacher is the personalised professional development that can be offered, which nurtures and stretches, is non-directive yet can also be direct.

Various perspectives of mentoring are covered in this book. Some represent mentoring as a focus on easing a new teacher's entry into teaching and helping with immediate questions and uncertainties that inevitably arise when a teacher enters the classroom for the first time. Others link to a vision of good teaching and a developmental view of learning to teach. Such mentoring still responds to new teachers' present needs while helping them to interpret what their students say and do and to figure out how to move their learning forward. This is called 'educative' mentoring to distinguish it from technical advice and emotional support, and to suggest that mentoring can be a form of individualised professional development (Langdon and Ward, 2015; Lofthouse, 2018). It is the stance adopted in chapter.

The idea of educative mentoring builds on Dewey's (1938) concept of educative experiences, which are experiences that promote rather than retard future growth and lead to richer subsequent experiences. According to Dewey, the educator (or, in this case, the mentor) is responsible for arranging the physical and social conditions so that learners (beginning teachers) have growth-producing experiences.

> Every experience is a moving force. Its value can be judged only on the ground of what it moves toward and into ... It is the business of the educator to see in what direction an experience is heading ... so as to judge and direct it' (Dewey, 1938, p. 39)

The resources you, as a mentor, need to 'judge and direct' professional learning for others are also necessary for your own professional learning. Such a 'stance' will be shown to support both the resilient professional practitioner and the socio-cultural context in which they work. You and the beginning teacher are then more likely to be able to 'thrive' in the school context, rather than merely coping with the demands experienced in the current school system (Struthers, 2018). With such personal resources and attitudes, you and the beginning teacher will be agentic contributors and better able to maintain mental control over yourselves when faced with challenges. This chapter therefore invites you to actively engage with the ideas and activities offered with a view to being able to model resilient approaches to professional action and reaction.

Objectives

At the end of this chapter, you should be able to:

- Recognise a variety of ways that reflexive practices can support both you and the beginning teacher to develop a resilient stance
- Support beginning teachers to develop their own teacher agency by using specific strategies to find balance and achievement in the face of adversity
- Develop your own skills as a mentor and professional teacher to support a 'thriving' community of practice in your school context.

Before reading the chapter, you are invited to answer a brief Resilience Assessment Questionnaire (Task 11.1 and Table 11.1) to consider your current level of resilience. This will locate you in the context of beginning to contemplate the nature of resilience.

Task 11.1 How resilient am I?

Using Table 11.1, respond to the statements by entering the relevant number in the score column:

1 = No, never through to 5 = Yes, always

Table 11.1 Resilience level

Statement	*1*	*2*	*3*	*4*	*5*	*Score column*
I usually know how others perceive me.						
I am determined to achieve my lifetime ambitions.						
I can see my future clearly.						
I normally feel comfortable in new situations.						
I plan my next day in advance.						
I enjoy the challenge of unravelling puzzles and solving problems.						
In general, I like people.						
My most important relationships are my strongest.						

Any score of 3 and below indicates a need to strengthen this element of personal resilience.

Source: Mowbray (2012).

Now complete Task 11.2 and reflect upon your resilience score.

Task 11.2 Reflecting on my resilience

- What are the features in your own life to date that have influenced your score?
- Make a list - you will return to this list later in the chapter.

What is resilience?

Resilience is the capacity to maintain personal control and robust attitudes in the face of challenging events and behaviours. It is that capacity to face up to challenges that may threaten us in a manner that enables us to deal with the challenge without it having a detrimental impact on us. It is about forming robust attitudes and responses to adverse events and experiences (Mowbray, 2011).

Resilience is not a skill to make you cope, but the attitude required to help you overcome adverse events. Resilience turns emotional reactions (experiences) into judgements (attitudes) about what to do when faced with something that appears to threaten us. Pemberton's (2015, p. 2) definition encompasses the reminder that when we employ resilient strategies, we are likely to also move forward in more empowered and agentic ways: "The ability to remain flexible in our thoughts, feelings and behaviours, when faced by a life disruption or extended periods of pressure, so that we emerge from difficulty stronger, wiser and more able."

If you have previously thought that resilience was a personality trait, something that was not you, this definition reminds us that it is a choice. In other words, we can all work to reframe the way we think about and respond to situations and people. However, where personality has an influence on attitudes, is in the predispositions of that person towards certain activities. People drawn to the armed services are likely to be predisposed to combat. People drawn to teaching are more likely to be predisposed towards learning and helping others develop their own learning. We are likely therefore to have a tolerance towards the 'others' we are teaching, mindful too that there are factors that can support or negate engagement in learning, often based on our own experiences.

When the socio-cultural environment in which learning takes place is difficult for our pupils, teachers are challenged to find ways to broker and differentiate the context for the 'others' - our learners. Similarly, when our working environment becomes more challenging, it is likely that our predisposition towards the 'work' of a teacher can be tested. This is borne out in media reports about how working conditions for teachers have become more and more challenging (Hazell, 2018; Sims and Allen, 2018). We know that today's learners appear more distracted, while bureaucratic demands (paperwork, assessment regimes, school leadership), curriculum delivery, parent communication and classroom management are frequently cited as events and behaviours that trigger distress and disturb the psychological wellbeing and performance of the teaching force (Geiger and Pivovarova, 2018). Thus, being able to maintain mental control in the face of potential or actual threats, and to be able to form a strategy to meet any challenges, can determine the action we eventually take when feeling under threat or stressed.

Why do we need resilience?

Resilience is normally needed when we face events that challenge us. If we have experienced an adverse event previously and overcome it without experiencing distress, then we are unlikely to regard a similar event in the future as a threat. Do you recall that first lesson observation by your university or school tutor? That anxiety about your performance and how it made you feel? You might even recall the physical reaction you had on that first formal event - yet you survived it. You have gone on to experience more observations and now most likely accept that observations of your professional practice can be 'reframed' as a form of professional development and a way to enhance and extend your 'performance'; the threat has become a stimulus for professional learning. Task 11.3 asks you to consider potential threats.

Task 11.3 Identifying potential threats

- Have you ever experienced any threats that appear in Figure 11.1?
- What specific threats and potential events are you currently facing?
- Make a list - we will return to it later in the chapter.

Looking at your list from Task 11.3, consider how your mentee might answer this same question. Ask the beginning teacher to complete the same task. Were their answers as you might have imagined? Perhaps you have both talked about such threats as the 'stresses' in the school or even more generally the stresses in teaching. Here we see a problem, as the term 'stress' is used to describe a huge variation in how people feel and react; it is individual to us all. Stress generally refers to two things: the psychological perception of pressure on the one hand, and the body's response to it on the other. Stress is at the extreme end of a

Threats

Leaders
Head teacher
Senior
Leadership
People

The
Organisation
Culture
Organisation/structure
Managerial change
Curriculum changes
Targets
OFSTED
Government expectations
'Rules'/regulations
Assessment requirements
Ambiguity of role
Targets
Values

Work
Environment
Condition of building/
classroom/staffroom
Performance orientation
Irrelevant meetings
Uncontrollable time
Excess demands
Clashing expectation
Limited collegiality
Absence of support within
the classroom
Condition of resources
Budget restrictions
Quality of IT
Work–life balance
Car parking

People
Conflict relationships
Bullying/ harassment
Discrimination
Level of pupil engagement
Interaction
Difficult parents
Poor coping
Poor performance
Job insecurity
Fear
Intimidation
Insecurity
Isolation
Boredom
Loss/bereavement
Accidents/illness

Figure 11.1 Threats in the teaching profession
Source: Adapted with permission from Mowbray (2018).

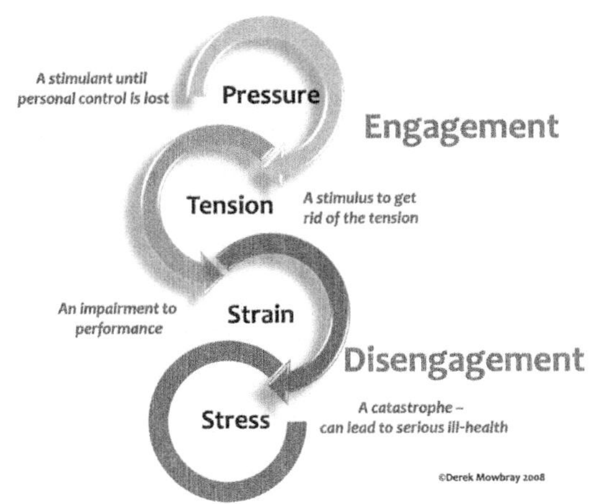

Figure 11.2 The pressure-stress continuum
Source: Mowbray (2008).

continuum where pressure (which can be good for us) is at one end and stress (which is catastrophic) is at the other. Figure 11.2 provides a more detailed overview of this.

As in other professions, pressure and tension can be strong stimulants to concentrate, but only when a person feels in control by knowing that the pressure and tension can come to an end if they take certain actions. Case study 11.1 provides an account from one student teacher who made a choice to ask for help.

Case study 11.1 Asking for help

My class has been unsettled for days, and I was very worried about this becoming a pattern. I knew I had to do something. I was close to breaking and I knew I needed help. Asking was my life saviour! My mentor suggested that I try out several changes to the organisation of the day, the groupings after lunchtime and how I deployed my Learning Support Assistant in the morning. Those suggestions changed everything.

This case study (11.1) example, could have been a story about the mentor coming to the rescue, solving the beginning teacher's problem by offering suggestions based on their own years of experience. However, it is the beginning teacher's own actions that we focus on here. They even acknowledge this themselves:'Asking was my life saviour'. Consequently, this beginning teacher changed their way of thinking about trying to appear competent and coping. Here, 'help-seeking' coined by Castro, Kelly and Shih, (2010), or the act of seeking assistance from others, became a way of self-preservation, of establishing one's own resilience.

Strain, on the other hand, is caused by our responses to ourselves, events and/or other people. For example, when the focus of our concentration is more on what others may have said or be expecting from us than our actual work with the learners, then it is our work performance that is impaired; our concentration is less, and our responses are more frayed and lacking the professional control on which we pride ourselves. When concentration gives way to total distraction, feeling completely overwhelmed by the situation and without fuel in the tank to support the everyday encounters we normally manage, then all sense of personal control and agency has been lost and physical illness is likely. Task 11.4 asks you to consider whether and when you have experienced such feelings and what strategies you undertook to cope with the situation and deal with the strain.

Task 11.4 'Help seeking'

Can you recall any times when you have felt that aspects of your work have not been in your own control?

What did you do on those occasions?

What strategies did you employ? Make a list and consider what the consequences of each may have been.

What have you said in the past to your mentee when they were feeling under pressure?

Contemplate how 'help seeking' is or could be encouraged in your school.

The process of being resilient

It has been suggested that mentoring and induction programmes might be one way to decrease the exodus of new teachers from the profession (Darling-Hammond, 2003; Farber,

2015; Geiger and Pivovarova, 2018). Such strategies attempt to either alter the negative working conditions found in school contexts or to provide additional resources for beginning teachers. However, others have noted that many teachers affected by the same conditions are not choosing to leave. Such teachers are exhibiting qualities of resilience, demonstrating the 'ability to adjust to varied situations and increase [their] competence in the face of adverse conditions' (Bobek, 2002, p. 202).

This reminds us that resilience is about the individual capacity to maintain cognitive or rational control in the face of potential or actual treats, and to then form an attitude towards the challenge that determines what action is to be taken. Personal control is heavily influenced by personal experiences combined with personal knowledge about ourselves – a metacognitive stance. Personal control is informed by:

- *Understanding self* – this refers to the *reflective sense* we make of our experiences, skills, relationships, the qualities of interaction we have with others and our general 'cultural or background' context. Understanding how these attributes inform and shape our decisions in response to our life experiences is a strong signifier of resilient ways of being.
- *Our thoughts* – how we think about events in our lives and how we manage and think about our feelings. An example is how we think about the observations our beginning teacher makes when we model practice – are we paranoid, insecure or lacking clear information about the rationale for the observations?
- *The standards or personal values that drive us* – this means our sense of ethical ways of behaving, the code of conduct by which we were brought up and/or choose to live. It also can refer to the internalisation of what it means to be a professional – for teachers in England, this is embodied in the Teacher Standards (DfE, 2011). The legal expectations as exemplified 'in loco parenthesis' are also included as well as our own personal integrity and meaning-making about being a teaching professional.
- *Emotions and the less intensive feelings* – these can boost one's attitude if they are positive at the time of the event. Such emotions include anger, fear, sadness, happiness, disgust and surprise. For example, if we lack information, we may become suspicious about the rationale and motives of the observation schedule being suggested. This suspicion can lead either to asking questions to clarify the position, or to paralysis, inaction and fear.
- *Our individual capacity* – this is our cognitive and physical ability to maintain control. It is often influenced by our self-knowledge and how we reflect on and react in situations, then the decisions we make about our physical health during these times of challenge – some may use more sleep, the gym, chocolate, food, nicotine or alcohol as supports.

These factors all add up to putting a person in a position to *evaluate* events, gain meaning from them and, from this sense-making, influence the choices made about what to do in the situation. Thus, when we evaluate an event or construct meaning about the event, we follow a process of collecting perspectives. We seek objective evidence and emotional evidence. We consult others (social proof) about what they might think and feel, all the while reviewing experiences and expectations, and determining whether the context is appropriate and whether it should be happening. We may also seek confirmation that what we are perceiving as a challenge to our sense of wellbeing is in proportion to what others might accept. This is a version of 'problem solving'. These factors work together and place us on high alert if something isn't 'quite right'.

Then comes the action we eventually take as a result of the evaluation of the event, together with a rapid assessment of the feasibility of adopting one of a choice of possible actions. Our choices could include:

- *action* - your evaluation may provide meaning and have stimulated a response, which could even be deciding not to act
- *inaction* - you may decide not to do anything, possibly stimulated by fear
- *enforced action* - coercive action, which is where we feel obliged to take action
- *learnt helplessness* - a type of inaction when we feel there is nothing we can do, so we do nothing.

As you can see, *choice* and subsequent *attitude or mindset* are dependent on your degree of *control*. Depending on how robust your self-awareness, thoughts, standards and emotions are, your sense of a degree of control can also be affected. Naturally, people who feel more in control feel more positive, and therefore are less likely to experience adverse responses to difficult events. When our attitude is positive, we usually find ways of facing up to and coping with an event with the intention of coming out of the experience stronger. We are also likely to have a more positive attitude towards similar events in the future. Task 11.5 asks you to consider how positive attitudes can be developed.

Task 11.5 'Every cloud has a silver lining'

- Have you been the one with the positive attitude to an adverse situation?
- Have you worked in contexts where maintaining a positive attitude has been difficult because of the attitudes of colleagues around you?
- What aspects of personal control have you relied on most in these situations?
- What helped your 'attitude' or mindset? How would you explain this to your mentee?
- What perceptions do you hold of your mentee's attitude?
- Are there ways in which you might respond differently?

Events or people don't disturb us; it is really our view of the event or person that does. This might come as a shock to some because it is so easy to first look externally for fault or blame. This is where reflection and reflexive practice are so valuable, not only when applied to our lesson plans and activities, but also to our own responses, judgements and ways of seeing. If our attitudes are rigid and not adaptable, then we will struggle to overcome adversity. Resilient attitudes are therefore flexible in nature to adapt to new or changing and demanding circumstances.

Reflective practice for strengthening personal control

You were probably introduced to the notion of 'reflective practice' during your induction/teacher education programme. Championed as a way to support improving practice, reflection and reflective practice have for many years offered a tool by which teacher educators could invite beginning teachers to pause, take stock and contemplate a range of possible options for engaging with and meeting the needs of their learners (Muijs and Reynolds, 2017;

Pollard et al., 2014; Schön, 1983). Participating in reflective practices also helps us focus on the rational options for both professional and personal action.

When we are challenged by a learner whose educational needs do not seem to be met, professionals do not collapse at the first hurdle. We have been inducted into a rational process of stepping back and weighing up a range of options, after we have first engaged in analysing the needs and circumstances. Our remit, we have been taught, is to not make quick and superficial judgements. One mentor colleague described her process (see Case study 11.2):

Case study 11.2 Weighing up the options

It is never easy when teaching and working with others. So much of what we do is about communication and relational professionalism. Many of the professional judgements I make are designed to have an impact on my learners and/or my colleagues. Therefore, I must weigh things up, seek advice and finally I have to feel comfortable with the actions I am about to propose so that I can follow through.

The action of reflective practice involves taking 'mental control' of what happens next. It is about making conscious decisions about behaviours and actions; some decisions will foreground 'the other' (our learners or colleagues) and some will help to anchor us to following procedures or processes with which we feel comfortable. Often, too, we may be aware of when a decision that is made in the best interests of the learner could be a challenge for us.

Operating in this agentic manner means that our choice is still a considered choice; a 'brain-engaged' outcome. Following through with actions from this standpoint and attitude means that we will be prepared for the 'uncertainty' that might result. Some people refer to this as 'thinking things through' in anticipation, so that we are ready for all eventualities, including how we might *feel* with different outcomes. Task 11.6 asks you to consider how you have approached such situations of stepping outside your comfort zone.

Task 11.6 Stepping out of your comfort zone

- Can you recall a time when you stepped out of your comfort zone to support or foreground the needs of others - for example, your learners?
- Was this a conscious and considered decision?
- How did you feel? Did you have to manage any feelings of discomfort?
- Was being out of your comfort zone not really a conscious decision but a reaction?
- What feelings and attitudes resulted? Were you annoyed and resentful, or perhaps surprised by your response?
- Consider what questions you might use to prompt your mentee to think about what supported their decisions in response to people or an adverse event.

You may recall doing this with your lesson planning. We contemplate options, and possible responses from our learners. We may imagine how adaptation will be needed for specific learners, such as modifications to resources, or additional adult support. We may also reimagine ourselves responding differently to an individual learner – you may have one who is a constant niggle to your patience. Everything described here is about a 'thought process' with which we engage.

Engaging with reflective writing

Reflection during initial teacher education programmes usually involves keeping a 'reflective journal' or having to write reflections after we have taught a lesson. Case study 11.3 provides a reflection for a beginning teacher about the value they see in such reflections. For many, they can seem like a chore, so what function might they serve? Perhaps as a mentor you have had cause to read them and add a signature?

How seriously have you taken the task? Writing down one's thoughts ideas, feelings, emotions, plans and even grandiose schemes helps us achieve what we want. The thinking process involved in writing means we evaluate what we write, in particular when we read what we have written (Brookfield, 2017; Cayley, 2011; Thompson and Thompson, 2018). However, it is also a way to make visible to others how we are framing our thinking. It is a form of externalising our ideas. This helps develop metacognition and can be a tool to support learning conversations. Bearing this in mind, what kind of conversations do you have with the beginning teacher after you have read their reflective journal? Task 11.7 asks you to consider how you engage with reflective journals.

Case study 11.3 Example of reflective writing

On my [school-based ITT] programme, I didn't have to keep a journal but I think I missed out somehow, because it was near the end of my year that I went to a conference and met others who had. They seem to understand much more about themselves in the classroom and why things were the way they were. I sort of envied their confidence and how they could talk about things. I have started to reflect this year and my mentor is good at picking up things ... half-baked ideas I may have talked about.

Task 11.7 Engaging with reflective writing

- How have you engaged with reflective journals in the past – for yourself or as a mentor?
- What can you recall about your own journal writing and lesson evaluations?
- Can you recall ever talking about your reflections with anyone?
- How does reflection help you in your day-to-day tasks?
- How might your mentee benefit from follow-up discussion to enable more conscious thinking in relation to what they have written?

- What questions could you ask a mentee to further invite more detailed interrogation of the ideas?
- Consider how you might engage differently with the beginning teacher's reflective journal and/or lesson reflections.
- What changes might you make in the way you read and respond to the beginning teacher?

Through such approaches, you can help beginning teachers to 'reframe' their views about diverse students, diagnose classroom challenges and develop alternative practices to meet the needs of students. This kind of mentoring is generally known as educative, and is conceptualised not only as a role, but also as 'a relationship and a process' (Feiman-Nemser, 2012, p.241).

However, mentors need the language to 'deconstruct their own practice, explain it to others, and in the process learn how to facilitate learning for (and with) their peers' (Lieberman and Pointer Mace, 2009, p. 460). Such a learning-focused approach requires you to take an educational 'inquiry stance' (Cochran-Smith and Lytle, 2009). In this sense, educational mentoring encapsulates knowledge-*of*-practice, a complex dynamic of transformational action whereby you become a learner yourself, continuing to develop your own knowledge while acting as an advocate for the beginning teacher, the school and the profession.

The language of critical reflection

Part of your challenge as a mentor at this point, is about what is required for this educative mentoring role. When a beginning teacher can reflect and contemplate options for professional practice, they are drawing on a repertoire of strategies and perspective that will not be the same as yours. Not only are their options less extensive, but they have had less experience of enacting approaches. They have a smaller set of conclusions from which to judge what might be most effective and when. As the mentor, you not only can bring your different repertoire of skills and understanding, but you have a far greater bank of experience and trials and tribulations on which to draw. How can you bridge the gap between the beginning teacher's practice and your knowledge? The short-circuit route might be to 'tell' the beginning teacher what they need to do, based on your evidence and the experience from your 'backpack'. Would this support the beginning teacher? 'Maybe in the short term,' you might reply, 'but how would such an approach help support the beginning teacher in the future to make a "brain-engaged" and considered choice about the way forward?' Cochran-Smith and Lytle (2009) coined the phrase 'knowledge-*for*-practice' as the formal knowledge and theory that teachers are taught. The acquisition of such knowledge is about helping teachers to know what is already known. However significant this knowledge is as a foundation, it should not be viewed as fixed or closed to critique. Practical knowledge or knowledge gained through experience is termed 'knowledge-*in*-practice'. It is generated by the individual teacher, who 'mediates ideas and constructs meaning and knowledge and acts upon them' (Cochran-Smith and Lytle 1999, p.267)

However, when teachers critique both theoretical and practical knowledge, their learning can be transformative (Meijer et al., 2017). When teachers are supported to rethink their own practice and to construct new roles for themselves as teachers, they are likely to also teach differently; they also have more agency over their decisions and actions. When knowledge and practice are problematised, and not taken for granted, teachers and mentors become agents of change. As a mentor, you are then involved with supporting the beginning teacher to develop their own 'knowledge-*of*-practice. The goal is that, as a mentor, you will focus on learning and on changing practice, rather than on maintaining the status quo.

Bridging reflection and resilience

As the chapter title suggests, the focus is on encouraging you to see your role as a mentor as facilitating the agentic and transformative professional learning of a beginning teacher to ensure that they 'thrive' in teaching. Case study 11.4 provides an indication of how this can look in practice.

Case study 11.4 Bridging reflection and resilience: A beginning teacher reflection

What I have started to do is act on evidence more. Before I used evidence as examples in [the mentee's] observation notes or taken from her own reflections. For example, I would note what I saw against the teaching standards. However, after a staff development day, I realised this meant nothing. 'So what?' Now I try to work together with her [my mentor] to use the evidence to build a new focus or goal. The evidence becomes our rationale to develop ideas further into practice. . It becomes the 'now what' in the discussion

Educative mentoring has been identified as a process that goes beyond an informal relationship of providing emotional and practice support, especially when the beginning teacher is stressed. Throughout this chapter, the significance of your attitudes, assumptions and the language you use has highlighted the agenda set with the beginning teacher. The continuum of teacher attitudes or orientations developed by Watkins (2010) is helpful here (see Table 11.2 for more information). Task 11.8 encourages you to focus on your personal orientation towards mentoring.

Task 11.8 Your preferred orientation as a teacher

- What is your preferred orientation as a teacher? Are you concerned with enabling the beginning teacher to prove their competence as a beginning teacher, or is your concern about them improving their competence in the classroom?
- What does this focus say about how you see your role as a mentor?
- What perspective might have the greatest impact on the beginning teacher's broader attitudes and engagement with the teaching profession and/or staying in your school?

Table 11.2 Learning orientations continuum

Learning orientation ← – – – – – – – –	*Performance orientation* – – – – – – – – →
A dimension along which we all vary as learners.	
We believe that effort can lead to success.	We believe that ability leads to success.
We believe in our ability to improve and learn and not be fixed or stuck.	We are concerned to be seen as able, and to perform well in other's eyes.
We prefer challenging tasks, the outcome of which reflects our approach.	We seek satisfaction from doing better than others.
We get satisfaction from personally defined success in different tasks.	We emphasise competition and public evaluation.
We talk to ourselves: when engaged in a task we talk ourselves through the options.	When the task it difficult, we display helplessness: 'I can't do X.'
A Concern for ***Improving*** one's competence	A Concern for ***Proving*** one's competence

Source: Watkins (2010).

Consider the statements in Table 11.2. First, where might you place yourself on this continuum? What would others see you do to accept your view of your practice? How do you see your mentee? What practices resonate from this continuum list? You will notice that each statement is suggestive of an attitude or a mindset. Drawing on earlier sections of this chapter, you will have good insight into what orientation may be problematic if an adverse situation were to occur. Would having a more highly driven performance orientation possibly inhibit resilient behaviours in the first instance? Moreover, what might be the implications for you as a mentor?

Whichever orientation you have considered to be your natural leaning, your own resilience will be a contributing factor to your 'stance' as a professional. Resilience comes from understanding your own achievement, success and where you have come unstuck before. When we consider the statements in the right-hand column, many of them are about external factors - forms of external judgement that are difficult to control. The statements in the left-hand column resemble areas over which we have some personal control, and that we form attitudes towards. It is this sense of agency and personal control that is crucial for sustaining a resilient outlook.

The process of being resilient highlights factors that contribute to ensuring we can have control over ourselves, control over our responses to others and control over our responses to events. The Mowbray (2010) Personal Resilience Development Framework (see Figure 11.3 for more detail) is based on influences of individual psychological distress. The approach is based on helping participants to strengthen their attitudes towards preventing distress in themselves.

- *Control over self.* People who know themselves well are mindful of their surroundings and behave with emotional intelligence towards others. They also have a sense of purpose. This helps the mind look forward in the face of threats that may halt their progress. Being able to control personal anxiety or the expectations of anxiety strengthens self-confidence.
- *Control over response to events.* People who are well organised can cope with the chaos of daily life better than those who do not pay enough attention to organising themselves,

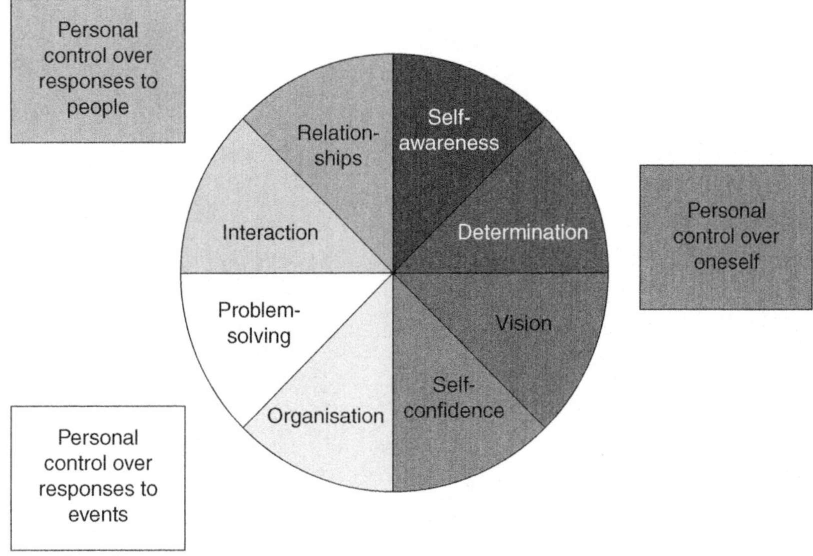

Figure 11.3 The Mowbray Personal Resilience Development Framework
Source: Adapted with permission from Mowbray (2010).

preferring to rely on memory or luck. When there are unforeseen circumstances, such people are able to remain flexible. People with the skills to create order from chaos know it is possible to deal with multiple demands effectively and are less likely to be anxious when others place demands on them.

- *Control over response to people*. In order for us to survive and prosper, we need to forge relationships. Resilient people have relationships that provide the appropriate reinforcement and support when they are required.

Finding your resilient voice

At the start of the chapter, you were encouraged to complete Task 11.1. Can you recall your responses to the initial questionnaire at the start of the chapter? Table 11.3 shows the links to the 'control' areas from the Personal Resilience Development Framework.

Table 11.3 Resilience Framework

I usually know how others perceive me. I am determined to achieve my lifetime ambitions. I can see my future clearly. I normally feel comfortable in new situations.	Personal control over oneself
I plan my next day in advance. I enjoy the challenge of unravelling puzzles and solving problems.	Personal control over responses to events
In general, I like people. My most important relationships are my strongest.	Personal control over responses to people

Now complete Task 11.9 and consider what resources you will draw on to ensure personal control over yourself and your responses to people and events.

Task 11.9 Reflecting back on the Resilience Framework

Look back at the Resilience Framework (Figure 11.3).

- What elements might need more attention to support your own resilience?
- Once you have been through this process, consider how you might invite your mentee to complete the same questions and how you might now support them further through educative mentoring.

Summary

To support and enable a resilient professional, educative mentoring offers processes that go beyond the often-expected mentor role of pastoral care when times are tough. As an educative mentor, you will be able to shift from talking about what you both know (or transmitting knowledge-*for*-practice) to having more collaborative conversations to develop knowledge-*of*-practice with the beginning teacher. As a result, you will give less advice and ask more questions so that the beginning teacher can talk about their own beliefs, attitudes and values, and you will be able to support the beginning teacher to make their own decisions regarding teaching.

In order to do this, you will need to engage in active listening and open-ended questioning as well as model self-reflection and metacognition as you respond to challenges in your practice or the demands within the school, and work alongside your mentee in a learning partnership.

Having read this chapter, you should have developed confidence in your ability to discuss the processes of resilience and wellbeing with the beginning teacher - both from a reflexive/personal perspective and in relation to the school context in which you both work. You should see the beginning teacher's reflective tasks/journals as starting points to engage with the five areas of personal control that are required to support resilient professionals.

Using effective coaching questions, you will enable the beginning teacher to have agency in reframing their challenges and articulating their developing learning. Take time to listen and carefully weigh up what aspects of practice the beginning teacher is discussing that might be not be well thought through - almost naive in their construction. Invite reflection on the elements in the day-to-day life of a teacher over which we can have personal control and then revisit the orientations and language used to describe the pressures of the profession.

Further reading

Lofthouse, R.M. (2018) Re-imagining mentoring as a dynamic hub in the transformation of initial teacher education: The role of mentors and teacher educators, *International Journal of Mentoring and Coaching in Education*, 7(3), pp. 248–60.

Mowbray, D. (2018) *Guide to Personal Resilience* (3rd ed.), London: MAS Publishing.

Struthers, D. (2018) Professional Resilience and wellbeing. In J.-L. Dutaut and L. Rycroft-Smith (eds), *Flip the System UK: A Teachers' Manifesto*, London: Routledge.

SECTION 3

Mentoring in specialist areas

12 Mentoring for art and design

Claire March

Introduction

As mentors, our first role is to support beginning teachers to understand this powerful cornerstone of the arts and its centrality to society. It is not just a subject that teaches children to manipulate the pencil or the paint to record objects in a realistic form; rather, it can inform our thinking of who we are, our identity and how we associate with the world. Art plays a central role in the world around us and how it shapes our understanding of who we are, including our cultural identity and history, through designs and visual records, as well as informing us about world cultures. Often when we consider another culture, the identifying markers are created by the arts. For example, if we consider Indian culture we would consider such iconic items as the Taj Mahal, classical Indian dancing, rich vibrant fabrics in a raft of strong colours and the distinctive music style. These art forms all enable the teacher or mentee to start to form an understanding of India, its history and the expressive nature of the country as a whole. Eisner (2002) suggests that art provides us with a window into who we are as individuals and where and what we hold important in our lives and culture, ensuring the development of empathy or understanding of difference. Eisner (2002) also identifies a number of other important aspects that engaging in art can teach pupils. These include central skills for life, such as an ability to problem solve, to make good judgements and to understand and celebrate different perspectives. Importantly, the arts give pupils a voice to communicate thoughts, feelings, emotions and personal expression in a non-language or mathematical base. Art enables the freedom to take risks to communicate to the world and voice our social commentary, which in turn leaves a marker for the next person to learn and understand (Hickman 2014).

Objectives

At the end of the chapter, you should be able to:

- Support your mentee to identify the key elements to consider for good art and design practice

- Support your mentee to consider strategies to help them with their reflective analysis of their art and design teaching
- Support mentees to develop and enhance their art and design teaching.

What are the essential elements of good practice in primary art and design?

First consider your own practice and complete Task 12.1, to establish what you think are key elements of good practice for art and design.

Task 12.1 Key elements of good art and design practice

1. Create a list of key elements of good art and design practice. This can be from prior knowledge, your own experience or observations.
2. Consider what opportunities there are for you to observe art and design. Could you and the beginning teacher observe a lesson together, and discuss the key elements of good practice?

It is important to recognise and to be mindful as mentors that most beginning teachers have had limited time in initial teacher education to engage in the pedagogy of art and design, with some programmes having as little as three hours dedicated to the subject area. Therefore, the role of mentoring professional practice is particularly important to enable mentees to develop their art and design teaching, so pupils can learn within the subject. It is key as a mentor to understand the beginning teacher's experience in the subject, their core knowledge of mediums and their confidence levels. This will allow you to consider appropriate approaches to develop their knowledge. You could consider setting up opportunities across your school from early years through to key stage 2 for the beginning teacher to observe art and design, to help them develop their understanding of progression and to enable a discussion of the art and design curriculum.

Within the National Curriculum in England, the purpose of study for art and design proposes that the curriculum should engage, inspire and equip pupils with the skills and knowledge to experiment (DfE, 2013). March (2020) identifies these key skills of art and design as invention, analysis, imagination, expression and observation, and suggests that these are developed through teaching and learning within art lessons; however, these skills are not solely the domain of the arts, as they are also vital transferable skills, highlighting the importance of learning within art as it impacts numerous skills. As the mentor, you can support the beginning teacher through considering where in an art and design lesson or series of lessons these skills of invention, analysis imagination, expression and observation can be developed. This is not to say that all these skills will be addressed in any one lesson; rather, across the curriculum there should be an opportunity to develop all these skills.

Task 12.2 Observing the beginning teacher

- What types of planning conversations and refocusing exercises did the beginning teacher use to scaffold the pupils' observations?
- What different types of questions did they use, why did they select them and how did they enhance the pupils' learning?
- What conversations, exercises or questions could they have used that could now be added into future lessons?

Art and design skills can also support learning using a cross-curricular approach. The most important aspect is for the mentor to support the beginning teacher to understand what these skills look like within a lesson. Some of them are clearly more obvious, such as observation, while the skill of effective analysis may require further support to develop subject knowledge. While observation seems quite a simple skill at first glance, within art and design you can support your mentee to ensure a greater appreciation of deep learning that takes place through effective questioning and refocusing exercises within the lesson. You could plan to discuss the use of questioning and refocusing exercises within your mentor and mentee conversations (see Task 12.2). Encouraging the beginning teacher to plan for questioning and refocusing activities will help to support and scaffold the pupils' observations and help them to consider and reconsider the object they are observing and interpreting within the art and design lesson.

Analysis of an artist's work can be challenging for beginning teachers, who may not be familiar with the artist, or their canon of work, or the period of history when the work was created. To help support your beginning teacher to overcome these challenges, you could signpost resources available to support subject knowledge development. An example of signposting resources is the National Gallery's Take One Picture, www.nationalgallery.org.uk/learning/teachers-and-schools/take-one-picture, which is a useful set of resources for primary teachers as it has a range of images within the collection that are all supported with teachers' notes and questions to support the analysis of the piece of work. These resources would not only help the beginning teacher when discussing these works with the pupils, but also help them to consider and develop a repertoire of questions to support the analysis of a range of artworks. If we examine Paolo Uccello's painting *Saint George and the Dragon* (1470), such questions arise about the storytelling within the image and the compositional structure, as pupils consider questions such as, 'How has the artist created the illusion of depth within the painting?" and, 'Who was the image created for?' The questions are all supported through detailed teachers' notes. Pupils will naturally develop their own questions as they become curious about the images, and such questions can often be a useful reflective starting point for discussion of the work. It can also highlight pupils' knowledge and understanding of the work.

What do beginning teachers need to help them optimise learning in art and design?

Within art and design there are a number of key areas in which beginning teachers will need support to optimise pupils' learning. These can be identified in three key areas:

- knowledge of great artists, designer and architects as stated within the National Curriculum in England (DfE, 2013a)
- understanding artistic processes
- knowledge of appropriate mediums and resources, including health and safety considerations.

The National Curriculum (DfE, 2013a) states that pupils should learn about great artists, craft makers, architects and designers, but makes no reference to which particularly significant artists, time periods or movements should be taught about. Identification of artists across art history and world culture can be exciting, but this is often a particularly daunting task for a beginning teacher, and also at times for the non-arts specialist's mentor, as there are so many potential works that could be explored. It is important to acknowledge here that the canon of artists most commonly encountered in the primary classroom stems from white European male artists, who are mainly painters from the late nineteenth and early twentieth centuries (Gregory et al., 2020; Watts, 2019) - the likes of Monet, Van Gogh and Picasso, with the occasional female artists from a later period, usually Frida Kahlo and Georgia O'Keeffe. There is also limited evidence of architects or designers taught within the current curriculum. Pause for a moment and in Task 12.3 reflect on your own practice.

Task 12.3 Reflecting on your own practice

- Which artists, designers and architects have you included in your own teaching?
- Are they white European males from the late nineteenth and early twentieth centuries?
- How often do you refer to women?
- How could you use a wider cross-section of artists, including contemporary examples?

As a mentor, it is important to consider your knowledge, and to reflect on why this particular canon of artists are used and whether this is indeed the case. The National Curriculum (DfE, 2013) also implies that pupils should gain a broad and balanced view of great artists. As a mentor, you might consider supporting and prompting the mentee to develop knowledge of artists beyond this canon, and to consider artists from different artforms, such as photographers, sculptors or textile artists, along with artists from a range of cultural backgrounds, and contemporary artists working with a range of mediums, such as the work of Nick Cave or Grayson Perry. It would be good to provide a wider representation of female artists, such as Cornelia Parker, Katie Paterson or Sheila Hicks. Consider which designers and architects could be considered, from key historical figures to more contemporary figures such as Norman Foster, Philippe Starck or Zaha Hadid. These contemporary artists, architects and designers are key to sharing aspirational figures with pupils, while creating a greater awareness of potential careers within the art world. Artists, architects and designers from your local community can also support the curriculum. Invite them to come and share their work with the children to help the pupils develop their understanding of processes and mediums. Your role as a mentor could be to support your mentee in the analysis of their current art and design offer, and thus pupils' learning, through signposting other key artists to the beginning teacher; they could be incorporated to create a broader curriculum with greater relevance to pupils.

In art and design lessons, process is key to ensuring pupil progress. At times, art lessons can focus on one-off pieces of work simply created for display, but process is the central point to effective learning within art and design. Process supports the development of the learning of new skills and an ability to express oneself. You may need to support the beginning teacher to consider the process involved within a single lesson and how this same process might build across a series of lessons, in a similar way to developing skills in literacy or other subject areas. This understanding of process could be achieved through sharing medium-terms plans from a range of classes and discussing how process is used to achieve learning. You could suggest that the beginning teacher arranges a time with the school subject leader to discuss progression across the school. Art and design can sometimes lack progression of skills, due to stand-alone lessons that are used to support other curriculum areas and that are not seen as a subject within its own right (Gregory 2020, cited in Gregory et al. 2020). The beginning teacher will need your guidance and that of the art specialist in your school to analyse and consider how one lesson may develop into a second and then into a series of lessons, not always using only one medium. Next, complete Task 12.4.

Task 12.4 Progression across lesson

- Consider the progression from one lesson to the next. How did you build on the process and skills?
- Can you share with the beginning teacher your mapping of process and skills?
- Was the lesson part of series of lessons, or a stand-alone lesson?
- Can you articulate the reasons why?

Case study 12.1 illustrates a series of lessons developing processes over a term, focusing on the topic of 'Who am I?' It is designed to develop pupils' self-expression and to build skills and knowledge related to the use of mixed media and clay. The pupils all had significant special educational needs (SEN), so the accessibility of the process and how this needed to be adapted were considered.

Case study 12.1 The process within the topic area of 'Who am I?'

Pupils started by considering a range of artists' self-portraits, which were purposefully selected with both contemporary and historical artists representing a range of backgrounds. It is important to note that it was difficult to find examples of artists represented with SEN. Pupils could select examples that interested them, and pupils who were able to communicate verbally were able to express elements of what they liked about the self-portraits. Pupils then worked on photographic images of themselves, adding colour and mixed media to reflect themselves as individuals (Figure 12.1).

From the pupils' self-portraits, they developed their ideas into three-dimensional forms, creating masks (Figure 12.2) reflecting their perceived self and how they wished to be perceived. Some pupils gave themselves mythical qualities, such as superheroes or unicorn appearances. Pupils then had the opportunity to place themselves into a story environment, creating scenes for them to divide into. These were then taken into a green screen session, where pupils wore their masks and moved through their story/landscape drawings that they had developed.

Pupils then progressed their masks in clay; here the skills relating to working with clay were important for the pupils to understand. It is recommended that a mentor might need to be explicit about specific subject knowledge related to the use of clay with the beginning teacher - for example, the importance of using slip, as this is the glue that joins two pieces of clay.

The pupils in the case study used buff clay, not air-hardening clay; the latter is often seen in school. Air hardening clay is very limiting and not cost effective, and has few benefits for the primary pupil. Pupils had to understand how to roll and manipulate the clay, and how to use slip throughout the mask-making to support features being added onto the mask. The knowledge of the medium directly impacts the success of the outcome, so scaffolding the beginning teacher's knowledge during such a process is vital.

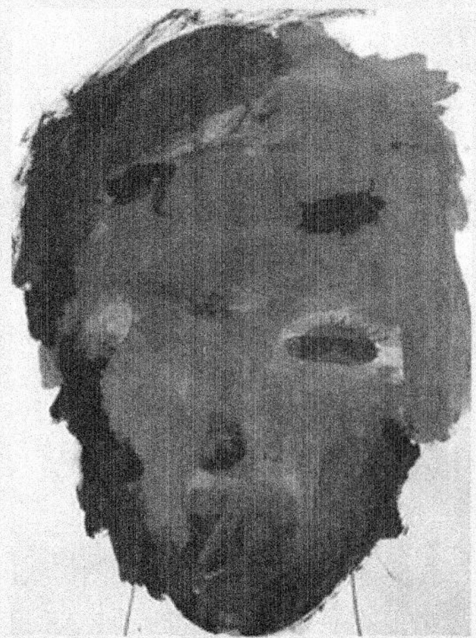

Figure 12.1 Portrait

Figure 12.2 Mask

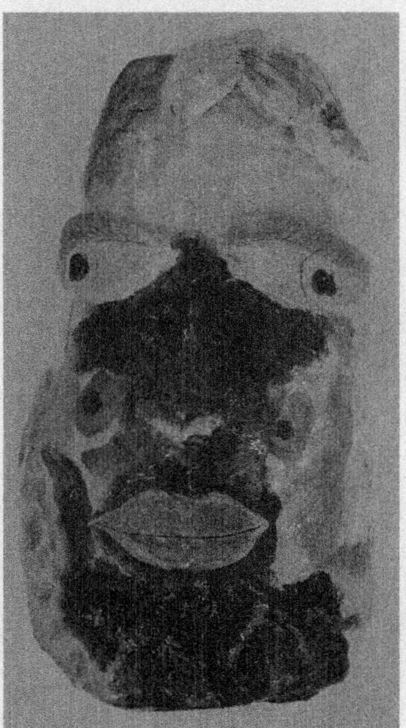

Figure 12.3 Glazed clay mask

Pupils at a later stage were given the chance to glaze their masks, adding colour prior to firing. It is worth considering here that the materials were suited to the pupils and the task. The glazes selected were chalk glazes, which could be hand held and were representational of the fired colour. These glazes were selected as a number of the pupils had challenges with fine motor skills and their ability to apply glaze in a similar way to using a pen or pencil supported the pupils (Figure 12.3).

The overall sequence of lessons built on a range of skills and knowledge related to the use of clay, mixed media and self-expression. A stand-alone lesson on portraits would have not enabled such depth of engagement and quality outcomes as a series of lessons enabling pupils to reflect and revisit the creative process. The knowledge and use of a range of mediums are something developed with time; beginning teachers in some cases will have limited knowledge of mediums available and how best to use them. Ensure there is plenty of time for the beginning teacher to observe practice in other classes to understand a range of materials; these opportunities will help to develop their knowledge and expertise. You could discuss the progression of mediums within the school, such as printing within the early years, and how this might develop and change within and across key stages 1 and 2, leading to more complex prints, layering up colours and designs.

For older primary pupils, I recommend that beginning teachers should not be afraid to use images such as Marc Quinn's 'Self' (1991), as it is a provocative piece that would extend and develop older children. Pupils often find the notion of this portrait by Quinn challenging, because it was made using the artist's blood and frozen in a cast of his head. The artist has then repeated this process at key points in his life, with a new cast of his face as it changed with age.

What help do beginning teachers need to teach art and design more effectively?

Key areas that the beginning teacher may find useful to explore with either the mentor or a knowledgeable other such as the art and design lead can easily be linked to 'the Teaching Standards (DfE, 2011) and consist of: ensuring all children can access the learning with high expectations; an ability set appropriate targets for learning and progression; and ensuring a safe and engaging learning environment. Each of these areas will be discussed and suggestions offered for how mentors can support the beginning teacher to teach art and design more effectively.

Access to the art and design curriculum

With relation to accessing the art and design curriculum, a number of factors need to be considered, such as pupils' prior experience and ability, and the physical ability to manipulate and engage with the resources. The beginning teacher needs to take into account the age and physical coordination of the pupils, as well as the current provision of resources and how these resources are organised within the classroom. In Task 12.5, consider how you and the beginning teacher could organise the resources in the classroom.

Task 12.5 Organising your resources

- Consider the children in the class, and discuss with the beginning teacher the pupils' physical abilities relating to fine and gross motor skills.
- How do you organise or adapt your organisation of resources within your classroom to make them accessible for all learners? Why do you organise them in this way? Discuss this with your mentee.

The beginning teacher may not have had experience in considering how and why they should organise the resources within an art and design lesson. It can help to support the beginning teacher's confidence to discuss the logistics and pragmatic reasons for organising the resources and materials available within the school and classroom in the way you -for example, why you use particular paints, where they are available, how the children access central resources, such as drying racks or storage space, and the expectations and availability of aprons and table covers.

The first time your mentee is planning an art lesson, discuss classroom layout and how resources can be made accessible. How do you, as the mentor or the subject lead, set the room up? How can they minimise spillages or accidents? Suggest demonstrating that water pots only require being a third full of water as this will prevent spillages. Also consider organising resources in trays that are easy to hand out and collect, and can also contain messy items. Are mentees aware of protocols around cleaning up? Do children wash up paint pots? Or is it the school policy that this is something that only adults are expected to do? All of this will potentially depend on the age and physical abilities of the children, so it can be helpful for you as the mentor to draw a layout for the art lesson, which could then support the beginning teacher to think through the logistics of the lesson. Alternatively, you could identify on the plan/layout all the key transition points, such as for moving wet prints around the room.

Differentiation for art and design lessons can be considered through adapting the task, or the medium, or the support or the tools to ensure pupils are able to engage in the task at the appropriate level. This might be to stretch pupils or support them with particular learning or physical adaptation requirements. Adapting the tools provided for children can be very important. Consider your class: are all children going to work best with the same-size paint brush or pencil? Do certain children need to use thicker or finer brushes? Is the handle length aiding their control? Would a sponge brush be a better option? With pencils, again consider pupils' fine motor skills and ability to grasp the tool - would a much chunkier drawing tool aid them? Or would the use of an iPad or tablet allow them to draw with their fingers as an alternative means?

You might consider such aspects as the size and colour of paper the child is working on. I recently worked with a group of children in a specialist setting, all attempting to draw self-portraits on A5 paper with charcoal, as nearly all the children found fine motor skills difficult. The size of the paper added to the challenge of the task. The small paper limited the size of the drawings, so the ability to add detail became a greater challenge. These pupils may have been aided if thicker charcoal had been provided and/or charcoal in pencil form used to limit the challenge of charcoal and the sensory nature and impact of charcoal-covered hands. Some children will find certain mediums difficult to work with, such as clay or modroc, because of their sensory nature, or even the risk of the child consuming the medium. Instead, you might consider using a modelling material that is safer, such a dough - although not salt dough, as this will make children sick. To support your mentee, discuss each aspect of differentiation, as identified above: the outcomes, mediums, tools and support. This is not to suggest all elements have to change, but some consideration and adaption to the lesson will support access to learning and pupil progress.

Assessment within the art and design lesson

Assessment within art and design can be a more challenging area than in subjects such as numeracy or literacy. Beginning teachers are often unsure about, or lacking in confidence in, how to assess or what to assess. It can be difficult to make a judgement on personal expression so, as both Ogier (2017) and Gregory et al. (2020) agree, it is important to highlight the importance of assessing the learning journey of each child and not the finished product. By assessing the learning journey, you should be able to identify the skills and concepts that require assessment and ensure that these are the focus of your assessment and feedback.

You may need to support the beginning teacher to identify within their planning the skills and concepts to be developed over the lesson or sequence of lessons, and then how and when they will be assessing these. This will enable the beginning teacher to become more proficient in assessing a skill and working on the feedback, development and progression within that skill. Enabling the beginning teacher to develop effective self- and peer-evaluation strategies for the children will support the pupils' learning and their critical analytical skills. Once pupils become confident about assessing their own skills and discussing these with other pupils, they will start to develop their own targets for improvement.

March (in Gregory, March and Tutchell 2020) suggests that a sketchbook is a particularly useful tool for observing progress over time. This can be used throughout the year to develop skills, record ideas and revisit work, creating a bank of ideas and critical thinking that pupils are able to revisit. The National Curriculum (DfE, 2013a) clearly identifies the expectation that pupils will use sketchbooks in key stage 2, as this mirrors similar behaviour to that of an artist.

You can support your mentee in considering strategies best suited to self- and peer-assessment within their planning. They should be mindful that children are protective of their own work and can often become demotivated or distressed if someone writes on or corrects an image. When correcting a view or interpretation of a medium, encourage the beginning teacher to be mindful, to complete any assessment on a separate piece of paper rather than in the pupils' sketchbook or individual piece of work. Children's peer evaluation can also be added to the work indirectly, either through sharing comments or using post-it notes.

Safe and engaging learning environment

When considering health and safety within an art lesson, Ogier (2017) suggests considering aspects of behaviour for learning, ensuring that pupils are engaged, with clear expectations about the learning environment and ways to engage with the resources. In some settings, art can even be seen as a treat that can lead to increased levels of appropriate behaviour. However, there may still be times when children have to stop an activity or task if they are putting others or themselves in danger. There are certain mediums that potentially have greater risks for consideration, such as sewing, batik (hot wax drawing), clay or modroc, glue guns or even painting, due to spills that might occur on the floor. It is important for beginning teachers to consider these risks within their planning, and to reflect on how they have mitigated against the risk. This might be through the organisation of resources, some pre-teaching of the risks, a higher adult support ratio or smaller groups engaging with the task on a rotation basis.

If the beginning teacher feels particularly unconfident about teaching through a specific medium, due to the risks involved, perhaps use a team teaching approach, where both you and the beginning teacher teach together or you plan the lesson and then you and the beginning teacher teach the lesson together. You may need to spend time with your mentee looking at your school risk assessments for art and design, as they need to get used to completing and sharing these within school for any medium that you and they feel has an increased level of harm.

How can mentors best support beginning teachers in their teaching of art and design?

Modelling within an art lesson can be just as important as doing so within numeracy or literacy lessons. Beginning teachers need to feel confident to model themselves or understand strategies for using the pupils or other adults to model. This requires an element of understanding and knowing their pupils, as well as knowing the skills and knowledge of other adults with whom they are working. There are many highly skilled teaching assistants working within our schools, and we need to use and celebrate their skills on a more regular basis.

When pupils engage in a task such as using clay for the first time, if the beginning teacher models the task, pupils will be clearer about expectations or techniques. This could be something as simple as how to join pieces of clay or more complex in relation to drawing a portrait, where you would expect the beginning teacher to touch on proportion. As a mentor, you should encourage your mentee to practise modelling prior to the lesson to ensure that they have fully understood the skill required or the elements of the process. Also encourage the beginning teacher to model to ensure that they are familiar with subject-specific language and vocabulary, as these are also key parts of art and design. Are there any specific terms that pupils would need explaining to them or should learn, such as a 'slip' or 'leather hard', which are used when working with clay? This vocabulary should be highlighted within the medium-term plans and the beginning teacher's short-term planning. You could share your own art and design vocabulary lists (or the school vocabulary list, if it is present in your school policies) with the beginning teacher. If you do not have vocabulary lists, why not suggest to the beginning teacher that they start to develop their own? You can suggest certain texts or websites that could also support their subject knowledge development.

When introducing new mediums to pupils, beginning teachers need to understand themselves, the abilities of the medium and the importance of time for exploration. Pupils can only understand the potential of charcoal as a drawing medium by first exploring the types of marks that can be created from charcoal. Exploration is a key component of any art lesson; this might be exploration of the medium or the process, or the students' own feelings and emotions. Exploration through paint medium is illustrated by Case study 12.2.

Case study 12.2 Exploration through paint medium

The notion of exploration is a central aspect of art and design, and can be linked to the process of invention (Adams 2016; March, in Gregory, March and Tutchell 2020). The term 'invention' might not mean something original to the world, but rather new to the child, such as a way to apply paint or mix a particular colour. For exploration to occur, pupils need to have freedom in either the application or the medium, or both. When I teach student teachers in initial teacher education art subject-specific sessions about different types of paint, the first task is to make marks with all the different types of paint, with no rules or limitations. Student teachers can apply them in any way they wish and they are encouraged to try adding water, glue or sand to understand how the paint behaves with the additives. While they are doing this, I ask them to consider the quality of the opacity and intensity of colour of the marks. Student teachers have a range of application tools from traditional brushes through to sponges, sticks, feathers and even cotton reels. Student teachers nearly always also choose to apply paint with fingers, and images often become abstract in nature (Figure 12.4).

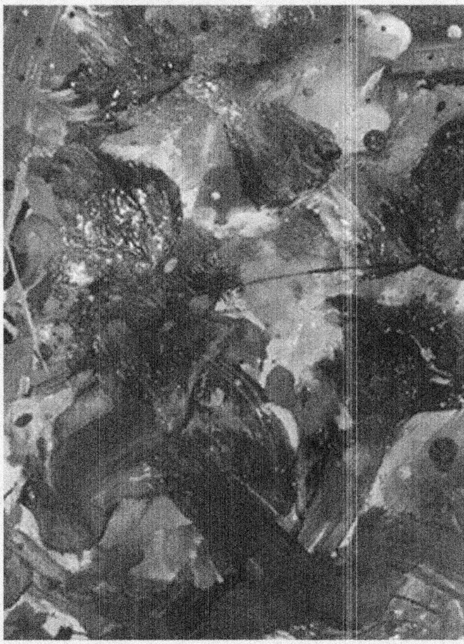

Figure 12.4 Exploration of art

Once student teachers have explored the paint, an analysis of the types of paints and effects is shared within the group, gaining an understanding of when and what each paint type might be used for, considering the consistency of the paint and even the practicalities. Then, with the knowledge gained, student teachers are asked to select a certain paint - such as watercolour or acrylic - and develop a piece of work using and exploring it in depth. This introduces student teachers to the potential range available in the classroom and supports them in selecting the most appropriate paint medium for the activity or materials with which they are working.

Pupils and beginning teachers alike cannot achieve the best from a medium if they lack an understanding of the potential it has to offer, so encourage the beginning teacher to spend time exploring materials with which they are less familiar. They are then more likely to involve their pupils in such exploration. Mentors should be mindful that although the activity in Case study 12.2 allows for exploration, it is by no means exhaustive and new ways of working with the paints can always be discovered, as can new ways of developing the process.

Summary

In this chapter, I have been mindful that although mentors have strong coaching strategies, they may not always feel that they are the expert in the field of art and design. The suggestions within this chapter may offer both you, as the mentor, and the beginning teacher opportunities to develop practice, subject knowledge and skills of art and design. The chapter has offered an understanding of the vast nature of the subject and an awareness that to develop confidence it is vital to spend time practising with materials and mediums. The more aware the beginning teacher is of the materials and mediums available, the more confident they will become and the more possibilities they will be able to use, thus enhancing the children's learning. The beginning teacher should always be discovering new artists, designers and architects, and adding to their existing canon of great artists. It is important that they hang this new knowledge onto existing structures by linking processes, timeframes or expressive skills together.

Further reading

Eisner, E.W. (2002) *The Arts and the Creation of the Mind*, Chicago, IL: Donnelley and Sons.

Gregory, P., March, C. and Tutchell, S. (2020) *Mastering Primary Art and Design*, London: Bloomsbury.

Ogier, S. (2017) *Teaching Primary Art and Design*, London: Sage.

13 Mentoring for mathematics

Hazel King, Gina Donaldson and Sonia Tomlinson

Introduction

This chapter will support you in mentoring beginning teachers by exploring the nature of high-quality teaching and learning in the area of primary mathematics. It will allow you to identify features of teaching and learning to promote with your mentee, and to challenge your mentee's knowledge of teaching. The ultimate aim is for your mentee to be able to articulate and justify their own philosophy of teaching mathematics, and to continue to develop their practice throughout their career. We will explore a range of practical and research-based ideas to help you to reflect on your role. You will be supported in considering how to support your mentee to enhance their teaching so that the children they teach become confident mathematicians.

Objectives

At the end of the chapter, you should be able to:

- Support beginning teachers to recognise good teaching and learning in primary mathematics
- Understand some of the particular issues of supporting mentees in their teaching of primary mathematics
- Support beginning teachers' development in primary mathematics
- Provide mathematics-specific feedback.

Task 13.1 focuses on you and your teaching and learning within mathematics.

Task 13.1 What makes good teaching and learning in mathematics

Think about a mathematics lesson that you have taught and that has gone well. What was good about the teaching and learning?

What is good teaching and learning of primary mathematics?

In this section, we explore some of the ways in which good teaching and learning of mathematics have been defined in the literature. A common argument across mathematics education is that children should understand mathematics. For example, the aims of the National Curriculum in England (DfE, 2013a) state that children should develop conceptual understanding of the mathematical ideas appropriate to their year group. International comparisons tend to show that countries that adopt mastery approaches, which focus on deep understanding, are the most successful in international tests (Jerrim and Vignoles, 2016).

Writers such as Skemp (1989) and Hiebert and Carpenter (1992) distinguish between different sorts of understanding and these texts can help to elucidate what it is to have conceptual understanding. For example, Skemp (1989) uses the context of travelling around a familiar place to explore what it means to have what he describes as relational understanding: you have knowledge of several routes and how these routes connect together, as opposed to an area where you only have the confidence to stick to one route. Applying this to understanding mathematics, a child might have a surface level of understanding of odd and even numbers in that they can identify them by looking at the ones digit. Or they might have a much deeper or conceptual understanding of odd and even numbers in that they understand how to identify whether a number is odd or even by sharing them by two or making groups of two. They might talk about the sequence of odd and even numbers in counting numbers. They might explore what happens when they add two odd or even numbers and explain why they can predict if the total is odd or even. This would indicate a deeper, more conceptual understanding.

The aim of enabling all children to achieve depth of understanding sets the backdrop for analysing the knowledge and practices of the beginning teacher. You might reflect, with your mentee, on the depth of their own mathematical understanding and the way they promote conceptual understanding. For example, when they introduce a new concept to their class, do they take time to explore it, looking at aspects of the idea in small steps starting with easier aspects and slowly progressing to more complex aspects? In establishing conceptual understanding, you will want your mentee to develop strategies to assess understanding and address errors. You might support your mentee to establish positive attitudes to mathematics and a growth mindset so that errors are seen as the starting point towards greater understanding (Boaler, 2016).

Teachers often use manipulatives and images to promote conceptual understanding. This stems from the theory of Bruner (1966), who identifies how learners can engage with representations of ideas that might be enactive, iconic and symbolic. You might consider with your mentee how to represent the ideas they are teaching to their class, how to choose representations that show the essential features of the idea and how to support progress from engaging with manipulatives, pictures and symbols. Context also supports children's development (Nunes, Carraher and Schliemann, 1993), and you might discuss with the beginning teacher which real-life contexts might be used to engage children in problem-solving that will deepen their understanding. This context might be a 'hook' for your mentee's lesson.

The National Curriculum in England stresses the importance of fluency in mathematics (DfE, 2013a). Fluency can be defined as rapid recall of number facts and the ability to use efficient calculation procedures. However, writers such as Russell (2000) and Boaler (2016) suggest that it also requires depth of understanding, including making links between number facts. For example, you might challenge your mentee to go beyond teaching table facts separately to linking them. As well as knowing 6 x 8, children could be supported to link this fact with 48 ÷ 6, or 3 x 16. A way to support and challenge the beginning teacher would be to work with them to consider how to develop fluency in the children they teach.

A further feature of teaching mathematics on which you might want to focus with your mentee is reasoning. Explaining thinking, giving reasons, convincing others and engaging in simple proofs of ideas deepens understanding (Askew, 2012). Therefore, your mentoring and coaching conversations might address your mentee's understanding of the place of reasoning in learning, what reasoning might look like for the age of the children they are teaching and strategies they can use to promote reasoning. For example, you might talk to your mentee about the topics they are planning to teach to ensure they can identify opportunities for reasoning, and can confidently model the reasoning they hope their children will develop. Task 13.2 looks at applying the ideas within this section to the original lesson you reflected upon in Task 13.1.

Task 13.2 What makes a lesson successful?

- Can you apply the ideas discussed here to articulate what made the lesson you reflected on in Task 13.1 successful?
- Did the lesson promote understanding, fluency and reasoning?

What are the issues with mentoring and mathematics?

As a mentor, you may face challenges with supporting beginning teachers in the teaching and learning of mathematics. The mentee will have their own preconceptions of what effective teaching of mathematics is, arising from their own personal experiences, which may not always align with good practice in the school. Your role as the mentor is to challenge these practices and preconceptions to enable the mentee to gain a deeper understanding of the teaching and learning of mathematics and apply this knowledge to their own practice. A further issue for mentors is the mentee's attitude towards mathematics. As with all subjects, your role as the mentor is to encourage the mentee to show a love for mathematics, as this supports a positive learning environment for the children.

Research carried out by Norton (2017) shows that many beginning teachers are anxious about teaching mathematics, lacking confidence in both their pedagogical knowledge of mathematics and how to apply it within the classroom. In turn, meaningful mathematical discussions with children are avoided, minimalising opportunities for children to reason. With this lack of pedagogical knowledge, the mentee will struggle with teaching for relational or conceptual understanding (Skemp, 1989), which then has a negative impact on the learning environment and the children's understanding of mathematics. According to Skemp (1989), a teacher with only instrumental understanding of mathematics will only teach for instrumental understanding and will not enable children to deepen their understanding and be able to apply knowledge to different situations. With a lack of subject knowledge, the mentee will struggle to make the connections between different areas of mathematics that Askew et al. (1997) argue are key for teaching to be effective. To begin supporting a mentee with low subject knowledge of mathematics, it is important that you, as the mentor, have a secure understanding yourself. Working on building the mentee's confidence can help reduce anxiety and motivate the mentee. Provide opportunities for the mentee to develop their subject and/ or pedagogical knowledge through observations, discussions with colleagues and directing them towards appropriate textbooks. This also provides you, as the mentor, an opportunity to develop your knowledge alongside the mentee. Read Case study 13.1 and then in Task 13.3, try to apply the ideas discussed in the case study of Sue and how you would support her.

Case study 13.1 Examples of Sue's teaching

Sue is a mature beginning teacher who is teaching subtracting a three-digit and two-digit number using the formal written column method to a Year 3 class. Sue demonstrated to the children how to subtract 125 - 57 on the interactive whiteboard.

$$\begin{array}{r} 125 \\ -57 \\ \hline \end{array}$$

She started in the ones column and told the children that they could not do 5 - 7, as they did not have enough, so they needed to borrow from the tens column. She crossed out the 2 in the tens column and wrote a 1 instead. Then she put the 1 by the 5, making it 15. She then demonstrated 15 - 7 which was 8.

$$\begin{array}{r} {}^{1}\,{}^{1} \\ 1\not{2}5 \\ -57 \\ \hline 8 \\ \hline \end{array}$$

Sue then repeated the process for the tens column, 'borrowing' the one from the hundreds column (crossing this out) and putting the 1 in the tens column to make 11. She then subtracted 11 - 5 which was 6.

Task 13.3 Supporting practice

- How would you now support Sue in your mentoring in moving her practice forward?
- How would you address the vocabulary that Sue is using in her lesson?
- How can you support Sue in developing the children's conceptual understanding of subtraction?
- What questions could you ask Sue to encourage her to reflect on her own teaching and how to change this to move her practice forward?

Some mentees may have a 'fixed mindset' (Boaler, 2016) when they begin teaching. They may believe that their ability to understand or teach mathematics is limited, and that they are powerless to develop their own understanding. They may even have chosen to teach in a younger year group due to the perceived challenges of teaching mathematics at a higher level. A fixed mindset may mean that the mentee is reluctant to take risks and prefers to teach in a way with which they are comfortable. They may simply replicate the teaching of mathematics that they received, even though they know these approaches did not work for them (Pound and Lee, 2011). This can then result in these negative dispositions towards mathematics being perpetuated in the beliefs of the next generation of learners. On the other hand, if the mentee is able to develop a 'growth mindset' (Boaler, 2016), the beginning teacher will be empowered to take risks in developing and improving their own practice. They can see themselves on a journey towards a deeper understanding of mathematics and how it should be taught. They can then apply this growth mindset to their expectations of children's learning. Such a change is likely to require the mentee to rethink their understanding of what counts as mathematics and how it should be taught, so they will need support and guidance through this process. In Task 13.4, consider your mentee's mindset and how you could help support and develop their mindset towards mathematics.

Task 13.4 Mathematical mindset

- What ideas about learning and teaching mathematics have you noticed in your mentee?
- What is their current mathematical mindset?
- How could you create a safe environment in which to discuss the mentee's beliefs about teaching and learning mathematics?

To help support and guide your mentee, you could, for example, read an accessible research article together on a topic that might fuel discussion and cause the mentee to rethink their assumptions. Fruitful conversations could be had by exploring whether there is evidence that the way children are grouped (Education Endowment Foundation, 2018) or even the temperature of the classroom (Barrett et al., 2015) can have an impact on children's achievement in mathematics. Could you go on a learning walk with your mentee, visiting a number of classrooms to see whether you can deduce the observed teachers' beliefs about mathematics from the way they teach the subject and set up their classrooms? Could you carry out a piece of action research together where you explore something you want to change in the classroom in terms of the teaching and learning of mathematics? Topics for exploration might stem from targets that your mentee has identified for their own practice. You could research the children's views of what helps them most when they are stuck in their mathematics learning. For example, do the children value using manipulatives or particular images (such as a tens frame, number line or hundred square)? Do the children value working with a partner to talk through mathematics? King (2013) used action research to explore how the children in her Year 3 class thought they could help each other learn. These children also explained the many ways they could help each other, including demonstrating the use of equipment and giving each other ideas of how to proceed. This teacher was then able to incorporate these approaches in her teaching.

Supporting beginning teachers' development in mathematics

There are many ways to support the development of the teaching of mathematics. Some of these may be very similar to the ways you would support a teacher in any other area of the curriculum, but others will relate specifically to the teaching of mathematics. For example, consider the following strategies:

- *Use of manipulatives and images.* Go through the maths cupboard and discuss the mathematical ideas that are represented by each manipulative, and how these can be represented as simple pictures to support progression. Ask your mentee to show you exactly how they would model a concept using manipulatives. This will emphasise how challenging it can be to do this succinctly and clearly for children, using accurate vocabulary and mathematical explanations. Time spent in this way will enable the mentee to make progress in their practice and understand the importance of thinking through the use of representations when planning.
- *Understanding progression.* Ask your mentee to observe the teaching of one particular area of mathematics across the school - for example, place value or multiplication. Ask them to describe to you how the learning of this area progresses from the youngest to the oldest children, with a focus on when key ideas are introduced and how they become more complex and abstract as the children progress.
- *Shared book scrutiny of some maths books from the mentee's class and/or across the school.* Work with your mentee to look for key features such as the development of fluency, understanding, reasoning and problem-solving. Ask them to consider how marking is used to support progression, but in a way that is time effective for the teacher. While looking at the books, children's misconceptions may become apparent and a useful conversation can be held to discuss how such misconceptions can be addressed in subsequent lessons. Activities such as these can be useful for all the staff to undertake together, with the mathematics subject lead directing discussions. Observing such discussions taking place might be more valuable at this stage than the mentee undertaking the task themselves, since they will be able to access the wealth of experience of the teaching staff as a whole. Look for opportunities when this might be taking place as part of school development, such as at moderation meetings across schools, so your mentee might be able to witness these rich discussions and consider the implications for their own practice.
- *Articulating good practice in teaching mathematics.* Through joint observation of mathematics teaching - perhaps in your school or using video footage of mathematics lessons - you can draw up a shared understanding of what good mathematics teaching and learning looks like. As a basis for this discussion, you might use your school's maths policy or a set of prompts based on the philosophy and practices of the school. These

prompts can then be used as a basis for setting targets for the mentee's development. Prompt questions might include:

- How has the lesson been designed to enable all children to master the mathematical concepts being explored?
- Has the teacher included opportunities for the children to articulate their reasoning?
- Has the teacher used manipulatives and/or visual images to support children's understanding? Why have they chosen these particular representations?
- How has the teacher dealt with any misconceptions?
- Has the lesson progressed in small, coherent steps?

- *Supporting with planning for mathematics.* Discuss planning with your mentee to see if learning is organised in blocks so that the children have the chance to master ideas before moving on. Are they planning the correct use of vocabulary, the ordering of sequences of examples to support progression, the use of manipulatives and visual images alongside more formal notation and opportunities for talk? Have they built in reasoning and problem-solving opportunities for all children, not just those who finish early, and is there a clear and consistent focus on fluency that includes rapid recall but also linking facts? It is important to discuss how the mentee might be using planning resources such as a scheme of work or textbook. A plan for a single lesson taken from a scheme could be dissected together to help the mentee to see how the content has been designed to develop understanding, and to build the mentee's confidence in adapting plans to the needs of their children. In Task 13.5, consider the feedback you would give to the lesson that has been planned by the beginning teacher.

Task 13.5 What feedback do I give?

You can tell a great deal about your mentee's subject knowledge and understanding of effective teaching approaches by close examination of their planning.

- Look at the lesson plan written by a beginning teacher (see Figure 13.1).
- Make a note of what feedback you might give.

Now reflect in Task 13.6 about the different aspects of your feedback and compare your response with the illustrated example of the lesson plan in Figure 13.2.

Task 13.6 Identifying the focus of my feedback

- Which aspects of your feedback are about general pedagogy?
- Which aspects of your feedback are mathematics-specific?
- Compare your feedback to the example lesson plan with mentor feedback (Figure 13.2).
- Consider why the mentor has chosen to focus on these particular issues.

Context	One-hour lesson for a class of 9–10-year-old pupils.
Learning intention	To use long multiplication to multiply decimal numbers up to four digits by one- or two-digit numbers.
Implications from previous learning	The class practised long multiplication in the last lesson and the higher-ability group was introduced to decimal numbers. As all the children practise their multiplication tables regularly, they should be able to work out these answers easily.
Possible misconceptions	The children might try to use short multiplication instead of long multiplication. When using long multiplication (e.g. multiply by 38), they might think that they are multiplying by 3 instead of 30 in this row. They might not know where to put the decimal point.
Teaching input (25 mins)	Ask the children what long multiplication is. Remind them of this week's work. Question: How is long multiplication different from short multiplication? Whiteboards: Show me 17×14 using long multiplication. 10×4 = 40/7×4 = 28/10×7 = 70/10×10 = 100 40+28+70+100 = 238 Introduce that we will complete long multiplication with decimals today. Important: We must use the layout I put on the board. Write column headings and sum on board. Don't forget decimal point. Whiteboard: Write 1.6×6 Ask children what they notice about my layout: 6×6 = 36/10×6 = 60 36+60 = 96 Have to put the decimal point back in! One number after the decimal point in question so need to make sure there is one number after the decimal point in the answer. So the answer is 9.6.
Development (25 mins)	*Worksheet* Differentiation: Greater depth group: Different set of questions including numbers to two decimal places.
Plenary (10 mins)	Questions on PowerPoint (multiplying decimals) Five minutes against the clock. Peer-mark.

Figure 13.1 Lesson plan written by a beginning teacher

		Mentor feedback
Context	One-hour lesson for a class of 9–10-year-old pupils.	
Learning intention	To use long multiplication to multiply decimal numbers up to four digits by one- or two-digit numbers.	
Implications from previous learning	The class practised long multiplication in the last lesson and the higher-ability group was introduced to decimal numbers. As all the children practise their multiplication tables regularly, they should be able to work out these answers easily.	Do they have any conceptual understanding of multiplication as well as this procedural understanding?
Possible misconceptions	The children might try to use short multiplication instead of long multiplication. When using long multiplication (e.g. multiply by 38) they might think that they are multiplying by 3 instead of 30 in this row. They might not know where to put the decimal point.	Have you addressed all of these in your input?
Teaching input (25 mins)	Ask the children what long multiplication is. Remind them of this week's work. Question: How is long multiplication different from short multiplication? Whiteboards: Show me 17×14 using long multiplication. 10×4 = 40/7×4 = 28/10×7 = 70/10×10 = 100 40+28+70+100 = 238	This looks like you are asking the children to complete an 'expanded long multiplication' method. It's hard to tell as I'm not sure how you want them to write this? 17 × 14 40 28 70 100 238 This layout is an expanded long multiplication.
	Introduce that we will complete long multiplication with decimals today. Important: We must use the layout I put on the board. Write column headings and sum on board. Don't forget decimal point. Whiteboard: Write 1.6×6 Ask children what they notice about my layout: 6×6 = 36/10×6 = 60 36+60 = 96 Have to put the decimal point back in! One number after the decimal point in question so need to make sure there is one number after the decimal point in the answer. So answer is 9.6.	This looks like you are teaching procedurally. How will you get the children to have a conceptual understanding? Will the children use manipulatives alongside, for example? How will you help them to understand the value of the digits? 'Sum' means multiplication. Use the word 'calculation' instead. Careful! If you are doing this method, please explain that you are doing the similar calculation of 16×6 first, or you will confuse the children. Then you will use the answer to 16×6 to help you to answer 1.6×6.
Development (25 mins)	*Worksheet* Differentiation: Greater depth group: Different set of questions including numbers to two decimal places.	
Plenary (10 mins)	Questions on PowerPoint (multiplying decimals) Five minutes against the clock. Peer-mark.	Are you going to be getting the children to do any reasoning in this plenary?

Figure 13.2 Lesson plan with mentor feedback

Mathematics-specific feedback

Trainee teachers need enough subject-specific feedback to improve their expertise in teaching mathematics (Office for Standards in Education (Ofsted), 2013). Therefore, mentoring in mathematics must to some extent be focused on the mathematical. As we have argued, there are some issues that are distinct to learning to teach mathematics. Any discussion between mentor and mentee should include some mathematical content. For example, a discussion following a lesson observation might include generic comments relating to, say, the time the children sat on the carpet, the way transitions were handled and how behaviour for learning was promoted, but this would not be subject-specific. As well, you would expect the discussion to include, for example, a reflection on the choice of manipulatives or pictures used, and the way variation was used in the questioning so that the children's attention was directed to the key mathematical idea to allow the mentee to continue to develop their mathematics subject-specific expertise.

One way to ensure this is to consider the sort of knowledge you are hoping to promote as a mentor. This might be knowledge you actually impart or develop in your mentee, or knowledge that you explore together or that you support your mentee in developing in a coaching situation. The knowledge on which teachers draw in their teaching has long been a subject for debate. Shulman (1986, 1987) was one of the first people to articulate the sort of knowledge teachers use in their teaching. He listed seven types of knowledge teachers need. Three of these can be useful for a reflection on mentoring. He distinguished between subject or content knowledge - in this case, mathematical knowledge - and pedagogical content knowledge and curriculum knowledge (Shulman, 1986, 1987). This might be a useful way to consider your mentee's progress. For example:

- Does your mentee appear to be drawing on secure subject knowledge? Can they recall facts accurately and rapidly? Do they make links between addition and subtraction, showing these as inverses? Do they use mathematical terms accurately? Can they spot links between calculations, such as linking 3 x 18 to 6 x 9? Can they identify misconceptions?
- Does your mentee appear to have secure pedagogical content knowledge? For example, do they choose appropriate manipulatives and images to represent the mathematical idea they want the children to focus on? Can they plan a sequence of examples which take children gradually from something they are familiar with to a new idea? Do they understand how to challenge misconceptions? For example, a teacher might always place the equal sign in the same place and encourage children to think of its meaning as 'makes' rather than 'is the same as'. This means that children find it difficult to understand the equals sign in a problem such as 10 = ? + 3. Does the mentee understand that we might use representations in different ways? For example, we might use the array to introduce multiplication and in particular the commutative law, such as 3 x 4 = 4 x 3, with younger children. We can use it again to show the distributive law, such as 12 x 7 = 10 x 7 add 2 x 7, or to show that 3 x 8 = 6 x 4 with older children.
- Does your mentee have a secure knowledge of the curriculum and expectations for the year group they are teaching? Is the work and learning at the appropriate level? When children struggle to access mathematical activities, can they trace learning back to a

spot where there might be a gap in the children's understanding, or where a misconception might have been established? Do they teach in such a way as to provide a secure foundation for later learning? For example, a teacher who teaches children to multiply by ten by 'adding a zero' would contribute to a misconception when the children learn to multiply numbers with digits after the decimal point by ten at a later stage.

In Task 13.7, considering your last observation, reflect on the different types of knowledge that your mentee demonstrated in their teaching.

Task 13.7 Types of knowledge demonstrated

- What sort of knowledge did the beginning teacher draw on in planning and teaching?
- Can you separate out the knowledge they drew on into the three areas:
    - subject knowledge
    - pedagogical knowledge
    - curriculum knowledge?
- Can you see any reasons why it might be useful to separate knowledge in this way?

Although Shulman's (1986, 1987) model is a useful one to unpick the knowledge teachers need to develop to teach mathematics well, it is not written specifically for the teaching of primary mathematics. Other models have been developed to articulate the knowledge teachers need to teach primary mathematics well, and these can be much more specific and therefore more valuable to your role as a mentor. One particularly useful model is called the Knowledge Quartet (Rowland et al., 2009). The model is based on research undertaken by a team of researchers based at Cambridge University. They worked with postgraduate trainee teachers and teachers at the beginning of their careers, videoing lessons and interviewing them. They searched for evidence of the sort of knowledge drawn on by the teachers, and explored how it was evident in lessons and planning. In particular, the research aimed to identify ways in which teachers' mathematical and pedagogical content knowledge 'played out' (Rowland et al., 2009, p.26) in their teaching. Their findings resulted in four areas of knowledge, or domains, on which the trainee and early career teachers drew. These domains are similar to Shulman's (1986, 1987) categories of knowledge, but much more specific to teaching primary mathematics. The four areas of knowledge, summarised here, are:

1. *The foundation domain.* This domain includes the knowledge and understanding that the researchers (Rowland et al., 2009) argue is fundamental to decision-making when planning and teaching mathematics. It includes the teacher's personal knowledge of mathematics - demonstrated, for example, by their ability to identify errors in children's work and thinking, and their accurate use of mathematical terminology. The domain also includes the teacher's beliefs regarding the nature of mathematics and its purpose in the curriculum, and the teacher's knowledge of general pedagogy and how to use this in a mathematics lesson. It might be evident in the teacher's decisions about the best way to introduce

mathematical ideas to children, thinking about the amount of time spent listening on the carpet, or in practical work, or in discussion. Knowledge of the foundation domain can be evident in teachers' planning and seen from observation of their mathematics lessons.

2. *The transformation domain.* This domain includes the knowledge on which teachers draw in their planning and teaching, which relates to the way they transform the mathematical knowledge they have so it can be learned by the children in their class. This includes the teacher's choice and use of representations, examples, demonstrations, resources and activities. It is evident in the way teachers use manipulatives and pictures, and choose tasks for children to complete. For example, when teaching place value, a mentee might make use of different representations, such as bundles of straws, sweets that come in packets of ten, bead bars, Dienes, place value counters or place value cards. If a beginning teacher has developed a good level of transformation knowledge, they should be able to justify why they chose to use particular manipulatives. For example straws, in bundles of ten, sweets in packets of ten, and Dienes all show clearly that ten ones make a ten, and then ten tens make a hundred. Place value counters are more abstract as the ones, tens and hundreds counters are all the same size. Place value cards do not show this aspect of place value, but they do show the way numbers are written and challenge a number of common misconceptions around zero being used as a placeholder. Your mentee might also be able to explain their justification for using manipulatives and images in their teaching generally, referring perhaps to theory such as that of Bruner's modes of representation: enactive, iconic and symbolic (Bruner, 1966). As you observe your mentee and talk to them about why they choose certain examples, you will be able to get a feel for their level of transformation knowledge.
3. *The connection domain.* This domain includes the knowledge of the connections that teachers make with children. These connections can relate to progression. Such connections might be evident in the sequencing of mathematical ideas across an activity, lesson or a series of lessons in a unit of work. For example, teachers use this knowledge to order ideas coherently as they plan for mathematics topics over the year, recognising the importance of counting and place value and how the teaching of written methods of addition, subtraction, multiplication and division build on these. Teachers also build connections over a unit of work, and in their planning and teaching for progression. For example, they might make links between number bonds to 10 and number bonds to 20 then 100. They also build connections between ideas in mathematics lessons, for example linking counting in twos to doubling. Knowledge from the connection domain is evident in your monitoring of your mentee's planning, in your observation of their lessons and discussion with them.
4. *The contingency domain.* This domain includes the knowledge teachers draw on to respond to ideas from the children that have not been anticipated. This area of knowledge underpins the beginning teacher's decision to act on or ignore the unexpected, and their ability to modify planning unexpectedly. For example, they might start a lesson and uncover a misconception held by a significant number of children and have to change their plans. Or a child might offer an idea that could lead into a different area of learning, such as a child who notices when working on the 8 times table, that all the multiples of 8 are even. The teacher then quickly has to make a decision as to what to do next. The knowledge from this domain is only evident in teaching and not in planning.

However, you may be able to unpick your mentee's level of contingency knowledge in your discussion with them as they reflect on their teaching.

Using the same lesson that you previously reflected upon in Task 13.1, in Task 13.8 consider the lesson from the viewpoint of the four domains of the Knowledge Quartet.

Task 13.8 The Knowledge Quartet

- Does this Knowledge Quartet framework enable you to analyse the lesson in a significantly different way from your previous response?
- Can the model help you to identify what sort of knowledge your mentee has and needs to develop, and therefore plan for their professional development?

Summary

This chapter has highlighted the particular support a beginning teacher may need to become an effective teacher of primary mathematics. You will need to develop a supportive relationship with the mentee as they explore subject and pedagogical knowledge. A positive attitude towards mathematics is important in teachers, and mentors will have to handle these discussions with sensitivity. It may be that the mentor will need to support the mentee in changing their mindset towards mathematics and how children learn. This will be well worth the investment because effective teachers of mathematics inspire children to develop a love of the subject too. Good primary mathematics teaching builds children's conceptual understanding and will include opportunities to develop fluency and reasoning. As well as sound subject and pedagogical knowledge, good teachers of primary mathematics have positive attitudes towards the subject and believe their understanding can develop. This enables them to support children's positive attitudes towards learning mathematics. Beginning teachers can be supported in their development of teaching mathematics by joint activities with a mentor, such as book scrutinies and discussing how manipulatives and images can represent mathematical ideas. It is important that you give your mentee mathematics-specific feedback to support their development as a primary mathematics teacher. The Knowledge Quartet (Rowland et al., 2009) is a useful model for analysing the specific knowledge needed by an effective teacher of primary mathematics and can be used to guide the support you give to your mentee.

Further reading

Askew, M. (2007) *Transforming Primary Mathematics*, Abingdon: Routledge.

Boaler, J. (2016) *Mathematical Mindsets*, San Francisco: Jossey-Bass.

Rowland, T., Turner, F., Thwaites, A. and Huckstep, P. (2009) *Developing Primary Mathematics Teaching: Reflecting on Practice with the Knowledge Quartet*. London: Sage.

14 Mentoring for physical education

Kristy Howells

Introduction

Primary physical education is one of the few places that takes the children outside from their 'normal' classroom-based learning environment to enable them to explore a world of learning that can occur inside in the school hall, or outside on a variety of surfaces, such as the playground or the school field. This can be a scary time for the beginning teacher as it may be the lesson that takes them out of their comfort zone. Yet this escape can instil a sense of adventure, a sense of excitement, and can inspire children to learn through, within and about their own bodies as they learn to physically develop, physically move. Children will learn skills and abilities beyond just the physical. They will also learn socially, morally, emotionally and spiritually. The National Curriculum in England states that the physical education curriculum will 'inspire all pupils to succeed and excel' (DfE, 2013a, p.198). Within the key stage 2 subject content, there is an emphasis on the children's capacity to 'enjoy communicating, collaborating and competing with each other' (2013a, p.199). Therefore, it is important as a mentor to support the beginning teacher to be confident and competent to enable children to 'enjoy' physical education, especially as it is the role of the teacher to provide opportunities for the children to become 'physically confident' (2013a, p.198). This chapter will consider how to help you as a mentor to support your beginning teacher to develop their understanding of physical confidence and how to think more through movement and develop a love for movement within their teaching.

Objectives

At the end of this chapter, you should be able to:

- Support your beginning teacher to foster curiosity and confidence in the essential elements of good practice in primary physical education
- Support your beginning teacher to optimise learning within primary physical education
- Support your beginning teacher to adopt strategies to continue to develop your own teaching and mentoring of primary physical education.

What are the essential elements of good practice in primary physical education?

To start the chapter off, Task 14.1 looks at the essential elements of physical education.

Task 14.1 Elements of physical education

- Write a list of what you consider to be the essential elements of physical education.
- Ask your mentee to also complete a list, then compare and discuss the similarities and differences in your lists.

In my earlier work (Howells 2015, 2018) I identified that there are four essential areas for good practice in primary physical education:

- pace
- structure
- transferable skills
- competition.

Pace

Pace is the number one element of good practice in primary physical education. On numerous occasions, children will enter the physical learning environment and then sit on the floor or stand in the playground for the first instructions. Instead, there is often time while the children are getting changed for practitioners to set the first instructions in the classroom, so the children are focused and ready to learn immediately. Beginning teachers may not realise this, and need to be encouraged to be brave and try it. They might also feel it is a brave thing to do, but through your encouragement your mentee could start to set individual targets and challenges for the children within the classroom that are linked to the upcoming lesson, so they work on these within the lesson and achieve more. You may need to make your mentees aware of how long, for example, they are talking during the physical part of the lesson at the expense of activity. Quite often, the best way for beginning teachers to develop awareness is to actually have you, or another colleague, observe and time how long the mentee talks for or how long it takes the mentee to share instructions. They may well be surprised how long they take to share instructions. Another way would be to video them teaching physical education, so they can see how much they talk and the children are static. This will help them review their pace and allow them to reflect on whether what they were saying was necessary, and whether the children needed to be static while they were talking.

The National Curriculum for Physical Education in England states that children need to be 'physically active for sustained periods of time' (DfE, 2013a, p.198), so it is important to consider the impact of the beginning teacher and how often they are stopping and starting activities, rather than having sustained periods of activity. One way to help support your mentee would be to encourage them to state timings on their plans for each part of the lesson, just as in other lessons, as this will help them to develop a good pace. This is particularly important to ensure that there is time for a cool-down period at the end of the lesson, and that this is not lost, forgotten or rushed. A cool-down is key to ensuring time for recapping the learning that has taken place within the lesson, exploring the impact of the children's learning and celebrating the achievements of the children within the lesson. This can also act as a calming moment for the children before they return to the more enclosed classroom setting. Task 14.2 focuses on pace within the cool-down by observing the beginning teacher's cool-down and discussing with them the different aspects that are involved in a cool-down in terms of physical education learning.

Task 14.2 Focusing on pace

- How did the beginning teacher use questions within the cool-down to recap knowledge and understanding learnt within the lesson?
- How did they celebrate movement progressions within the cool-down?
- How did they explain the progressions?
- Did the beginning teacher share with the children the next steps and the next lessons?

Structure

The next essential element is structure. This links to pace in that, if the beginning teacher has good structure, the children will see the flow between one activity and the next and this will enhance the progression of their learning and in turn the progression of the mentee's learning. All teachers, including beginning teachers, need to consider whether the structure of each lesson is similar or whether they vary the structure according to the learning that is occurring within the lesson. The key to developing ownership and individual structure of the lesson is to make sure that warm-up activities link to the focus or theme of the lesson. For example, if the focus is on gymnastics activities such as balance and coordination, then the warm-up should have a gymnastics element to it and/or a balance and coordination element to it. Quite often there is a tendency to 'just play a warm-up game' that does not link to the lesson intentions. It can disappoint children and reduce their enjoyment levels if the teacher moves from, say, a games-based warm-up to gymnastics. Instead, it is important to consider what gymnastics games and/or activities could be played at the beginning of the lesson and show the focus of the game - for example, balance and coordination - to then follow on and link to the whole structure of the lesson. This will allow the children to be focused, which helps enhance their learning. If you encourage this approach with the beginning teacher, it will allow them to make the most of the potentially limited allocated time that they have for physical education within the school week.

Within your mentee's lesson plans you need to ensure that they have mapped out how they will organise the activities. Are they starting as a whole class then moving into pair, or group work, or are they starting small as individual or pair for exploratory work, then building up to a whole class? This mapping out will make transitions quicker and easier for the beginning teacher. You need to encourage mentees to *always* plan to have a trio when they are planning for pair work, as they will often have an odd number of pupils in their class. Rather than be flummoxed by their planned numbers not working, they need to plan for the unexpected so that they will be confident in their delivery as they have already planned for this obstacle.

Within structure, another key aspect of planning to consider is teaching points. Rather than just planning to teach, say, a teddy bear roll, the plans a beginning teacher will have structured will include details about the key words, phrases and detailed teaching points that they will actually use to articulate the teddy bear roll to all abilities. This may seem like extra planning to the beginning teacher, but it will actually help them with their assessment, as they will be able to clearly see where the children need support and where they need extra support (e.g. legs getting stuck in the air). If your mentee has not focused on identifying the key teaching points, they will not be able to give immediate formative feedback, and this is when the children can get bored within the lessons and disruption can occur.

Children rely on formative feedback, especially in primary physical education. Physical education is one of those subjects in which children find it really difficult to see what they are doing and to be able to know and understand their own progression. Therefore, the teacher is vital in assessing, observing and giving productive formative feedback that will help progression. Your mentees need to plan the areas that you will be looking for within your structure – this is vital and a key resource in progression. Case study 14.1 shows photographs for illustration of the teddy bear roll and the appropriate teaching points for each stage.

Case study 14.1 Amelia completing a teddy bear roll and the key teaching points of each stage

Key teaching points

Stage 1: Sit in straddle position (toes pointed, body tall).

Stage 2: Lean to your favourite side (keeping the straddle position).

Stage 3: Kick the leg in the air down towards the floor.

Stage 4: Sit back up.

Transferable skills

Transferable skills are really useful to include in lesson planning. They can help children make sense of the world, their movement and their development physically, cognitively and socially. A child needs to understand – and, similarly, beginning teachers need to understand – how the balance they are learning to control within, for example, dance can help to support them in their games activities or swimming activities. The children will not be able to spot or identify the skills that are transferable, so the teacher needs to identify those for them. The easiest way to do this is for your mentee to put transferable skills into their plans so they are able to remember to share with the children, to recap previous learning and also to extend next steps. This is essential so children can see that they are doing the same activity, skills and abilities within different situations. Within the National Curriculum for Physical Education (DfE, 2013a, p.199), pupils should be 'developing balance, agility and coordination, and begin to apply these in a range of activities'. Mentees are going to need to identify the multiple times they will be working on the A, B, Cs (Howells, 2019) of simple, complex and functional movements as these early A, B, Cs continue to develop into key stage 2 and link to developing 'flexibility, strength, technique, control and balance' (DfE, 2013a, p.200).

The National Curriculum (DfE, 2013a) focuses on multiple transferable skills, which are the elements that the children have to learn within physical education; however, they are often forgotten in planning. They are easy to identify and easy to map within mentees' plans so they know where they have covered them with their children, how they are progressing, how they are linked and how they can be used to identify areas on which the children still need to work. These could include body tension, extension, control, coordination, stability, timing, spatial awareness, focus, flow and clarity of dynamics, to name a few. Discuss with the beginning teacher, how, where and what transferable skills they could add to their lesson plan to enhance the physical education learning. Task 14.3 will help you to identify these skills.

Task 14.3 Identifying transferable skills

In their lesson plan, can the beginning teacher identify the following skills?

- collaboration
- competition
- balance
- stability
- challenge
- timing
- travelling (with/without a ball)
- confidence
- fluidity/flow
- body tension
- extension
- control
- spatial awareness
- focus
- sending
- receiving
- agility
- flexibility
- strength.

Competition

The fourth essential element is competition, which could be considered quite prominent within the primary physical education curriculum (DfE, 2013a) as competition features within the curriculum multiple times. The Purpose of Study states that 'opportunities to compete in sport and other activities build character and help to embed values such as fairness and respect' (2013a, p. 198). This is repeated in the Aims, which states that all pupils should 'engage in competitive sports and activities' (2013a, p. 198). In key stage 1 subject content, teachers should be getting the children to 'engage in competitive (both against self and others)' (2013a, p. 199) physical activities, while in Key Stage 2 subject content, children now need to 'enjoy ... competing with each other' (2013a, p. 199). Within key stage 1, the focus could be on developing emotional resilience linked to competition, and how the children cope with winning and losing. So your mentees do not have the five- to seven-year-olds running round shouting 'losers' at each other for the rest of the day, the beginning teacher may need help in embedding fairness and respect into their lesson planning. This is where their structure and the importance of timing and pace for the cool-down can help them as a beginning teacher. This can be their space to recognise the success, but not just who won - also why, and how. This can also be a place to recognise particularly good performances, or performances that have improved within the lesson. Crucially, this is where the teacher's, and especially the beginning teacher's, observational skills are important. It is also is important for you to encourage your mentees to keep records of performance. This will aid the children in developing their cognitive skills, through comparing their performances and demonstrating improvement as well as understanding how they have physically improved. In Task 14.4, reflect on how you currently record improvement then read Case study 14.2, which illustrates a way to recognise improvement that may be greater than the actual 'winner'.

Task 14.4 Recording improvement

- What objective measurements do you use to help children compare their performances and analyse their improvements?
- Discuss with your mentee how they and you could record performances to help learning within physical education.
- Use Case study 14.2 to discuss with your mentee ways to record and assess pupils' performance.

Case study 14.2 The importance of recording objective measurements

Child's name	*Week 1 - first attempts at throwing a foam javelin, using a guided discovery approach.*	*Week 2 - focused on transferring weight from the back foot forwards as the foam javelin was thrown*
Jonny	3.00 m	3.10 m
Gloria	2.15 m	2.65 m

The table illustrates both the distance thrown and the teaching points that were given to the children.

Jonny threw a foam javelin in Week 1 to a distance of 3 m and in Week 2 he went beyond this and threw a foam javelin 3.10 m. He may be regarded as the overall winner when he is competing against others.

However, while Gloria's improvements from 2.15 m to 2.65 m from Week 1 to Week 2 is greater than Jonny's improvements, her improvements still keep her in second place (in this example); however, in terms of competing against herself, she has improved dramatically. Gloria's improvements were due to her really focusing on transferring the weight of her body within the throw, which she had not achieved within the first week's attempts. The extra teaching points and assessment points helped her improve.

In terms of the sports man/woman of the day, I would award this to Gloria due to her improvements. This will help Jonny develop his respect for others even though he still 'won' the overall distance. This example also shows the importance of record-keeping from one week to the next, including of the extra teaching points that helped with the improvements. This will help not only the planning, but also to help the children to understand their learning and progression.

What do beginning teachers need to help them to optimise learning in physical education?

One of the ways in which beginning teachers can help to optimise pupil learning in physical education is to develop their own observation skills through understanding and analysing what really happens in a physical education lesson. A beginning teacher needs to consider what to observe and how to observe it, and also consider how to observe equipment that the pupils are using, as this can be key to understanding the whole movement process. Alongside observations, questions that are used by the teacher will help to develop the children's learning. Planning for observations and planning for questions are key elements that will help the beginning teacher to be confident in observing the whole class, as well as focus children and individual children. Observing a whole class can be overwhelming when a beginning teacher first starts, but with preparation and templates it can be made a great deal more efficient and easier. Encourage your mentee not to be afraid to ask the children to repeat the skill or activity while they are observing, so they get to see the movement more than once. Children can quite easily be doing something 'funny' as a one off and correct things themselves.

There are two main ways to observe movement and skills in isolation and then one combined way to observe (Howells et al., 2017). The first is the biomechanical way in which the focus is on body parts - what is happening at the head and eyes; the arms; the body; the legs; and finally the feet. If your mentee is using equipment, how does each of these body parts interlink with equipment - for example, how is the child holding the tennis racket and how are they holding the ball prior to serving? Being aware of what is happening with each body part can help feed into the mentee's teaching points. This in turn feeds into the information that they will question and share with the children while they are giving them formative feedback. Ultimately, this feeds into their assessment of the lesson, movement and skills. This is the easiest of the two ways to observe, and helps the beginning teacher to start to learn and develop their understanding and knowledge of movement, which for some is an incredibly difficult skill to master (see Table 14.1). Allow time for your mentee to observe you, other colleagues and children moving during break times so they can become familiar with observing different parts of the body and deciding whether or not that movement is accurate.

Table 14.1 Body parts and skill observation template

Body part	*Observation of the skill*
Head/eyes	
Body	
Arms/hands	
Legs/feet	

The second way to observe is to focus on the parts of the skill. This links back to skills acquisition theory, where the skill is broken down into the preparation phase - essentially, everything that is done with the body and equipment before the movement occurs. This is sometimes referred to by children as the readiness phase. Next comes the action phase, which includes all the movement that occurs within the skills; this is normally the largest part of the observation. Finally comes the recovery phase, which is the end part of the movement, where the child is regaining balance to finish the movement or return to the readiness stance, ready to go again.

The combined method is to use the biomechanical method within the skill base in order to combine and break down the skill not only into the parts of the skill but also into what each of the body parts is doing within that skill. You could use this style of observation with beginning teachers who have specialised in physical education within their initial teacher education.

Below is a three-stage process that a beginning teacher is able to work through to help support their own development of observation skills that will be used within a primary physical education lesson. It is possible to work through the three stages and the checklists as a mentor with your mentee, as well as using others' observation techniques to help develop their physical education pedagogies. It is important for a mentee to identify whether they are seeing and observing the same movements, skills and abilities that the children are demonstrating as other colleagues observe. Ideally, your mentee should practise observations of children's movement alongside someone else, or by using video so that they can then discuss the skills/activities they are observing.

The stages are set out as tasks (Tasks 14.5 to 14.7), for you to complete, to help your mentoring. The first stage of the mentoring role focuses on unpicking how a lesson has been planned, how the mentee is observing the whole lesson - not just individual skills - and beginning to develop individual skill/tactic observation (Task 14.5). The second stage of observation is based more on consecutive lessons. Can they see, for example, how the lessons are linked together and built upon, and how progression of the learning is developed? How are key questions planned for and used? Also, Stage 2 considers how children with special educational needs and disability (SEND) are planned for and engaged within the lesson (Task 14.6). Stage 3 focuses on identifying differences between EYFS and KS1 or between KS1 and KS2, and looking at how specific movement skills are developed (Task 14.7).

Table 14.2 Stage 1 checklist for critiquing observed physical education lessons

Skills being learnt
What physical skills were being learnt and how?
Beyond the physical skills, what other skills were being learnt?

Structure of lesson
How was the lesson structured?
Why was the lesson structured in this way?
Were the children successful at developing their skills?
How were the children grouped?

Progression
How were skills/tactics developed within one lesson?
What was the role of the teacher?
What questions did they use and when?

Assessment
How were the children assessed?
What questions were used by the teacher?
How would you record/assess the children? Compare with the class teacher.

Task 14.5 Stage 1: Planning the lesson

- Ask your mentee to observe your own physical education lesson, or if possible video your lesson and then critique it using the checklist in Table 14.2. Then discuss with your mentee what they observed in terms of how you planned the lesson - structure, assessment, questioning, teaching styles.
- Ask your mentee to then plan and teach the warm-up with you or another member of staff, or to team teach a skill or activity. Discuss with your mentee the planning process and how they planned for structure, assessment, questioning and teaching styles.

Task 14.6 Stage 2: Considering consecutive lessons with your mentee

- Ask your mentee to observe your physical education lessons in consecutive weeks, or video them and critique them using the checklist in Table 14.3.
- Discuss with your mentee how they think their children are progressing in their physical education learning from one week to the next. How did they know they were progressing?
- Ask your mentee to observe and record how children with SEND are planned for. Do they ensure that all children are planned for and engaged in learning within physical education lessons?
- Critique the observations and records together.

Table 14.3 Stage 2 task checklist for critiquing physical education lessons

Progression

What have children learnt from one week to the next?
How did the children remember what they had learnt? What type of questions did the teacher use?
What difficulties have the children had in remembering what they had learnt previously?
What do you need to plan for them to overcome such difficulties?

Skills being learnt

Can you identify from either observations or planning the practical, cognitive and personal skills (see below) that were planned for within the physical education lesson to ensure the children were physically educated and how these were developed over the weeks?

Physical skills

Psycho-motor; visual-spatial; potential for skill learning and performance (fitness)

Cognitive skills

Planning; analysis; evaluation; creativity; knowledge and understanding; health

Social skills

Interpersonal: social; leadership; intrapersonal; moral; motivation

Task 14.7 Stage 3: Considering different age phases

- Ask your mentee to observe a variety of different physical education lessons throughout the school. Are they able to identify the differences between EYFS and KS1 or KS1 and KS2 lesson and observe specific movement skills (checklist for observing movement skills)?
- Discuss their observations with them.
- Focus your mentee on how groups are used within physical education lessons and why they have grouped this way. How does it help the learning of all children?

Use Table 14.4 for support.

What help do beginning teachers need to teach physical education more effectively?

Strategies exist that can be used to help beginning teachers teach physical education more effectively. One strategy used within physical education is to 'put on the act' even if, for example, dancing is not their favourite area. Mentees need to provide that inspirational role model to their children. They need to put on their dancing shoes and show them how to do it. You wouldn't expect the beginning teacher to go into a literacy lesson not excited about the activity, so it is important to remind them that they need to be engaged and that they also need to be excited in physical education lessons. If mentees are really worried about teaching a particular dance, they need to think back to the curriculum where the requirements are to 'perform dances using simple movement patterns' (KS1) (DfE, 2013a, p. 199) or 'using a range of movement patterns' (KS2) (DfE, 2013a, p. 199). Your mentee doesn't have to be like the dancers on *Strictly Come Dancing* or *Britain's Got Talent*, or be the greatest dancer

Table 14.4 Stage 3 task checklist for your mentee to use to observe movement skills within different age phases in physical education lessons

Observe

What are you observing - skill, individual, team?
Watch the whole movement.
Watch the whole movement more than once.

Analyse

Did the whole movement look right?
Was the outcome of the movement effective?
Is the movement repeatable?
Does it match criteria? If so, how?
What criteria are you using?
Can you describe the movement using the preparation phase, action phase and recovery phase?
Can you describe the movement using the head, arms, body, legs/feet?
What improvements (teaching points) would you suggest?
Can you phrase the improvements and teaching points so it is the next positive challenge for the child?
Does the pupil improve during the session and if so, how?
Where did the children give any feedback?
What type of feedback were they given and by whom?

themselves - they don't need six months' training - but they may feel they need to be. To boost their own confidence, you could suggest that your mentee attends a local Zumba, jive, hip-hop, line dancing or a street dance class. Perhaps hold a staff session after school so they can see that there is no expectation for them to be an amazing dancer. Alternatively, you could suggest to your mentee that they watch videos on YouTube and then bring these into their teaching with the children. They can take what they learn and focus on how to break down the skill, what the teaching points are and how to put the dances together. Some of the best dances I have done with my primary-aged children have come from watching choreography on YouTube, then drawing my own pictures, my own choreography and planning to help me visualise how to teach it to the children. One particular favourite is 'Everything Is Awesome', the song from *The Lego Movie*. Case study 14.3 illustrates the song 'Everything is Awesome' and how to choreograph this song into a dance.

Case study 14.3 Everything is awesome choreography

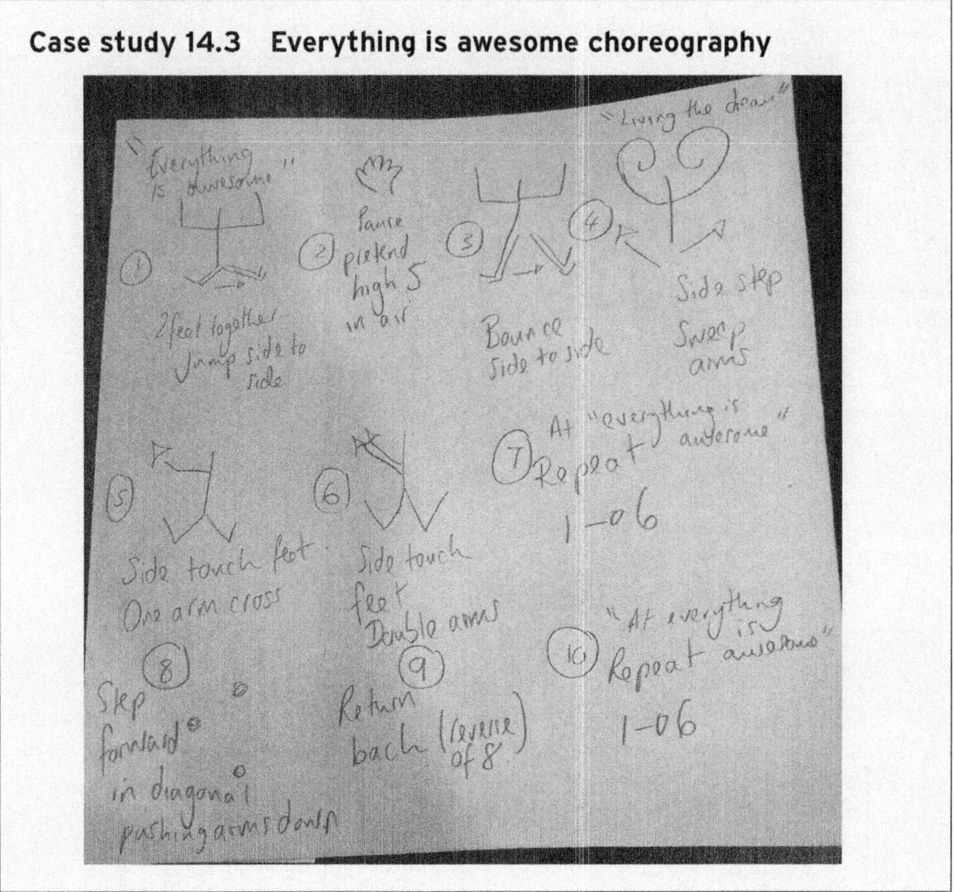

Another example of the use of films to enhance dance is illustrated in Case study 14.4.

Case study 14.4 Dance linked to films and music

The fight scene in *Star Wars: The Phantom Menace* is a good choice – like *The Lego Movie*, the film is rated as U, so suitable for all your children. The fight scene is often referred to as a dance, as the characters are reacting and acting to their movements with balance, coordination, stability, and links between actions and motifs (for KS2). These film clips can be used as a stimulus or used as whole songs to develop the aims and content of the National Curriculum. You need to allow time and space for children to review, develop and enhance their performances, as these are important aspects of the development and progression of learning. Although brilliant to move to and respond to, I have to admit the 'crazy frog song' was one that I regretted after using it for several consecutive lessons. The children, however, loved it as it was very popular with them at the time, so it is important to use meaningful and timely music and stimulus to enhance your teaching.

Another strategy is the need for detailed planning, especially at the beginning of a career, so your mentee knows how the lesson is flowing and what happens next. They will need to plan in detail for the next challenges, to differentiate. In thinking about how they are going to group the children, Pickup et al. (2008) proposed different ways to group: by physical ability (high, middle and low ability); by mixed ability; randomly; by friendship group; and by grouping non-performers. When considering grouping, the beginning teacher needs to think about the aim of the group: does the teacher want them to cooperate, collaborate or compete, as these 3Cs (cooperate, collaborate, compete) may influence the way and style used to group the children.

There are many pros and cons for each type of grouping, and these can be explored further through the resources in the Further reading section at the end of the chapter. To help build your confidence in mentoring physical education, you could use sports coaches or an expert coordinator who you may have within your school. Sports coaches or other experienced colleagues within your school can also help to develop the confidence and competence of your beginning teacher, encouraging them to work on their physical education teaching if it is not as strong as their other subject areas. You would not want your mentee to miss that moment when Freddie scores his first-ever goal or when Georgia balances across the beam for the first time. Mentees need to teach and see these moments, rather than avoiding and stepping away from physical education. Encourage them to love physical education, even if they do not see themselves as an expert.

If you do not have sports coaches within your school and you are the expert coordinator, then it is important to share with your mentee how you develop your plans. Ask them to come and watch you. Encourage them to ask you for advice on how to progress learning in consecutive lessons, especially when they change to new topic areas or focused areas within the curriculum. When they are learning how to identify faults and begin to offer feedback and next step progressions to the children, ensure that you have encouraged them to only identify one fault at a time. Trying to identify everything, even though they may now be able to see movement and see that everything that is wrong, won't work! The key here is that your mentee knows how to preserve children's motivation and excitement within physical education. Although it is sometimes easier to do so, they must not be tempted to tell children that everything is rubbish or needs lots of improvement. Instead, ask them to focus on positives and *why* the movements are right. Beginning teachers need to identify which part will make the most difference and then focus on this, thus giving the children clear directions and guidance on how to progress – the HOW of movement. Your mentees need to be detailed in their progression of the movement in their feedback, as shown in Case study 14.5.

Case study 14.5 How to extend feedback focusing on the *how* of movement for Jonny undertaking a handstand

You can't just tell Jonny, 'You need your legs higher in your handstand'.

You need to tell him *how* to get his legs higher: he can't see his legs, and he may think that his legs are really high! If mentees don't know how, they need to ask and seek support from their mentors and physical education coordinators.

You could support Jonny with the extra details of the how: 'Jonny, as you put your hands down on the floor, shoulder width apart, focus on pushing down hard with your hands as you kick the legs up towards the ceiling, with toes pointed.'

That way, Jonny has a clear target and goal to be working on: the pressure of the hands, the direction of the legs and the extension and tension of the toes. You can then come back, question and reassess his progression later. Some visual guidance may be needed, such as demonstrations from your mentee or from Jonny's peers, as well as verbal guidance to help show where the fault is and how to improve it.

Be clear and concise in your feedback, so the mentee can step away from this child with them fully understanding what the beginning teacher would like them to do next and what they are expecting from them. Don't be afraid to ask them to repeat back to the beginning teacher what their next challenge is. If the phrase 'the next challenge' is used, the child has a goal and purpose, and it will help them to remain positive.

If you acknowledge the importance and value of physical education, then your mentees will too. Howells (2012) identifies that primary schools are places where habits, likes and dislikes are formed, and therefore the value of physical activity, physical education and school sport can have an impact on children continuing to be active and healthy later into life. Therefore, be a role model and show the importance of activity; do not treat physical education as a moveable item, or miss physical education if it is raining or due to the nativity play. Physical education is a statutory compulsory subject through all key stages, from the age of four until the age of sixteen. Although it is the responsibility of schools to determine the amount of time per week allocated to physical education, the government and Ofsted recommend two hours of high-quality physical education a week. It should be given the same value as literacy, mathematics, science and computing. It is therefore recommended that it is not taken away due to poor behaviour within other subject lessons and is not used as a time to practise the school play or because the choir needs the space. These excuses are inexcusable!

For some children, physical education will be their only structured time of physical activity. Bailey, Howells and Glibo (2018, p.2) identify that 'physical activity has an important part to play in protecting young children from mental illness, and has the potential to save lives through helping to reduce feelings of hopelessness, suicide and self-harm'. Howells and Bowen (2016) state that physical education and physical activity have a positive influence on self-esteem of primary aged children. School and physical education lessons are often seen as the vehicle to provide opportunities for children to be physically active and to solve the obesity crisis. Pate, O'Neill and McIver (2011) propose that physical education lessons are often claimed to be the key place to provide 'important benefits to public health' and the World Health Organization (WHO) has previously suggested that one way of increasing children's physical activity levels could be to increase the number of physical education lessons – as long as children do not spend longer in a queue than they do participating!

Physical education can also be a time and place where other holistic skills are developed, not just physical skills, so it is important a beginning teacher recognises how and where these skills are being developed. Kirk (1993) and later Laker (2000) developed domains of

Table 14.5 Domains of learning applied to the National Curriculum for physical education in England

Practical	*Cognitive*	*Social*
Mastering basic movements Running Jumping Throwing and catching Balance Agility Coordination and control Dance Strength Flexibility	Tactics and principles for attacking and defending Applying and developing skills to link to make actions and sequences Understand how to improve Recognising success Compare performances and demonstrate improvements	Communicating Collaborating Challenges both individually and within a team Compete with self and with team against others Cope with not winning Confidence

Source: Howells (2015).

Table 14.6 Domains of learning applied to the Early Years Foundation Stage curriculum in England

Practical	*Cognitive*	*Social*
Controlled effort Active games Energetic play Use of beanbags, cones, balls and hoops Stand on one foot Move freely Climb Negotiate space, adjust speed, direction, avoid obstacles Catching, rolling Draw lines and circles Experiment with ways of moving Jumping off objects Increasing control over objects Kick Balance Target throwing	Create different moods and talk about feelings Use key movement vocabulary Use key manipulation vocabulary Pose challenging questions Follow sensible rules Understand how body feels and express how it feels Know why you get hot	Confidence Collaborative throwing, rolling, fetching, receiving Play with one another Understand boundaries of self and others Match activity to interests.

Source: Howells (2017).

learning to include physical/practical, cognitive and social (including emotional) elements of learning that take place within a physical education lesson and that teachers can focus on. Howells (2015) applied these domains of learning to the National Curriculum for Physical Education (DfE, 2013a) (Table 14.5) and later in 2017 they were applied (Howells, 2017) to the Early Years Foundation Stage framework (EYFS) (DfE, 2014) (Table 14.6). The aim was to be able to share and to show experienced teachers, mentors and beginning teachers how they were already thinking in the domains of learning within the planning they were undertaking. In a very similar way to adding transferable skills to plans, these domains of learning can also be applied.

How can mentors best support mentees in their teaching of physical education?

Given that children's physical education lessons occur in most schools for only two hours a week, it may be that most/some beginning teachers have limited experience of teaching physical education. It is therefore likely that mentees are in great need of your support. For many, sports coaches may have taken physical education lessons, or perhaps the mentee had their planning, preparation and assessment (PPA) time allocated during physical education time during their initial teacher education.

It may have been that they were not in a year group or the right time of year when classes went swimming, so may have missed teaching any swimming. Even though their initial teacher education gives them the best opportunities to learn and develop, they may not have had many opportunities. However, there are also beginning teachers who specialise in physical education during their initial teacher education. Such beginning teachers need challenging and developing, perhaps through peer tutoring of others. They need to share and to be asked questions about what their dissertations and independent research projects focused on. This could lead to enhanced practice at a whole-school level.

Summary

This chapter has identified that you, as a mentor, need to spend time with your mentee to check on their confidence as well as competence levels, and to support them in their planning. In particular, it is important to check that real learning is taking place within the lessons - that is, that their identified teaching points ensure progression of learning is occurring rather than just doing activities/skills. Ideally, mentors need to challenge the beginning teacher in discussion about how they go about planning, in particular, for consecutive lessons and how they are planning for the range of abilities within the class, including children with SEND. The latter can be an area of which many beginning teachers are fearful, and some may not know where to start. It is also important to have discussions with the beginning teacher about what else other than physical learning is occurring within the physical education lessons.

Spending time watching your mentee teach, but with a specific focus on, for example, the length of time it takes to give instructions, how to stop the children or how to learn on the playground vs the field are all areas that would benefit the mentee. You should offer physical education-specific related advice linked to the focus that the mentee has requested or negotiated, as sometimes mentees do not know what they need. They also need guidance on, or discussions about, how to record assessments so they can develop children's learning from one lesson to another, so they can pass information onto the next year's class teacher to continue the children's progression in physical education. This means the children are never in a position where they may be bored.

Physical education can provide a wonderful learning opportunity for children and also for teachers, although it is recognised that many teachers - beginners and experienced educators - are worried or fearful about teaching physical education. There are so many opportunities in physical education to help support children to lead healthy, active lives, to build character, to build children to be the next generation of Olympians, Paralympians, sport reporters, sport analysts, all through inspiring and motivating them during their formative years within primary school settings. All this needs is you and your mentee to support the children to fulfil their potential.

Further reading

Howells, K., with Carney, A., Castle, N., and Little, R. (2017) *Mastering Primary Physical Education,* London: Bloomsbury.

Pickup, I., Price, L., Shaughnessey, J., Spence, J. and Trace, M. (2008) *Learning to Teach Primary PE*, London: Sage.

Sewell, K. (ed.) (2018) *Planning the Primary National Curriculum: A Complete Guide for Trainees and Teachers*. 2nd ed., London: Sage, pp. 266-80.

15 Mentoring for reading

Rachael Stone

Introduction

This chapter will support you in mentoring beginning teachers by developing their understanding of what it means to teach reading. What constitutes the teaching of reading may be perceived differently by teachers of different key stages, but this chapter will be helpful for mentors of mentees teaching from Reception to Year 6. Reading is viewed as a holistic activity within this chapter, which draws on what is considered to be best practice for teaching reading. The chapter focuses on developing your awareness of what it means to teach reading, and how to then develop the understanding of your mentee. It provides extracts from case studies to illustrate how prompt statements on the teaching of reading can develop your mentee's understanding.

Objectives

At the end of the chapter, you should be able to:

- Support your beginning teacher to adopt a holistic understanding of the best practice for teaching reading
- Understand how to support and develop your mentee's understanding of teaching reading
- Use strategies effectively for supporting the development of your mentee with the teaching of reading.

To start the chapter, Task 15.1 asks you to consider your own definition of reading and to reflect upon your own practice of teaching reading.

Task 15.1 Why read?

- How do you define reading?
- What is important for you in the teaching of reading?

The definition of reading used in this chapter

The teaching of reading in primary schools in England is often linked with raising national standards. Therefore, the focus of attention for teaching reading often deals with the business of what needs to be done to improve, with perhaps too much attention given to methods and materials (Bearne and Reedy, 2018). However, teaching reading involves more than simply instructing children with quick-fix methods to evidence progress. The teaching of reading to primary school children should be about developing a far more extensive range of literary understandings than focusing solely on skills. Bowtell, Holding and Bearne (2014) suggest that reading as an act requires a variety of cueing systems to make sense of print, but becoming a reader involves the interaction between the text and the reader. This chimes with Roche's (2015) belief that the reading process can stimulate the exchange of thoughts and ideas. Reading is a holistic activity that draws its influences far more widely than the confines of the National Curriculum. Reading traverses the traditional boundaries of literacy and draws on social, cultural, historical and political influences to expand children's ability to understand, interrogate and challenge what they have read in order to explore and deepen their understanding of the worlds of factual information and fiction (Larson and Marsh, 2015; Roche, 2015).

Mentoring for good teaching and learning of reading

Without question, being able to read is an essential skill for everyday life, but learning to read the words on the page is only part of the process of becoming a reader. Teaching children to read involves developing children's skills so that they are able to interrogate and understand authentic and meaningful social, political and cultural issues (Roche, 2015). At the heart of good teaching and learning of reading in primary schools should be the use of real books to facilitate and develop discussion skills. Through children's literature, children create an understanding and knowledge about the world that surrounds them. Often, children's worlds are limited by their social and cultural experiences, and these can frequently exclude children from experiencing and knowing much wider opportunities. However, through children's literature, they may find access to worlds from which they are excluded, awaiting them within the pages of narrative and within the rich descriptions of non-fiction. Children's literature is more than a mechanism to learn to read; it is also quality literature that can develop children's interest in the world around them and enrich their lives in considerable ways (Cliff-Hodges, 2010). Overlooking the inclusion of children's literature to teach children to read creates more than a void in their reading development; it also means missed opportunities to understand and question the world. This chimes with the concerns raised by Roche (2015) about the National Curriculum in England's (DfE, 2013a) focus on teaching reading by separating reading skills out into isolated teaching episodes and moving towards teaching from templates and pre-prepared materials: these are lost opportunities for children to question what they are reading (Leland, Harste and Huber, 2005).

Support your mentee by encouraging them to create opportunities in the classroom for the young critical reader to develop the skills to question the media-driven world in which they are growing up. The current generation of children learning to read require encouragement and skills to develop a critical voice to ask the big questions about texts (Brookfield, 2012). Big questions you could encourage your mentee to use with the children include: What effects does this have on me as a reader? Who has produced the text? How could it be told differently? What's missing from this account? Jewett and Smith (2003) argue that effective literacy draws on a repertoire of practices that allow learners to engage in reading to act as code-breakers, meaning-makers, text users and text critics. The 'text critics' element appears to have no analogue in the National Curriculum (DfE, 2013a), yet I would argue it is an essential skill to achieve well, both in becoming a reader and in achieving in the national reading tests.

The current National Curriculum for England (DfE, 2013a) model follows a linear scheme in which reading concepts are introduced at specific ages. This model draws on the work of the cognitive psychologist Ehri (1987, 1995), among others, and assumes that all children acquire specific skills in a fixed, linear sequence. Larson and Marsh (2015) suggest that there are limitations to the linear model. They argue that the current curriculum guidance model for reading is a reductionist pedagogical framework unsuited to the holistic nature of the acquisition of literacy, in which the importance of communication is a recognised tool grounded in social, cultural, historical and political practices. Capturing the complexity of teaching reading with your mentee in the classroom may involve traversing the traditional boundaries of literacy teaching and exploring alternative frameworks. This has the potential to create authentic learning experiences for children. Consider Task 15.2.

Task 15.2 Communication and learning to read

Discuss with your mentee how important communication is for learning to read.

In many respects, teaching reading draws on the notion that reading is far more extensive than merely decoding the written word. Teaching reading recognises that a knowledge of the world and personal experience are as important as the influence of intertwining cultural and social differences. However, one of the most notable attributes of critical reading is that it is strongly influenced by raising the critical consciousness of learners. Critical reading is underpinned by the principle that dialogue is at the heart of learning, and that analysis and interrogation of texts encourage children to draw on critical insights from their world to engage with their reading without the prior need to acquire a set of print-based literacy skills (Comber, Nixon and Reid, 2007).

As the world responds to new technological environments, the development of digital literacy enables children to participate in meaningful, creative and authentic tasks, which develop the skills, knowledge and understanding needed to analyse and produce multimodal, multimedia texts. Larson and Marsh (2015) highlight the importance of digital literacy and acknowledge that there are challenges to the more traditional role of the class teacher in adopting digital literacies in the classroom. This is an aspect of reading that you may need to constantly develop your expertise as technology advances to enable you to support your mentee in then aiding the children. In the ever-changing world of literacy, texts and images are becoming increasingly specialised. The variety of screens continues to become more and more sophisticated and more prevalent relative to traditional print media such as books (Kress, 2010). However, Burnett and Merchant (2018) suggest merging the boundaries between screens and print-based texts and stress the importance of encouraging opportunities for children to move fluidly between online and offline spaces.

The role and the influence of the community should also not be overlooked when teaching reading. The community is not just the immediacy of the classroom but is expanded to include wider society, defined by Rogoff (2003) as groups of people with shared understandings, culture, values and history. Larson and Marsh (2015) recognise that there are challenges for teachers to build and maintain a meaningful learning community in the short timeframe of an academic year. However, they reveal how the shared engagement of children's literature can quickly provide a shared experience and can encourage children to make connections with much broader communities. By placing children's literature at the centre of lessons, the children engage with common communities and draw on cultural, institutional and historical aspects to make connections with their own lives.

By presenting reading as a holistic activity that is far wider than that implied by the reductionist pedagogy of the National Curriculum in England (DfE, 2013a), you could consider with your mentee how reading can be taught, and what needs to be understood by the beginning teacher in order to teach reading. Learning to read is a far more social and complex practice than simply decoding words, and as Hall (2003) argues, literacy cannot be simplified to just one model. In accordance with Hall's perspective, Larson and Marsh (2015) view reading as a complex social practice in which children need opportunities to draw on personal experiences and to engage with wider communities to build and rebuild their knowledge and understanding in their reading. This implies the need for a move away from the isolated practice of children silently reading and answering questions, and a move towards a sense that learning to read is about communication, culture, community and collaboration. The possibilities of teaching reading through a more holistic approach and exploring meaning through children's interactions and engagement with a wide range of modes and media enrich the children's experience of learning to become a reader (Burnett et al., 2014).

Supporting a beginning teacher to teach reading

The prospect of teaching children to read, whether they are four or eleven years old, can be quite daunting for your mentee, especially as their main experience of teaching reading will be drawn from their own reading journey. Hence, you may need to challenge their perceptions. Trying to establish what is important for teaching reading is a good starting point, and can be a way to encourage your mentee to draw on the experience of colleagues across the school. Case studies 15.1 and 15.2 (Stone, 2018) illustrate teachers' responses to focused reflections on reading provision in different age phases. These reflections include considering a literacy-rich environment; opportunities to talk; bringing personal experiences to help with understanding texts; non-fiction texts; seeing others reading - children and adults. Read Case studies 15.1 to 15.5, then complete Task 15.3.

Case study 15.1 Emily (Reception teacher) responding to the statement 'a literacy-rich environment'

We are lucky here that we are still allowed to encourage child-initiated learning with the children, which gives me a chance to offer the children a much richer experience of learning to read.

It is really important for me to provide the children with an environment that is rich with language. We talk a lot! Any opportunity to talk and we do. I try to make sure that books have a big presence in the classroom ... book corner, boxes, and stories whenever I can squeeze one in. I like to start the day with a story. It sets the tone for the day and gives a shared experience we can all talk about. Learning to read takes time, and that is something I recognise, but it can sometimes be overlooked by others.

The children who attend here ... almost all of the children start school unable to read and very few have interacted with books. We are up against it from the start. I have to find time to get them interested in reading.

So yeah ... I try to make the environment literacy rich, and squeeze in where possible role-play, oral storytelling, talking about story endings and changing them, that sort of thing. It's not ideal or best practice for me, as it's not enough! Especially as they don't get any kind of stimulus at home. I do what I can to get them interested.

Case study 15.2 Flo (Year 1 teacher) responding to the statement 'opportunities to talk'

The children love to talk so I always make sure that they get opportunities to talk. We talk about books, listen to individual stories, play games, that sort of thing. Interestingly ... now we are at the end of the Year 1, the children are enjoying and listening to longer stories, and they enjoy talking about what has happened before. Stories in the early part of the school year were always being interrupted with other timetable expectations, so I was finding that slightly longer stories were being left unfinished. We've found a way around that though ... with chat. We talk about what we can remember and use pictures under the visualiser. It's a challenge for some of the children to remember, but with pictures and the talk it seems to be working. I wouldn't have done it this way before, but because of the pressure of time, I've had to find a way around it. It works and I'm pleased the kids are getting something from it.

Case study 15.3 Ruby (Year 2 teacher) responding to the statement 'seeing others reading – children and adults'

Reading, it's easy to forget how important it is and how we can get it so wrong ... I think this is so important if you consider what it means. It means this is something that is achievable and that you can do it too, you can learn to read. That self-belief in children is so important for children to learn to read and something that can be overlooked. I've put the statement right in the centre of the map, as I think together with early experiences of reading can sow the seed of a successful reading journey. Sometimes we have the expectation that we can teach reading without considering what the child thinks about the task in front of them.

Case study 15.4 Edward (Year 3 teacher) responding to the statement 'non-fiction texts'

Non-fiction for example, I am not as enthusiastic about non-fiction, not like I am with fiction. I read a lot of fiction, both children's literature and books, for my own pleasure. I think I have probably talked about fiction books every day in school with the children, but can't recall doing the same with non-fiction.

I am not sure I have any decent non-fiction books – I need to make a list of what I've got ... and perhaps think about getting some new books in ... and how to bring them into the learning. Perhaps to link with the topics we are doing next term. That would be a start, wouldn't it?

We have a school library, which we only use for booster groups. There are lots of non-fiction books in there. I'll have a look at what we have got – this is a good time to be thinking like this.

We can choose the texts we use for English lessons, but have less autonomy for guided reading. It is very prescriptive and really just about comprehension, getting the right answers. There are non-fiction texts in the guided reading programme ... it's not very exciting though ... no, not much excitement with those texts or tasks. I might have a think about making some links with non-fiction books in the library ... put a bit of energy into it.

Case study 15.5 Nancy (Year 5 teacher) responding to the statement 'bringing personal experiences to help with understanding texts'

Gosh! ... This is a massive oversight on my part. I've never considered drawing on the children's personal experience. I've perhaps made links with my own experience ... but never considered giving the children opportunities to draw on theirs. I feel a bit ashamed about that now ... something I need to think about that's for sure. The last book we read, as a class, I'd chosen because they potentially could relate to the characters, but not given them the opportunity to do it. I need to think about how I might do that at the start of next year ... with my new class.

Task 15.3 Reflection on practice

Explore with your mentee their practice in relation to these five pointers for reflection:

- a literacy-rich environment
- opportunities to talk
- seeing others reading - children and adults
- non-fiction texts
- bringing personal experiences to help with understanding texts (ask your mentee do they ask the children to bring personal experiences to help their understanding, if so ask them to provide examples).

Developing your mentee's understanding of teaching reading

During Task 15.4, observe your mentee teaching and then explore Case study 15.6; this will prompt their thinking on the teaching of reading. Your involvement in this process is an important step in supporting the mentee to develop their understanding of teaching reading. You will be able to keep discussions on track and ensure the smooth flow of ideas through questioning and perhaps drawing on your personal understanding of teaching reading. During the discussion, ask your mentee to reflect on their current practice and consider how the thinking around the statement can be used in their teaching. As in Case studies 15.1 to 15.5, the mentee will question their current practice and begin to put in place ideas for their future practice.

Task 15.4 Future practice

Discuss ideas around how this might be included in a reading lesson. For example, if the statement is *bringing personal experiences to help with understanding texts,* you might want to ask the children questions such as:

- How is the character like you?
- How are they different from you?
- Have you experienced some of the problems faced by the character in the story?

Case study 15.6 Example of Ruby's response to the task and statement 'bringing personal experiences to help with understanding texts'

This is really important too ... Children need to make early connections with books. Ok, for example, oh ... I don't know ... if they haven't had a life experience of going to a shopping mall then the Biff and Chip book about going up and down the escalators is not going to be funny to them ... or interesting ... You can teach understanding, of course you can, but the immediateness of their enjoyment and understanding is just not there ... it also removes the pleasure from reading too.

Summary

This chapter has considered how to support yourself as a mentor. We have looked at strategies to develop the understanding of your mentee and their teaching of reading. We have also considered ways to involve the knowledge and understanding of other colleagues across the school to support your mentee in developing their understanding of teaching reading. The approach suggested of using pointers for reflection can be a starting point for continued discussions on the teaching of reading and will provide multiple professional development opportunities for teaching reading between you and your mentee.

Further reading

Burnett, C., Davies, J., Merchant, G. and Rowsell, J. (2014) *New Literacies Around the Globe*, London: Routledge.

Hempel-Jorgensen, A., Cremin, T., Harris, T. and Chamberlain, L. (2018) Pedagogy for reading for pleasure in low socio-economic primary schools: Beyond 'pedagogy of poverty'? *Literacy*, 52(2), pp. 86–94.

Larson, J. and Marsh, J. (2015) *Making Literacy Real: Theories and Practices for Learning and Teaching*, 2nd ed., London: Sage.

16 Mentoring for science, technology, engineering and mathematics (STEM)

Hellen Ward

Introduction

In this chapter, I develop ideas about STEM mentoring and how you will support your beginning teacher in STEM, from the perspective of being the director of a large STEM Hub. This hub encompasses much of the South-East of England, and includes more than 5000 schools and 3000 STEM Ambassadors. I work with scientists, technologists, engineers and mathematicians from industry and higher education who volunteer in secondary and primary schools. They use their skills and knowledge to promote STEM Insight in young people. I was a science educator who believed that science provided the answer, whatever the question. However, over the last decade through working with STEM professionals, I have realised that school science and STEM in the workplace are very different. This chapter uses everyday examples and is written from my vision of 'STEM for all'.

Objectives

At the end of this chapter, you should be able to:

- Support your mentee to understand what is STEM, know why STEM is important
- Support your beginning teacher to know how and where STEM can be incorporated within and across the curriculum
- Support your beginning teacher to develop their awareness of the numerous opportunities and resources to enhance both their knowledge and understanding of STEM
- Know how to mentor your mentee to develop their STEM teaching.

As many beginning teachers may not have experienced STEM as an area within teacher training, the following sections offer context for you as a mentor to help support your mentee to engage with the questions 'What is STEM?' and 'Why STEM?'

What is STEM?

STEM is short for science, technology, engineering and mathematics. The STEM agenda has a focus on future skills shortages and this 'pipeline' argument was reiterated by Lord Rees in his foreword to the Royal Society's (2010) *State of the Nation* report. His view was that the role of science education was to close the STEM skills shortage gap. This economic argument was one of the main drivers in the latest National Curriculum for primary science in England (DfE, 2013a). Historically, the launch of Sputnik by the Russians in 1957 is often seen as the key event that focused the American education system on STEM opportunities. England and Wales followed, but at a slower pace, and science education in primary schools only became mandatory with the *Education Reform Act* of 1988. Even now, what STEM education looks like and how it is perceived by different stakeholders demonstrates that many diverse perspectives remain. To some, STEM means mirroring the types of projects that real-life engineers or scientists conduct. For others, it is about expanding the talent pool by improving pupils' mathematics and science scores. A further group takes the view that it is about creative approaches to education (Breiner et al., 2012). In America STEM education was developed as a drive to provide critical thinking skills and make students into creative problem solvers.

Why STEM?

Today's digital technology provides greater demand for, and access to, science knowledge via media and electronic sources. The composition of effective provision is debated and there are many suggestions about what this might involve: the CBI (2015) identifies industry links; the Royal Society favours practical activity; Nesta Policy and Research Unit (2006) suggests scientific inquiry; the current National Curriculum in England has a focus on knowledge (Oates, 2011); or authentic activities (Friesen and Scott, 2013). Perhaps understanding 'the whole game' is beneficial (Perkins, 2009b). The metaphor of learning being a whole game is useful, as it contains aspects that we will revisit in the section focusing on approaches to STEM. There is overlap within all the approaches, but identifying the reason for STEM might be as challenging as finding the philosopher's stone. The current 'one size fits all' approach is not effective if the number of students who will go on to study STEM subjects is considered.

A simple examination of the student population in the United States showed that only about 8 per cent of the general high school population end up with a STEM degree of one sort or another. But even if it were as high as 10 per cent, it is reasonable to ask what sort of science education we are providing to the other 90 per cent of our future citizens (Rudolph, 2014, p.1076). The issue is thought to be common across the developed world, and if it is true that 90 per cent of students leak out of the STEM pipeline, it is not surprising that there is an argument for the remainder of the pupils to have scientific literacy (Osborne, 1996).

The leaky pipeline

The leaky pipeline (Figure 16.1) is a very strong narrative, which is used as a driver to recruit STEM Ambassadors (www.stem.org.uk). There are some concerning issues with the UK STEM pipeline, one of which is the higher number of girls who leak out of the pipeline, compared with boys.

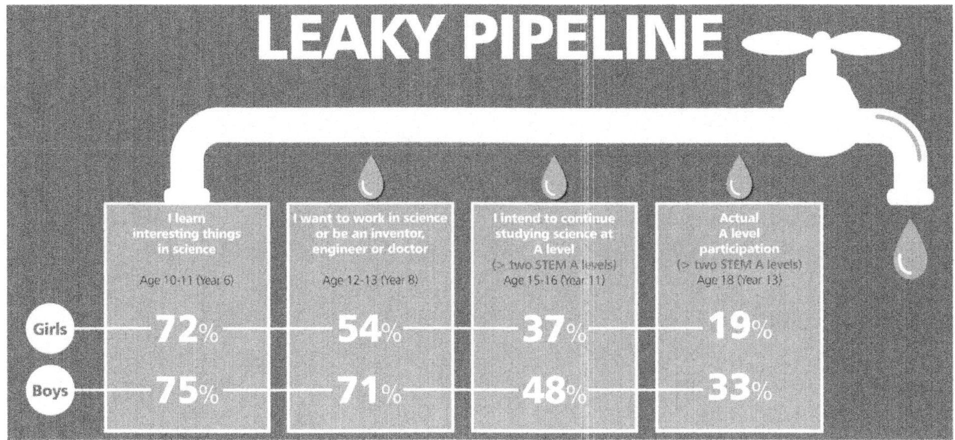

Figure 16.1 The leaky pipeline
Source: Remnant (2019). Adapted from Aspires 1 and 2 studies Kings College London and UPMAP study, UCL Institute of Education.

It is important to note that the questions asked of these pupils at each stage of the pipeline are not identical. There is evidence that if the question about liking science or thinking science is important to society was asked to A-level students, the data would look very different. Youngsters used in the Wellcome Trust (2011) Exploring Young People's Views on Science Education study identified that studying science contributed to their own personal development. The outcome of research does not identify that students do not like STEM or science, but that they do not see it as relevant for them in their future careers (Archer et al., 2015). You may wish to consider the importance that you place on STEM when you are mentoring. The ASPIRES project found that interest in science lessons was not the issue, a finding supported by OECD data (2007). The problem is that learners do not go on to science careers, suggesting that there is a mismatch with education practices and science in the world, which results in the leaky pipeline. Archer et al. (2015) determined that if learners are to go on to study science after the age of sixteen, they need to develop a science identity.

The pipeline, while a striking way to gain attention, only reflects the economic argument. It focuses directly on the needs of society rather than the needs of an individual. There is a continuum between society and the individual (Eisner and Vallance, 1974, cited in Pollard and Tann, 1993). At one end of this continuum is the role of science education to enable the individual to fit into society as it currently is, while at the other end is how students might change society. Roberts (1982) advises that 'what science is' depends on the interpretative frame of the teacher, which is bounded both by your own education and teacher training, and can ultimately influence your mentoring. This can result in an emphasis on science as a completed subject, rather than science as an unfinished, complex and multidimensional subject. Hodson (1985, p.220) suggests that myths about science and scientists abound because they were adopted by teachers as part of their apprenticeship (training to be a teacher and their own education in school) and the teachers in turn use these impressions in their future teaching (Lortie, 1975) and mentoring. The beginning teachers that you mentor will be influenced by the approaches you show them, and how you develop their understanding of STEM education. To support your mentoring, it is useful to be aware that these issues all influence how they, as future teachers, will address STEM and how they will manage STEM in the curriculum.

Curriculum emphasis

Mentoring within STEM may be needed more than in any other area, due to a lack of time that your beginning teachers may have spent focusing on STEM within the curriculum during their own training. Rudolph (2014) made an important point about the curriculum offered: if 90 per cent of the pupils are not going to take STEM roles, there may be an increased need to spend more time with your mentee focusing on STEM as a curriculum emphasis. Their lack of future STEM role is in line with the scientific literacy argument that even if a pupil is not going to study STEM, as a future citizen in a democratic society, they will have a role in making informed decisions about the impact on society of, for example, genetically modified crops, three-parent babies or laser technologies that can cure cancer. The education goals for future citizens are thought to be different from STEM education for procedural expertise and disciplinary knowledge - that is, becoming a STEM professional. These debates underpinned the revision of the National Curriculum in England (DfE, 2013a), where foundational knowledge - the subject-based material needed for future learning - became more important than 'how science works' and other science in society methods that had previously been prevalent. This is because STEM education in society is different from the education needed if students are going to go on to careers in STEM (Oates, 2011). These factors are important as a mentor, and to support your mentoring it is helpful to identify the different positions.

In this mentoring debate, it is useful to look at research into science education. Roberts (1982) originally developed seven curriculum emphases that were used as reasons for teaching science:

1. *everyday coping* - thinking about how learners will use knowledge in their everyday life
2. *the structure of science* - useful for those who would work with science in the future
3. *scientific skill development* - where skills are identified as transferable across subjects and more useful that knowledge
4. *science, technology and decisions* - how society makes STEM decisions that influence students, for example on the effects of deforestation or single-use plastics
5. *correct explanation* - about foundation knowledge and how science explains the world
6. *self as explainer* - an area not often taken as a focus, but one that is included in all curricula as a result of constructivist approaches to learning; it starts from students' ideas and how they explain the world
7. *solid foundations* - science as a set of ideas upon which later learning will be built.

After extensive research into science teaching schemes and published materials, Roberts went on to categorise these emphases into two visions (Roberts, 2007):

- Vision I comprises: the structure of science; correct explanation; scientific skill development; and solid foundations, where the focus is within the domain of the sciences towards the canonical notion of knowledge that will be required for future study.

- Vision II comprises: everyday coping; science, technology and decisions; and self as explainer, which looks outward towards society and imagines the learners as future citizens who will need to understand and make informed judgements about scientific endeavours. STEM education is currently more suited to this vision.

Traditional science education favours a Vision I approach and teaches science as a one-method, ultimate form of knowledge, something that Kritcher (1998) terms 'the legend'. Teachers with whom I work often say that they see STEM as an opportunity for pupils to gain understanding that will help them with everyday coping – for the pupils to understand and then control their environment and learn knowledge that they can apply outside school. Next, complete Task 16.1 and consider your current role.

Task 16.1 Your role in relation to STEM

- What is the role of STEM education in your children's learning?
- What is the role of STEM education in your school?
- How do you currently mentor within STEM?

What you perceive as the role of STEM education in children's learning is an important feature of being a teacher, and will influence what you promote to the beginning teachers you mentor. The answer to this question will help you identify what types of STEM you encourage your mentee to become involved in and how you go on to influence the way they will deliver STEM in the future.

In school, science and an effective STEM curriculum have more in common with the approaches of Ziman (1978) and Feyerabend (1993), both of whom viewed science as having many outcomes rather than as a subject that seeks predetermined truth. In STEM pupils have the advantage of meeting practising scientists, engineers and technologists who can share their understanding of STEM and relate it to what the students are learning in school. As a result, STEM-based learning could provide an opportunity to increase science literacy for all pupils. I think that everyone should have a working understanding of science as a right (OECD, 2000). This is an important aim of STEM education.

This section has used scientific research to examine the pipeline argument. In part, this is because in primary education there is little explicit teaching of engineering, and technology is an under-represented subject. Research into mathematics has focused on teaching methods and, as a subject taught daily, the focus is often on the knowledge rather than the ways in which mathematical truths are derived. What is clear is that the educational vision of the teacher influences the approaches they go on to use. A teacher's own education and the effectiveness of their mentor will promote or limit what they see as possible. In the next section, the position of STEM in the curriculum is debated and suggestions made.

The where of STEM

We start the where of STEM with Task 16.2.

Task 16.2 The where of STEM

- Where do you currently identify STEM in the curriculum you teach?
- How has your mentoring changed as STEM has become more important?
- How has STEM been considered within your school?

This section is the largest in this chapter, and it signposts you to resources and ideas that will aid you in how you support your mentee. STEM education is constantly changing, so be aware that some of the ideas will evolve and be replaced. STEM education might take place in a focused week where the normal curriculum timetable is collapsed, and enrichment and enhancement activities are provided. This is an opportunity to use project work, to expand the time given to creating a solution to a problem. There is also more flexibility to include outside visitors and visits than might be possible in the normal timetable. There are obvious disadvantages to this because there is little connection to the rest of the learning experience, and STEM becomes different; while special, it is not thought of as a part of everyday life. This approach can also be problematic for a beginning teacher, who might never be in school when these events take place. To support the beginning teacher as a mentor, you need to identify at least one STEM opportunity for them while they work with you.

In primary schools in the geographical area that the STEM Hub (www.thestemhub.org.uk) supports, the approach is very varied. More than 70 per cent (2018/19) of the primary schools across the region do not request any external support and the reasons given generally focus on the need to teach basic skills (this is usually a code for phonics, English and mathematics). Those teachers who do ask for support provide a starting point for other teachers in their school to build upon. To support your mentoring, it is important to remember that there is a good deal of free support for you and the beginning teachers with whom you work. STEM Ambassadors are a free resource for all teachers in all state-maintained schools in the United Kingdom. In the next section I provide some examples of activities designed to develop STEM in primary schools, with suggestions of how they might be used in developing a STEM curriculum that you could then use with your mentee. The next section is divided into regular inputs and special events, and the role of professional institutions. These ideas are just starting points to support your mentoring as you and the beginning teacher gain more exposure to STEM professionals.

Regular input in addition to curriculum time

Ask a STEM Ambassador to lunch or to work alongside your beginning teacher

This is an easy starter activity, where someone from industry comes and eats lunch with the children, sharing some of their stories and ideas with them about the role they undertake.

With more than 33,000 registered trained and DBS-checked STEM professionals across the country, this is a great starter resource for your beginning teacher, encouraging them to use this resource, which is accessible to any primary school. Requests can be made by registering for a free STEM account www.stem.org.uk. These sessions are funded by organisations such as the Institution of Engineering and Technology (IET) and the Institution of Mechanical Engineers (IMechE), and they have pre- planned experiments or activities that you can do with your pupils about the environment and how animals are suited to where they live. STEM Ambassadors are normal people - for example, Kerry, who works in the South-East. Case study 16.1 contains some information about who she is and what she offers schools.

Case study 16.1 Example of geologist Kerry Henderson, STEM Ambassador

In my work, I have undertaken a lot of site work so have a lot of practical knowledge of my subject. I have had to make interpretations of results for consultancy purposes. I also have various rock samples that I could use as an Ambassador to give a visual and tactile experience.

I am a Chartered Geologist and Associate Fellow of the Remote Sensing Society with degrees in Geophysics. I have worked in industry for over seventeen years as a geologist, engineering geologist and engineering geophysicist. I enjoy working with children (my second job is trampoline coaching), inspiring them and getting a buzz out of them being excited about a topic. Last academic year, my son did rocks as one of his science topics. I think the STEM scheme is exciting as it helps teachers and enthuses pupils.

A day in my life

Encourage your mentee to talk to the parents of the children in their class and find out more about them: it may be that some are STEM professionals who could come and talk about what they do in their jobs. Research suggests that if external visitors come into school, it will result in fewer pupils becoming NEET (Not in Education, Employment or Training). One self-reporting study with teenagers found that those who engaged with people in industry on four or more occasions were less likely to become NEET. Australian research by Tytler et al. (2008, p. 9) states that STEM needs to be adopted in primary schools, as 'for the majority of students, their life aspirations are formed before the age of 14', so what happens in your classroom can impact later life chances.

One off event

The collapsed curriculum

During weeks like Science Week (March), Tomorrow's Engineering Week (November) or Space Week (October), the requests for STEM Ambassadors increase, as every school seems to want to use these weeks to let their pupils know about STEM. For Science Week, the British Science Association has money available for schools, which must be requested before November each year. www.britishscienceweek.org/about-us/grants. Mentor your beginning teacher to source the resources that can be found with such weeks as Science Week - for example, teachers can download packs of materials and undertake some STEM-based teaching in their classrooms. Some schools ask all teachers to each run a workshop and then let the pupils move around the various activities during the day. To support your mentee, team teaching is a great opportunity to mentor the beginning teacher and provides new skills as mixed-age pupils can all work together.

Projects

There are always a range of projects and awards with which the pupils can get involved. Listed below are only a few of the hundreds that are available to support your mentoring. It is important that, as a mentor, you help the beginning teacher by supporting them, so they do not become overwhelmed. Also, not all STEM-based support is free or impartial, so it is important that in order to support the beginning teacher as a mentor, you need to help them with this often-bewildering area. Mission X is one project currently available. Mission X: Train like an Astronaut is (at time of writing) a free educational programme with the aim of using space exploration, and the excitement around it, to inspire young people to learn about science, nutrition, exercise and space. It has been developed with expertise from space scientists, fitness professionals, astronauts and space agencies from all over the world: www.stem.org.uk/missionx.

There are many similar projects that can be used, and there are many ways in which these events can support your mentoring. STEM Learning has a bank of resources that can help you to explore how engineering can be used to enrich the primary curriculum and equip you with ways to get started, topics for engineering projects, books as hooks into engineering and additional support and inspiration. For more information visit their website: www.stem.org.uk/engineering-resources/primary.

Professional institutions

There are also professional institutions that can help with support with your mentoring. They offer a variety of resources. Some institutions provide in-school support for teachers, while others come and teach the children for you, and provide resources for you to download. There are more than 50 professional bodies for engineering alone, so I will only highlight a few of the institutions that provide the most opportunities across the whole country. One such professional body is the IET, which is accessible at: https://education.theiet.org/primary/teaching-resources. The site is easy to navigate, with filtering of opportunities by age range and time available to spend on an activity. To support your beginning teacher as a mentor, you could share this site with them and then support them to deliver a STEM-based lesson with the children. The session includes design and technology, science and mathematics, and is written with an integrated STEM perspective, which may suit the way your primary school is operating.

Another professional institution is the Institution of Mechanical Engineers (IMechE), who have primary resources accessible at: www.imeche.org/careers-education/supporting-teachers/resources-and-activities. The only problem with the IMechE site is the amount of material on it, which can potentially be a bit overwhelming for your beginning teacher. To support the beginning teacher, as their mentor, use the above link, which will take you to the Toolkit site. Here you can book an activity, and a local IMechE professional will come and bring the kit (enough to teach 30 children) with them. Make the request on the www.stem.org.uk site and make it clear that you want an IMechE tool kit activity.

I was fortunate enough to observe a pilot class activity run by an IMechE STEM Ambassador. The children were all Year 5 and many thought engineers were people who fixed engines and got dirty. None of the pupils wanted to be an engineer at the start. The pupils undertook the bridge-building activity where they had to construct the longest bridge that held the greatest weight. The pupils worked in groups and all managed to create a bridge by the end of the session. All bridges were able to hold bags of stones, but the winning bridge was exceptional. After the event, the pupils had a better understanding of engineering and what engineers might do. It helped that the STEM Ambassador was supported by two young biomedical engineers who worked alongside the pupils and explained why they had been selected to train as engineers. Pupils ended the session knowing more about engineering but also having enjoyed their learning and developed resilience and group skills. This set of materials is a great opportunity to work with the beginning teachers. To support the beginning teacher as a mentor, you need to help them to identify that education is helping pupils become part of society and that our role as teachers is not just about helping pupils to be good at school.

The final professional institution is the Royal Academy of Engineering (RAE), which operates many different programmes, not all of them suited to primary-aged children. As a mentor, you may need to support your beginning teacher to find specific appropriate programmes for primary-aged children. One of my favourite programmes is the Connecting STEM Teachers (CST) programme, which was launched in 2011 and aims to create a national network of support for teachers across all STEM subjects, ensuring that they have the knowledge and confidence to engage a greater number and wider spectrum of school students with STEM. The teacher coordinators are all secondary, but three times a year they run events where training is provided for primary and secondary teachers and all teachers leave with equipment to run STEM activities in their classroom. This is an event worth taking the beginning teachers to. A list of teacher coordinators and their schools can be found on the RAE site: www.raeng.org.uk/education/schools/education-programmes/connecting-stem-teachers.

Summary

There are many free resources available for mentors and beginning teachers to help develop knowledge and competence in teaching STEM. Some of these opportunities can be planned to work within the curriculum and some are suited to special events. To support your mentoring, there are many opportunities to develop STEM across the curriculum and increase your pupils' opportunities to meet inspirational role models. This chapter has identified several opportunities from all the activities available. STEM is also an area where some consultants make money - so check before you book that there is no charge. Most national programmes are free. To support the beginning teacher as a mentor, you need to help them navigate the opportunities available. It is worth the time and effort both for you and the beginning teachers, because if you can engage pupils in a range of STEM opportunities then perhaps, when asked what they want to be, they will have more options to draw upon than a footballer, a hairdresser or a social media influencer.

Further reading

Lortie, D.C. (1975) *Schoolteacher:A Sociological Study*, Chicago, IL:University of Chicago Press.

Perkins, J. (2009) *Review of Engineering Skills*, London: Department for Business Innovation and Skills. Available at: https://www.raeng.org.uk/publications/other/perkins-review-of-engineering-skills. Accessed 12 January 2020.

Tytler, R., Osborne, J., Williams, G., Tytler, K. and Cripps, J. (2008) *Opening Up Pathways: Engagement in STEM Across the Primary-Secondary School Transition. A Review of the Literature Concerning Supports and Barriers to Science, Technology, Engineering and Mathematics Engagement at Primary-Secondary Transition*. Available at: https://pdfs.semanticscholar.org/26d3/9dde4d8dcb50de6855a3a4f229649dcce104.pdf Accessed 12 January 2020.

SECTION 4

Mentor development

17 The role of research in mentoring

Sandra Eady

Introduction

In this chapter, the focus is on how mentors can make the best use of research in their work with beginning teachers. A good analogy is planning a holiday. When we book a once-in-a-lifetime holiday, we take advice, we discuss and reflect with others, we read the latest holiday reviews, evaluating their credibility and reliability, and we reflect on all the information we have before taking action. We don't usually book a holiday based on our gut reactions, but we tend to adopt a critical stance, asking ourselves how we might maximise the quality of our experience and weigh this up in terms of the financial cost. We might consult with other members of the family and take into account their needs and preferences. In other words, we might engage in extensive 'research' about the place(s) we intend to visit, ultimately to maximise the likelihood of long-lasting memorable experiences. In many ways, a mentor might encourage the beginning teacher to view their approach to a teacher career in a similar way and to embed research within their normal practice. The goal is to engage in informed research and critical reflection about teaching and learning in order to make sense of, reflect on and inform future actions - ultimately, to improve the quality of learning for pupils. Ideally, mentors of beginning teachers should also consider how particular strategies adopted in the classroom also reflect their own and the beginning teacher's underlying beliefs and values about teaching and learning. Enabling beginning teachers to make research-informed choices about the teaching and learning strategies they use in the classroom can be far more effective than merely providing them with another teaching strategy for them to use. More importantly, this approach encourages beginning teachers to adopt a more questioning stance about the effectiveness of their actions.

Objectives

At the end of this chapter, you should be able to:

- Explain why mentors should engage with research
- Identify how mentors can engage with and make the best use of research
- Select the kinds of research mentors and beginning teachers should engage with about the mentoring relationship as well as teaching and learning.

A good starting point is to reflect in Task 17.1 on your own understanding of what educational research is/is not.

Task 17.1 What does research mean to you?

- Can you list five or so words that you associate with the word 'research'?
- Take a few moments to complete the following sentences:
  - Research is ...
  - Research is not ...
- Now jot down some research that has either influenced your teaching, or your own learning, or has influenced another aspect of your life, perhaps in a non-academic sense. Note, if you can, who did this research. Why was it influential?

Why mentors should engage with research and why educational research is important

There are convincing arguments for why mentors should engage with research. For example, it can help mentors to better understand the mentoring relationship and it can enlighten your own practice, it can throw new light on particular issues faced by beginning teachers. Providing differing perspectives on a particular problem or issue can encourage critical reflection about whether pupils really are benefiting from a particular approach.

The mentor's role, therefore, is to move the beginning teacher beyond focusing on the basics and technical issues of teaching to a more informed understanding of teaching and learning. A knowledge of research and related theory thus provides mentors with tools to support and develop a beginning teacher's understanding of the interwoven complexity of relationship building, teaching and learning.

Hendrick and Macpherson (2017) point out when useful research is given to teachers, it is often in the form of a list of strategies divorced from their original reasoning and theory. They give the example of the use of lollipop sticks in the classroom, where every pupil in the class has a number, and those numbers are also written on lollipop sticks. When asking a question, the teacher selects a lollipop stick and reads out the number (or name of the pupil) thus signifying which pupil should answer the question. This strategy originated from the research on assessment for learning (Black, 2003) and was originally used to increase pupil engagement but is now insisted on by some schools as the only way questions should be asked (Hendrick and Macpherson, 2017), with little or no reference to its origins. The lollipop stick example illustrates how teachers can often apply strategies in the classroom yet be unaware of the research context in which they were developed or the underlying theory of student engagement.

Another example is the use of reward systems that promote behaviourist strategies to encourage positive behaviour in the classroom through the use of marbles in a jar, a star chart, points leading to 'golden time' or more recently class dojo. Often these strategies are applied by beginning teachers, who then become more and more frustrated when they find that the strategy is not having the desired effect. Again such strategies have become decontextualised from the original research and underlying theory. Thus, beginning teachers are often not aware of the rationale for such approaches. What is needed is a more informed understanding and critical reflection of the research that resulted in particular strategies and how they have been informed by particular theoretical perspectives.

Often beginning teachers get hung up on always using a particular strategy in the classroom and become frustrated when it doesn't seem to work. Helping beginning teachers to make links between a common strategy, research and the underlying theory may help them to make more strategic choices, thus building in greater flexibility and informed choice of different strategies to support effective teaching and learning. Before continuing, reflect in Task 17.2 on a particular strategy you currently use on a regular basis in the classroom, and consider how it links to research evidence.

Task 17.2 Linking practice to research evidence

- What research evidence is this strategy based on?
- Now try to relate the strategy back to a particular piece of research theory or theorists.
- How does this underlying theory fit with your values?

Getting beginning teachers to question a strategy in terms of when it is/is not effective and why, who is it effective for, who benefits from this strategy, who does not benefit, how they know this is the right strategy and so on can be far more effective than providing them with another strategy that you commonly use yourself. More importantly, this approach encourages beginning teachers to adopt a more questioning stance about the effectiveness of their actions.

Using research to inform the mentor-mentee relationship

Cain (2009) suggests that the way mentors see their role tends to fall into two broad categories: whether a mentor should *offer advice* or *encourage reflection*. These categories are underpinned by different values and philosophies. Offering advice makes the assumption that the mentor has the knowledge and expertise, and an obligation to merely pass this on to the mentee, who then is expected to integrate it into practice without questioning whether it is appropriate. On the other hand, encouraging reflection makes the assumption that the mentor does not and should not have a ready answer, but adopts the role of a skilled facilitator, who places value on the existing knowledge and experience of the mentee with a view to supporting the mentee to reflect on their beliefs and values in relation to the issue/dilemmas that arise from practice and to take ownership of their actions. Making use of research about the mentoring relationship, and teaching and learning will enhance your understanding of these different perspectives, your role as mentor and the capacity of the beginning teacher to improve their practice.

In Task 17.3, consider how you could introduce and use research within your mentor meetings.

Task 17.3 Using research during mentor meetings

- To what extent do you envisage mentoring meetings to be largely concerned with practical matters of teaching rather than introducing, applying and reflecting on educational theory and research?
- What research or theory might you draw upon to inform reflections about the role of mentoring?

Another reason for engaging in research and theory is to better understand the mentoring relationship and how it can be a productive one with reciprocal benefits. Cain (2009) discusses different ways in which mentors might engage with research to inform their own practice - for example, where the mentor consciously bases teaching approaches on research findings or uses teaching materials that have been informed by research. Mentors can be explicit about the research underpinning these teaching approaches or teaching materials with the beginning teacher by building it into the mentoring conversations or encouraging beginning teachers to relate their practice back to research.

The mentor-mentee relationship can be better understood by engaging in research linked to theoretical frameworks derived from the literature. Hawkey (1997) suggests that frameworks could include *ideals* or aspirations, which the mentor and mentee could explore as part of the mentoring relationship and in light of these look at what factors might encourage or limit a move towards a particular ideal. For example, the mentor might want to explore ideas such as trust and communication, power balance, support and challenge with the beginning teacher. Hawkey (1997) suggests mentors might want to consider *polarities* - for example directive or inquiry-oriented approaches to mentoring. Mentors might use these concepts to explore their own beliefs about mentoring and learning to teach. They might examine their mentoring practice and change it in light of these polarities.

Exploring *theories* of adult learning will enable the mentor to better understand the mentee. Korthagen and Vasalos (2005) cite a theory of adult learning drawn from anthropology to better understand their mentee; the theory suggests that 'externally visible behaviours are closely related to inner beliefs, identity and mission'. If a mentee is struggling to manage a pupil's challenging behaviour, there might be greater value in getting the mentee to examine their beliefs about themselves, their sense of identity as a teacher, rather than just suggesting a list of strategies such as 'use of voice' or 'posture' to try out in the classroom. In this way, the mentee is likely to have a greater understanding of their actions and to know why they are using a particular strategy. In turn, a mentor might engage with the practical implications of this theory by asking, 'Can my mentee simply alter certain behaviours or is the cause of the problems more deeply rooted?' If the latter is the case, the mentor might engage the trainee in 'core reflection' (Cain 2009).

Frameworks for mentoring: Case studies

Cain (2009) suggests that in-depth case studies can be another way to help mentors understand their own experiences of mentoring in the light of other people's experiences. Case studies can help mentors to explore the power differentials that might exist between mentor and mentee. For example if the mentor holds a senior position in the school, how might this affect the mentoring relationship in terms of honesty, openness, trust and respect? Could the mentor be perceived to be favouring the mentee above other teachers? What level of confidentiality should be agreed if the mentee discloses poor practice within the school? The mentor might use the case study as a way to reflect on such scenarios and consider the extent to which they are able to break down these differentials.

Mentors might use case studies with mentees to help them explore their values and beliefs around inclusion, diversity and gender, and how these might influence preconceived ideas about teaching and learning that they use to judge the quality of others' teaching. Cain cites Graham's (1999) example where a student teacher's beliefs about good teaching are in contrast to those of their mentor but align more closely with those of another mentor in the school. Engaging in such professional dialogue also enables the mentor to explore the extent to which they would be willing for a beginning teacher to try out teaching approaches, knowing that they may be less inclusive and only benefit certain pupils.

Mentors who adopt an inquiry stance and use research methods themselves to inquire into their own practices are in a stronger position to support beginning teachers to critically assess their own practice and thoughtfully implement strategies and interventions arising from research evidence. The mentor can play a crucial role in helping beginning teachers to develop the skills of critical engagement with research evidence in order to improve the outcomes for their pupils (Rose and Eriksson-Lee 2017).

Promoting learning conversations

Earl and Timperley's (2009) notion of evidence-informed *learning conversations* (see also Chapter 8) could provide a foundation for mentor-mentee relationships and discussions about teaching and learning. The basis of learning conversations is the mutual understanding of each contributor's claims and values, together with the reasoning and data on which they are based. These processes relate to each aspect of improving practice, whether identifying the current situation and its merits and difficulties, deciding the goals of improvement, or working out how best to get there. Earl and Timperley's (2009) notion of 'evidence-informed conversations' provides mentors with a way to structure conversations with beginning teachers. These learning conversations are a combination of the following elements:

- *Using relevant data.* Generally, educators find local, anecdotal knowledge more powerful than knowledge developed through research because it is more personal and is perceived to relate directly to the context in which improvement is sought. If you, as a mentor, are going to be active in interpreting and using data, as well as challenging and disputing interpretations or uses that you believe are contestable, you must become knowledgeable about judging the value and quality of the evidence. You will need to be aware of the clarity of purpose of the data, agree the criteria to judge the quality of the evidence, have knowledge about statistical and measurement concepts and, most importantly, be willing to make interpretation paramount. All too often, educational decisions are made using data that are available, rather than data that are appropriate. You need to consider what other data could you draw upon, and what other data you could encourage your mentee to draw upon.

- *Inquiry habit of mind.* The notion of an inquiry habit of mind refers to an ongoing process of using evidence to make decisions. Inquiry is, very simply, a way of finding things out - collecting data and interpreting evidence in ways that enhance and advance understanding. You could encourage your mentee to consider what the data shows. How does it benefit the learners?
- *Relationships of respect and challenge.* If knowledge is to become more generic, it needs to be socially constructed by the key participants, the merits debated and the potential flaws exposed. In this context, 'respect' is not about taking the time to understand each other's viewpoints but rather about probing meanings and challenging each other's interpretations of the evidence and the reasoning on which the different viewpoints are based. Respect is as much about challenge as it is about support, with a key value being respect for the capacity of all involved to learn and improve. Remember to consider whether you both share the same understanding - is there another way of interpreting this evidence?
- *Developing professional scepticism.* The focus of learning conversations should be on mentors supporting new teachers to intelligently use evidence from their classrooms and use high-quality research - which has been (at least initially) selected or signposted - to inform teaching. While this suggests mentors need to encourage beginning teachers to adopt a questioning attitude and willingness to interrogate claims, it also assumes that both parties have a certain degree of background knowledge to inform this critical stance and have the skills to apply these two things to their practice in order to be an 'intelligent consumer of research' (Rose and Eriksson-Lee, 2017).

In Task 17.4, consider how you might use Earl and Timperley's (2009) questions to help construct a learning conversation.

Task 17.4 Constructing a learning conversation

- What other data could we draw upon?
- What do the data show us?
- How does this benefit the learners?
- Do we both share the same understanding?
- Is there another way to interpret this evidence?

How mentors can engage with and make the best use of research

Rose and Eriksson-Lee (2017, p. 7) highlight some of the tensions about beginning teachers accessing and using research by referring to the

> knowledge mobility problem: the process by which the evidence produced by research organisations is transformed into accessible and usable knowledge for teachers, and the implementation of this knowledge in order to develop practice and improve pupil outcomes.

Rose and Eriksson-Lee cite the findings of the Evidence Informed Teaching Report (Coldwell et al. 2017). Four of the key findings pertinent to the mentor/mentee relationship are summarised below.

1. The quality of research evidence is necessarily mixed, and accessing and assessing research evidence requires time, expertise and access to resources. To be usable by a wide range of teachers, available research evidence needs to be accessible and presented in plain language.
2. There are frequently new 'big ideas' in education emerging from research to which teachers do not necessarily have access or sufficient time to evaluate.
3. There is some evidence that teachers may lack the confidence to engage with research, sometimes due to a lack of prerequisite supporting knowledge - for example, not possessing the background in research methods or quantitative data analysis in order to assess the robustness of evidence.
4. Even those who are confident in their professional role can feel profoundly uncomfortable when what they hold to be true is challenged and they have to rethink their beliefs and practices.

The above issues are often compounded by the necessity for teachers to have sufficient time and opportunity to engage with key ideas and integrate these into a coherent theory of practice (Timperley et al. 2007). They struggle with what is robust and reliable research, and the extent to which it is based on theory (Hendrick and Macpherson 2017). There are a range of different kinds of research and the variety of methodologies adopted makes it hard to compare the findings of one study with another. Furthermore, the findings of research can be hard to translate to outcomes and strategies for the classroom. Hendrick and Macpherson (2017, p. 7) sum up the problem as follows:

> Educators in the UK and around the world are uniting behind the need for the profession to have access to more high-quality research and evidence to do their job more effectively. But every year thousands of research papers are published, some of which contradict each other. How can busy teachers know which research is worth investing time in reading and understanding?

Given the issues outlined above, it is not surprising that research does not always inform classroom practice. Both beginning teachers and mentors have little time to read and reflect on relevant research and embed this in practice. However, recently there have been attempts to address this by summarising key findings from research and the impact it is likely to have in the classroom.

Individual reading of user reviews to support research

Freely available user reviews such as the Education Endowment Foundation (EEF) https://educationendowmentfoundation.org.uk provide evidence-based resources that are designed to support teachers' practice in the classroom and enhance pupil learning. The aim of the EEF is to improve the educational attainment of the poorest pupils. It was established as an independent charity in 2011. On the EEF website, there is a teaching and learning toolkit where the latest research and interventions are evaluated in terms of impact and cost. The Big Picture pulls together evidence from the Teaching and Learning Toolkit and EEF-funded projects, which have been independently evaluated, focusing on fourteen high-priority issues or themes for schools. Next, complete Task 17.5.

Task 17.5 Using evidence-based research

- Using your earlier list of theory research and strategy, search the EEF website https://educationendowmentfoundation.org.uk to find at least one user review from the teaching and learning tool box that links to your list.
- Ask the beginning teacher to also complete this and then discuss the user reviews you have found.

The National Foundation for Educational Research (NFER), established in 1946, is a leading independent provider of educational research and insights. The 'Schools' tab on the NFER's drop-down menu on the website provides a link to its latest publications and research. There is also a link to Research in Schools: 'How to' Guides, which give advice on how to run your own in-school research project. The Assessment Hub link provides access to a collection of short-read articles on assessment.

The Evidence for Policy and Practice Information and Co-ordinating Centre (EPPI-Centre) conducts systematic reviews of research evidence across a range of different topic areas and provides support for others who are undertaking systematic reviews or using research evidence. Currently, there are a large number of systematic reviews in the fields of education, including initial teacher education, health promotion and public health, as well as social welfare and international development. The website offers two ways to access the findings of reviews:

1. The topic pages enable access to the key messages about a specific subject area - for example, obesity. These key messages are drawn from the total knowledge base within the EPPI-Centre and may come from multiple reviews.
2. The Chronological List is a complete list of all EPPI-Centre reviews, and is in alphabetical order within each year. EPPI Centre has been providing evidence based systematic reviews to inform policy and practice https://eppi.ioe.ac.uk/cms/

The Chartered College of Teaching in England provides a set of tools for schools and teachers that were developed by the UCL Institute of Education, Sheffield Hallam University and Durham University, based on the evidence-informed teaching project findings (Coldwell et al. 2017). These are designed as practical tools to encourage teachers and school leaders to consider their engagement with research evidence, and the areas needed to develop, deepen and embed this engagement. These tools can provide mentors and beginning teachers with the tools to stimulate conversation, reflection and joint decision-making; they are meant to be collaborative tools.

Features of evidence informed teaching include:

- awareness engagement and use
- phases of development
- starting out, deepening and embedding.

Now complete Task 17.6.

Task 17.6 Evidence-informed teaching

- Use the link https://chartered.college to download the evidence-informed teaching tools to gauge your phase of development as a mentor:
- In terms of whether you are starting out, deepening or embedding your use of evidence and research to underpin the mentoring relationship and your practice, consider how you could use evidence and research to continue to develop your mentor-mentee relationship.

In Scotland, the General Teaching Council for Scotland provides all fully registered teachers with free access to a range of peer reviewed education journals through EBSCO Resources (education journals, e-books and online resources). In this way, all schools and teachers have access to the latest articles.

Collaboration with universities

Evans, Waring and Christodou (2017) report on a project that promoted early career teachers' research literacy through establishing strong collaborative links between universities and practising teachers in schools. They showed that universities, in collaboration with schools, play an important role in supporting the sustainability of research and in enabling teachers to connect their own practice with the broader body of research knowledge. They show how teachers need to know not only how to locate and critically use research evidence, but also how to actively engage in research with their pupils as an integral part of their everyday practice; research should not be seen as a separate entity, but as a sustained and integral part of being a teaching professional. Case studies 17.1 and 17.2 illustrate different ways in which mentors might collaborate with universities to engage with educational research, through professional reading groups, and also through undertaking Masters-level qualifications or advanced mentoring qualifications.

Case study 17.1 Example of professional reading group

One university in Scotland set up a professional reading group for teachers. The group, facilitated by a university tutor, met six times a year on the university campus. It consisted of teacher mentors who were interested in reading and discussing research papers related to coaching and mentoring. The tutor, or someone in the group, would identify a paper and this would be distributed and read by the group prior to the meeting. The group would then spend time teasing out some of the themes or issues raised by the paper and discussing them in relation to their mentoring experiences and contexts. Through this experience, teachers felt they had a better understanding of models and frameworks of mentoring, the strengths and possible pitfalls of mentor-mentee relationships and a refreshed understanding of recent research underpinning teaching and learning. One teacher who enjoyed this experience decided to organise a similar professional reading group back in her school, which had adopted a whole-school approach to mentoring students and newly qualified teachers.

Case study 17.2 Example of further study undertaking an advanced mentoring or Masters-level qualification in mentoring

Undertaking further study at a university will lead to greater opportunities for mentors to discuss in more depth research related to supporting beginning teachers. In one university, a coaching and mentoring module brought together teachers from across primary and secondary schools in three different local authorities. The module encouraged the teachers to engage in a critical inquiry back at school. The critical inquiry had two interwoven strands: a reflection on how they as mentors through the mentoring relationship facilitated the professional learning of a beginning or early career teacher back in their school, and a reflection on their professional learning as a mentor facilitating that learning. The Masters-level module provided different 'spaces' for reflection on theory and research, both within the university seminar workshops with each other, as well as with their mentee back at school. This dual approach enabled mentors to use theory and research to critically evaluate different models of mentoring as well as different approaches to teaching and learning. Best of all, they were able to see how it was possible to improve the learning experiences and outcomes for pupils by directly engaging their mentees in reflecting on how different theory and research could inform practice.

Now, in Task 17.7, reflect on your own practice.

Task 17.7 Reflecting on your own practice

What could support you to engage with educational research in order to:

- deepen your understanding of the mentoring relationship
- support the beginning teacher to use research to inform their practice?

With what kinds of research should mentors engage?

One of the problems for mentors is knowing what kinds of research to engage with. There is a considerable range of educational related research to choose from, and it is difficult to know which research is credible and reliable. Here are some broad definitions.

- *Evidence-based research.* This implies that the outcomes of research should essentially override professional judgement and dictate what teachers do in the classroom - seen as unprofessional and a misconception, although some see it as relating more to whole-school initiatives.
- *Evidence-informed research.* This implies that a teacher is using empirical research to inform, challenge and refine their professional judgement. This kind of implementation involves applying informed professional judgement rather than implementing a specific intervention programme or package.
- *Practitioner based research.* This is where a teacher reflects on a particular aspect of practice, usually related to teaching and learning, with a view to making a change or intervention in order to improve practice and learning outcomes for pupils.

The above broad areas of research might draw on the following kinds of learning theories. Taylor and Hamdy (2013) provide a comprehensive grouping of adult learning theories into several categories:

- *Instrumental learning theories.* These focus on individual experience, and include the behaviourist and cognitive learning theories.
- *Behavioural theories.* These form the basis of many competency-based curricula and training programmes. A stimulus in the environment leads to a change in behaviour. Applying these theories usually results in learning that promotes standardisation of the outcome. This leads to the main issue with behavioural theories: who determines the outcomes and how they are measured.
- *Cognitive learning theories.* These focus learning in the mental and psychological processes of the mind, not on behaviour. They are concerned with perception and the processing of information.
- *Experiential learning.* This has influenced adult education by making educators responsible for creating, facilitating access to and organising experiences in order to facilitate learning.

Table 17.1 Types of research

Intelligent consumers of research	*Key areas of knowledge*
• Developing professional scepticism • Knowledge of curriculum and learning • Knowledge of research methods and data analysis • Implementation into classroom practice	• Data analysis and assessment • Knowledge of curriculum and learning • Cognitive science and understanding misconceptions • Summaries of educational research, e.g. EEF and What Works Clearinghouse' (WWC) in the US • Research methods practitioner enquiry

- *Humanistic theories.* These theories promote individual development and are more learner-centred. The goal is to produce individuals who have the potential for self-actualisation, and who are self-directed and internally motivated.
- *Transformative learning theory.* Transformative learning theory explores the way in which critical reflection can be used to challenge the learner's beliefs and assumptions. The process of perspective transformation includes *social theories of learning*. The two elements that are crucial to social theories of learning are context and community.
- *Motivational models.* Any theoretical model that attempts to explain and relates adult learning to an educational theory must have two critical elements - motivation and reflection.
- *Reflective models:* The reflection-change models consider that reflection leads to action and then change.

Rose and Eriksson-Lee (2017) identify four broad areas to help beginning teachers, which may also help mentors to support beginning teachers to become 'intelligent consumers of research', and key areas of knowledge that may act as a broad foundation for critical engagement with evidence-based and evidence-informed practice (Table 17.1). As a mentor, you could use Table 17.1 to discuss the different types of research and key areas of knowledge with which you are familiar with your beginning teacher.

Summary

This chapter has discussed why mentors should use research with beginning teachers and how it will help their mentees develop and question their own practices and the strategies they are using in the classroom. It examined how mentors can engage in research to support the mentoring relationship and develop beginning teachers' understanding of teaching and learning. If offered ideas, toolkits and resources to help the relationship and understanding. It also examined the variety of educational research that mentors should and could make use of to both enhance their own practice as a teacher, and help support their beginning teacher as a mentor.

Further reading

Aubrey, K, and Riley, A. (2017) *Understanding and Using Challenging Educational Theories*, London: Sage.

Earl, L., and Timperley, H. (2009) *Professional Learning Conversations: Challenges in Using Evidence for Improvement* Berlin: Springer.

Education Endowment Foundation (EEF) (2011) *Teaching and Learning Toolkit*. Available at: https://educationendowmentfoundation.org.uk Accessed February 2020.

18 Developing a community of mentoring and coaching in a school

Rebecca Heaton

Introduction

Creating a community of mentoring and coaching is concerned with developing a whole-school ethos that not only values the continued development of teachers as learners, but sees it as a key priority for school improvement. A school with a strong ethos of mentoring and coaching is one that encourages open discussions about teaching practice, values mistakes and has a relentless focus on improving teaching practice. The introduction of a robust programme of induction and mentoring then embedding it into the culture of a school are crucial for both developing and retaining new teachers (Portner, 2005). This chapter will explore how this ethos is created and maintained in schools, exploring the principles that underpin it and the actions, systems and procedures that ensure mentoring and coaching have a high impact on teacher practice.

This chapter specifically examines how lead mentors create a community of mentoring and coaching within the primary school. The chapter will begin with a focus on mentoring and the role of the lead mentor. The title of 'lead mentor' denotes the person with responsibility for leading a team of mentors within a school. The chapter will therefore be of particular use to those who are new to this role, or who are looking to develop it further. For those who have previous experience of being a mentor, and are transitioning to the lead mentor position, this is a significant shift from guiding an individual to creating a team of practitioners with a common set of principles and goals. Later in the chapter, the case for coaching will be considered, and how this fits into the wider picture of teacher development, alongside mentoring, will be examined.

Objectives

At the end of this chapter, you should be able to:

- Identify the role of the lead mentor, considering how the role can enhance mentor provision in the primary school
- Consider the issues that may arise in mentoring, and critically reflect upon the role of the lead mentor in successfully overcoming these
- Understand the wider picture of teacher development, considering how mentoring can contribute to creating a community of mentoring and coaching in a school.

The role of the lead mentor

The role of the lead mentor can significantly contribute to the success of new teachers in schools where there are multiple mentors. This role may not exist in some schools, where perhaps there is only one teacher who is new to the profession. In other schools the lead mentor may have a different title, such as 'Mentor Coordinator' - or may have no title at all. The lead mentor has several roles as discussed below.

Mentors are assigned carefully

Mentors are assigned on the basis of their experience, expertise and personal motivation to work closely with a new teacher, to ensure the best outcomes for the new teacher and their pupils. Research suggests that the success of the beginning primary teacher is partly dependent on the way mentors are selected and paired; the beginning teacher must have professional respect for their mentor, the mentor must be willing to share their classroom practice and they must have the appropriate personal characteristics, such as being supportive, trustworthy and a good listener (Hobson et al., 2009).

Mentors are prepared and supported appropriately

Mentors have appropriate professional development opportunities to ensure that they understand the role and responsibilities of the mentor. Research suggests that mentors are more likely to be effective when they have had the appropriate preparation (Hobson et al., 2009). Mentors have a thorough understanding of the particular training route of their beginning primary teacher, so they are able to support the beginning teacher in fulfilling the expectations of their training or newly qualified year - for example, timetable expectations, placements and commitments outside of the school, such as academic requirements.

Mentors are fully aware of the expectations of mentoring that are specific to the school - for example, how often the new teacher should be observing teaching elsewhere; who arranges these observations; and how the school monitors the progress of the new teacher. These should be considered and decided by the lead mentor, who needs to communicate them clearly at the beginning of the year. Mentors have the opportunity to share best practice throughout the school, through opportunities to discuss and review provision for their beginning primary teachers. Bullough and Draper's (2004a) study suggests that mentors can feel uncertainty, vulnerability and isolation in their roles. Therefore, to maximise mentors' growth and development, it is good practice for the lead mentor to create these opportunities throughout the school year.

Mentors have capacity, in some cases due to having additional time released from teaching, to ensure that they can fulfil all the obligations of the mentor, including time for regular meetings, time to observe and to give feedback and time to attend any continuing professional development (CPD) relevant to their development. This may rely on the goodwill of the mentor in allocating their own time, or it may be that additional time is given. For high-quality mentoring to truly be embedded in the ethos of a school, 'mentoring students is not an "add on" activity; space and time will need to be created' (Smith and West-Burnham,

1993, p.38). Whatever the expectations may be, they should be established with the mentors by the lead mentor at the beginning of the year.

Lead mentors see the 'big picture', ensuring consistency and high-quality mentor support

Lead mentors have an overview of all new teachers - their current stage of development and their progress - so additional support can be offered as appropriate. They have an overview of their mentors - their strengths and development needs - in order to best support their beginning primary teachers. The lead mentor is approachable and acts as a 'sounding board' for mentors and beginning primary teachers. There is a consistency in the expectations of mentoring across the school, through clear communication and regular discussions.

Mentoring has a recognised status as a key priority area in order to maintain and improve the quality of teaching across the school. Depending on the school, it might be that the role of the lead mentor has already been established, or the role of the lead mentor may have been newly created as a result of an influx of new teachers entering the workplace. In either case, it is vital that the role and responsibilities of the lead mentor are clearly defined. This needs to be explicit, and all stakeholders, including the beginning teacher, the mentor, the lead mentor, the leadership team and external agencies such as university tutors, need a clear understanding of who is accountable for the various aspects of in-school support. The role and responsibilities of the lead mentor, compared with the role of mentor, will vary from school to school - and rightly so. This will depend on the wider roles of the individuals, their time commitments, their personal interests and the wider logistical implications. Next complete Task 18.1.

Task 18.1 Whose responsibility is it?

Consider the following examples, which are likely to occur. In the context of your school, would these responsibilities be better led by the lead mentor or the mentor?

Placements

For new teachers who are unqualified and undertaking their training year in school, who will organise their placements - whether these be in other schools or an alternative key stage? Who will organise cover arrangements for the teacher's class while they are absent from their base class? When will placements be organised and how will the arrangements be communicated?

Communication between external agencies and the school

If new teachers are working with external agencies, such as universities or a provider of initial teacher training, who will be the primary contact? If not the primary contact, how will communication be ensured within the school to ensure all stakeholders are aware? How will visits by external personnel be arranged and communicated?

Timetables

If new teachers are working on reduced timetables, who will organise and arrange their timetable? Will there be any set expectations about how teachers use their additional timetabled time out of class (for example, to observe)? Will the use of this time be monitored; if so, how and by whom?

In addition to the questions in Task 18.1, a fundamental question related to the role of the lead mentor is *how will they retain an overview of the development of all beginning teachers?* This will be explored further later in this chapter.

Why is the role of the lead mentor important?

As mentioned previously, not all schools will have or need a lead mentor role. So what is the value gained from having this additional role or 'layer' to a school's mentoring provision? This is an important question for school leaders, in terms of the creation or retention of the role, but likewise for lead mentors to consider how they can improve outcomes for beginning teachers as a result of the position.

The lead mentor role provides an opportunity to drive the effectiveness of mentoring and school support, to maximise the impact beginning teachers have on the outcomes of pupils. They ensure consistency in standards of mentoring, and have the capacity to drive these standards up. As Rhodes, Stokes and Hampton (2004, p. 5) highlight, the 'seeds of non-retention' in teaching are sown at an early stage, so ensuring that the mentoring provision in a school for beginning teachers is of a consistently high quality can be pivotal to their attitudes and development.

The lead mentor is able to act as a collective voice for mentors, ensuring that mentoring is prioritised and valued in the school, and that the time commitment attached to mentoring is acknowledged and accounted for. Additionally, with the overall responsibility for mentoring, the lead mentor is in a strong position to consider how mentoring might be one piece of a wider programme of support for the beginning primary teacher, such as CPD provided specifically for teachers who are new to the school, and opportunities to observe outstanding teaching.

Case study 18.1 illustrates an example of a lead mentor's tasks throughout a year, from the initial contact made with the beginning teachers to the completion of their first year.

After reading through Case study 18.1, complete Task 18.2.

Case study 18.1 The role of the lead mentor – a year in review

Summer term	*Autumn term*	*Spring term*	*Summer term*
• Initial contact is made with all teachers. • A welcome email is sent and a visit to the school is arranged. • One-on-one meetings are held with each of the teachers; there is a tour of the school, meeting key members of staff, with an overview of their training year provided. • Teachers are allocated to classes. • Mentors are identified and allocated.	• A schedule of induction activities is planned for the Autumn term. • Placements are planned and arranged to take place across the year. • Mentors are supported where additional input for beginning teachers is needed. • Each beginning teacher is observed at an early point in the term by the lead mentor. • A brief 'drop in' is conducted at a later point in the term to gauge development over the term.	• All arrangements are confirmed with regard to the logistics and preparation for placements. • All beginning teachers are prepared for placements, through meeting with them as a collective beforehand, to outline the expectations of their role during placements, and as an opportunity to ask any questions. • There are regular 'check-ins' with all beginning teachers and their mentors during their placements.	• All mentors are supported in ensuring final assessments are completed. • The training year is reviewed and evaluated, with input from the mentors and beginning primary teachers, and amendments are made to the following year's plans, accordingly.
• An induction programme is organised and held for beginning primary teachers, during the summer term. • A mentor workshop is facilitated by the lead mentor.	• The lead mentor sends out information to all mentors and beginning teachers to support them in knowing how best to prepare for their first formal review meeting. • A mentor workshop is facilitated by the lead mentor, focused on sharing best practice, celebration and looking forwards to the next term. • An end-of-term reflection and celebration session is organised and facilitated for all new beginning teachers.	• Ongoing CPD opportunities are reviewed and planned. • 'Drop-ins' are conducted near the end of term, on all beginning primary teachers.	

Task 18.2 Reflecting on your actions

- Which of these actions in Case study 18.1 might normally be undertaken by the mentor?
- What is the added value of having a lead mentor?
- Which of these actions can be pre-planned, and which are reactive?
- How might these actions be similar or different in your setting?

Ongoing actions throughout the year

In addition to the actions illustrated in the table above, the lead mentor ensures that throughout the year:

- the successes and development areas for the beginning primary teachers are communicated with the school leadership team
- they liaise with the training agency to organise visits from tutors, where multiple mentors and beginning primary teachers are involved
- appropriate external CPD for mentors is arranged.

The role of the lead mentor in addressing potential challenges

For beginning primary teachers, their first year in teaching will be one of the most challenging in their careers. A lack of expertise and experience means that reflecting on how to improve their practice is a crucial part of their development. In the Department for Education's policy paper, *Teacher Recruitment and Retention Strategy* (2019), it is highlighted that not enough beginning teachers are receiving the level of high-quality support that they need to support a successful career in education. Therefore, ensuring high-quality mentoring that addresses the potential challenges which may arise during this process is a priority for the lead mentor. Earlier within the book, we have already considered the potential issues that might arise in the mentoring of the beginning primary teacher and solutions for the mentor were considered. The lead mentor may contribute to finding solutions to issues, and may have the flexibility and capacity to provide additional support for beginning teachers. As Hobson et al. (2009) identify, in some cases where mentors have not provided sufficient support for beginning primary teachers, particularly in terms of their emotional and psychological wellbeing, this has been due to mentors being unavailable. This is one example in which it may be appropriate for the lead mentor to provide additional support to the mentee.

When considering issues that may arise, a key question for the lead mentor is to consider not just how they may be addressed, but by whom. In many cases, the mentor who has a close working relationship with the beginning teacher will be the more appropriate person to directly work on the issue with them. For the lead mentor to become any more closely involved may cause increased pressure or stress for the beginning teacher, and a sense of disempowerment and frustration for the mentor. In such situations, being a 'sounding board' for mentors can be one of the small but effective ways in which to support the mitigation of issues.

Conversely, the lead mentor may need to be more heavily involved in addressing potential issues – for example, if they are needed to act as an impartial mediator. If a mentor does not have sufficient capacity to provide the additional support that is needed to support a mentee or if the gravity of the issue requires attention beyond that of the mentor, the lead mentor can step in. Addressing the potential issues that may arise in the training period of the beginning teacher is a process that should be balanced between the mentor and lead mentor. The key priority is to maintain the confidence of the beginning teacher, considering solutions that won't undermine or threaten them, but rather support them to be successful in their role. The lead mentor is pivotal and crucial in supporting the mentor, the mentee and consequently the progress of the learners involved.

The following stages should be considered when addressing issues that arise with beginning teachers' development.

Identifying the issue(s)

The lead mentor works alongside the mentor, and potentially professionals from external agencies (ITT/ITE providers, university tutors, etc.) to identify the present situation, considering:

- the current level of support the beginning teacher is receiving, and the effectiveness of this
- the specific issues that are impeding the development of the beginning teacher.

It is important to consider the involvement and input of the beginning teacher at this stage. It may be that where there is high confidence that planned interventions will be effective, the beginning teacher may not be privy to conversations that focus on the issues impeding their progress. This would help to prioritise and maintain the wellbeing and confidence of the mentee. On the other hand, it may be that the beginning teacher's involvement in this stage is necessary to equip them with the appropriate sense of urgency, so they can appropriately prioritise their development. Decisions about whether or not to include the mentee in such discussions is probably better made through discussions with the mentor and the lead mentor.

Planning the intervention

The mentor and lead mentor consider what actions could support the beginning teacher in addressing the specific issues that have been identified. This might include:

- team teaching with an experienced teacher
- planning support
- observations
- observing others
- self-reflection through video footage of teaching.

The lead mentor's role here is to consider the school's capacity to support. It may be that the mentor has the capacity to fully implement the interventions. Alternatively, it may be that the lead mentor supplements the role of the mentor in implementing the support. In some cases, it may be appropriate that the school utilises external agencies (ITT provider or university tutor) to deliver additional support.

Implementing and reviewing the intervention

The lead mentor ensures that the support is implemented as agreed. They then receive feedback to consider the impact of the support, how it has affected the overall progress of the beginning teacher and whether further intervention is needed.

Next, complete Task 18.3 using the three steps from above.

Task 18.3 Applying the three steps

A beginning teacher in your school has been teaching a Year 5 class since September. It is now November and he is still struggling to assert himself. During lessons, pupils are often off task and in books there is little evidence of progress.

The teacher is aware of his difficulties implementing effective behaviour for learning strategies and knows that his lessons are not having the desired impact on learning. At times, he is left visibly upset after lessons.

His mentor is a Year 6 teacher who is released one afternoon a week to support the mentee. She has been effective in regularly observing the beginning teacher and having regular mentor meetings, but is beginning to worry that this support is not having sufficient impact, and that the negative impact on the students and their learning is too high.

Monitoring the quality of mentoring

As a lead mentor, a key responsibility is ensuring that high-quality, consistent mentoring is being delivered across the school. While ultimately less time-consuming for the lead mentor, in some ways this aspect of the role is far trickier than directly mentoring beginning primary teachers. As a lead mentor, the role is to support the mentor in guiding a beginning primary teacher, so it can feel like a far more convoluted process to reach that final goal of impacting and improving the learning outcomes for pupils.

A key consideration for the lead mentor is that for mentors, involvement might well be voluntary, so the lead mentor is relying on their goodwill. Hobson et al., (2009) suggests that mentoring can result in mentors having an increased workload (which can become unmanageable) and even result in the mentor feeling nervous or anxious at the prospect of being observed and presenting their ideas to beginning teachers. The effective leadership of professional development requires the development of genuine professional trust (DfE,

2016a), and it is important to retain sight of this when considering methods of monitoring and evaluation.

Strategies to monitor the quality of mentoring

1. *Regular communication with the mentor and beginning teacher*. This is key. It does not need to be formal communication as much as regular interactions and opportunities to 'catch up'.
2. *Co-observing the beginning teacher.* This informs the lead mentor of the development of the beginning teacher and offers an insight into the relationship between mentor and beginning teacher. This can also be a valuable development opportunity for the mentor, through discussions after the observation, and it may be that the lead mentor gives (and therefore models for the mentor) feedback.
3. *Opportunities for mentors to discuss their own development, and the beginning teachers' development, through learning conversations.* Again, this strategy offers support for mentors in their role, while offering a 'window' for the lead mentor into the mentoring activities in the school.

Creating a successful community of mentoring and coaching

Having the one-on-one intensive support of a mentor is developmental, which is often reserved to the domain of the beginning teacher. However, the continued learning and professional development of teachers is what underpins school improvement, through raising achievement and attainment (Lofthouse, Leat and Towler, 2010). Therefore, for the lead mentor, establishing an effective and consistent programme of mentoring is one part of a larger picture of teacher CPD, which ensures that all teachers have a personalised approach to their development. It may be that the lead mentor has responsibility for both coaching and mentoring in the school, or it may be that there is another member of staff who leads the school's coaching provision. In either case, it needs to be considered how both forms of professional development will be integrated in the primary school to create an effective and cohesive programme of mentoring and coaching.

Coaching and mentoring

For beginning primary teachers, mentoring is used primarily as a tool to develop their knowledge and skills in teaching, guided by a more experienced colleague. It may be characterised by the 'expert-novice' relationship, whereby the expert develops the novice both professionally and personally (Atkinson et al., 2008). It may likewise be used at different stages of a teacher's development - for example, for progression, to support teachers in order to respond to the demands of a new role such as a leadership position - or for challenges - to support teachers to address significant issues (CUREE, 2005).

The terms 'mentoring' and 'coaching' have been defined in a number of different ways. The terms are sometimes used interchangeably (Lofthouse et al., 2010) due to the commonalities between the two forms of development. In the National Framework for Mentoring and Coaching, the distinction lies in the scope of the development, mentoring being focused upon 'supporting professional learners through significant career transitions', while coaching is focused upon, 'The development of a specific aspect of a professional learner's practice' (CUREE, 2005).

Questions to consider in developing whole-school mentoring and coaching

Who is the mentoring and coaching for?

As mentoring is a fundamental part of initial teacher training, having a coach or mentor to support your professional development can be viewed as being for teachers who have deficiencies, whether this is because they are beginning primary teachers, or more experienced teachers with identified weaknesses in their practice. This fallacy is reinforced in schools where coaching is used primarily as a tool for teachers who are deemed to be underperforming. As the Lofthouse et al. (2010, p. 18) observe, 'if it (coaching) is seen by teachers as aggressive remedial action, it will not be actively sought out'.

In schools where mentoring and coaching are truly valued, they need to be recognised for their potential in contributing to whole school improvement: *coaching and mentoring can positively impact all teachers' professional practice, no matter at what stage of their career it occurs*. This is the case not only for those who are being coached or mentored, but also for those who do the mentoring or coaching. In order to develop this principle, a key stipulation needs to be that coaching is not used primarily as a tool to combat under-performance. One suggestion to challenge its status is the use of a 'coaching champion'. This is a member of staff who is well regarded and influential within the school – for example, a senior member of staff – who can champion the process.

How flexible is your mentoring and coaching provision?

While developing a successful culture of coaching and mentoring depends on establishing clear expectations and non-negotiables for provision, it is also important that support is flexible, depending on the needs of the teacher. The development of every teacher is different, so while consistency and non-negotiables certainly have a place in the successful establishment of a community of mentoring and coaching, equal thought should be put into where flexibility should be embedded – for example, is it important that coaching begins at the start of the year or could the process be triggered at any point in the year, in response to need?

How will mentors and coaches be allocated in your school?

Allocating mentors and coaches needs to be considered thoughtfully to ensure a mentoring or coaching relationship in which both parties feel comfortable to have open and honest conversations. You may want to consider specific expertise – for example, year or phase group experience, or subject expertise – that may enhance the development of the individual. This is especially pertinent in the case of mentoring, where the mentor needs to have an appropriate level of working knowledge of the needs and context of the beginning primary teacher (CUREE, 2005). For coaches, you may want to consider how they will be allocated and whether there will be an application process. Will teachers be able to choose their own coaches? How will the school ensure it has capacity for all teachers who wish to have a coach?

How confidential are mentoring and coaching conversations?

In any mentoring or coaching partnership, professional trust is vital; however, the issue of confidentiality needs to be considered. Are conversations completely confidential, or in certain cases – for example, if information is disclosed that is significant to the individual's well-being, or may pose harm to pupils or the school – will conversations be shared? Establishing trust is vital in both mentoring and coaching capacities, and it is important that teachers are confident that their conversations will not become the topic of 'staffroom gossip' (Lofthouse et al. 2010). However, equally there needs to be an acknowledgement that under certain circumstances information will need to go beyond the mentor or coaching pair. This may be something that is spoken about with all staff, but it should also be discussed on an individual basis when establishing the ground rules for the mentoring or coaching relationship.

Summary

The role of the lead mentor allows the capacity for schools to improve and refine their mentoring practices. Lead mentors need to define and outline their roles and responsibilities at an early stage, to ensure that they offer added value to the school, rather than convoluting the process of mentoring. Lead mentors can offer additional capacity and support for both beginning primary teachers and mentors, when issues arise. This needs to be handled sensitively on a case-by-case basis. Lead mentors are pivotal in the development of whole-school mentoring; however, this is just one aspect of a wider picture of teacher development. The development of a community of mentoring and coaching, in which every teacher has access to personalised professional development, allows for whole-school improvement.

Further reading

CUREE (2007) *National Framework for Mentoring and Coaching*, Coventry: CUREE.

Department for Education (2019) *Teacher Recruitment and Retention Strategy*. Available at: https://assets.publishing.service.gov.uk/government/uploads/system/uploads/attachment_data/file/786856/DFE_Teacher_Retention_Strategy_Report.pdf Accessed 22 February 2019.

Lofthouse, R.M., Leat, D. and Towler, C. (2010) *Improving Teacher Coaching in Schools: A Practical Guide*. London: National College for Teaching and Leadership.

19 The secrets of partnership working for mentors

Penny Webb, Hazel King and Sarah Goodwin

Introduction

This chapter considers how partnerships between higher education institutions and schools develop in teacher education programmes, and how these can support mentoring. We present examples of mentoring partnerships in England and the Netherlands to act as a lens when considering how good partnerships can enhance mentoring practices. The roles of structures and relationships are explored in relation to the working of successful partnerships.

Objectives

At the end of this chapter, you should be able to:

- Recognise how initial teacher education partnerships are conceptualised
- Understand that the secret of good partnership can be dependent on the philosophical approaches adopted by the higher education institution and school
- Understand what current research tells us about the importance of structures and relationships in partnerships
- Consider your role in developing partnership working.

To start, let's focus on your partnerships. Reflect on your own context in task 19.1.

Task 19.1 Partnerships

Make a list of the individuals and groups of people with whom you are in partnership when carrying out your mentoring role. This might include staff from a teacher education provider, school mentors, class teachers and trainee teachers.

What is partnership?

Partnerships are most commonly seen between teacher education institutes (such as those based in universities) and schools, where trainee teachers can hone their practice while being supported by mentors. Schools both in the United Kingdom and internationally have followed a 'goodwill' model, although schools do typically receive payments for placing trainee teachers (Aitken, Corkery and Jones, 2017). Sometimes referred to as the 'theory into practice' model, trainee teachers explore theoretical models within taught sessions and complete focused assignments set by the higher education institution, aiming to apply their theoretical learning when on school placements. School mentors are vital in supporting the next generation of trainee teachers. The number of higher education institution days to school experience days can vary. The model described by Aitken et al. (2017) is based in New Zealand and identifies how students have two days in school and two days on campus. There are key defined roles within these partnerships, including the mentor teacher who runs the school-based training days and who holds learning conversations with the trainee teacher, similar to those conversations you will be having with a beginning teacher you are mentoring. In addition, there will be a university tutor who makes links between the learning undertaken in the university and the practical experience, ensuring effective integration between both. Aitkin et al. (2017) identify that these partnerships between the university and the school are communities of practice, where goals and processes are shared. Next complete Task 19.2.

Task 19.2 Relationships

Read Case study 19.1, which considers the relationship between the mentor and the tutor from a higher education institution in England and consider the following questions:

- What supported this positive working relationship?
- Reflect on your own context and the experiences you have with your tutor from a higher education institution – is it similar to Case study 19.1?

Case study 19.1 Positive mentoring opportunities within the partnership in one English school from the perspective of a school mentor

A positive working relationship between the mentor and the university tutor is important when working with trainee teachers in our school. Detailed below are the opportunities the university has given to me in my role as a mentor.

Mentor development programme

Training sessions led by the university for new and experienced mentors allow for positive and developmental discussions and make the mentors feel valued in their role. These sessions offer me an opportunity to network and to clarify the role of the mentor within the teacher training programme. The training supported me in areas we may not have experienced within the classroom, such as tackling difficult conversations with trainee teachers.

Self-evaluation tool

Although this at first appeared to be another paperwork exercise in an already overloaded role, I have found that when used correctly this can be a valuable tool allowing for reflection, development of ideas and, in turn, an improvement in practice. An example of this is the induction procedures at my own school. This area was identified as an area for improvement through the self-evaluation tool so through honest discussions with the trainee teachers on placement and with the university tutor and us, we developed a trainee teacher handbook, which includes photographs of staff and their role within the school. As a school mentor, the self-evaluation tool has also led to opportunities to liaise with other schools where we have shared ideas and moderated our gradings of the student teachers.

Area meetings

Area meetings, where school mentors and university tutors meet for training, give another opportunity for networking. Here I was able to share ideas and also receive help for any challenges we may have been experiencing with our trainees. These meetings also highlighted opportunities for personal development for mentors, including attending university grading meetings and interviewing students for the initial teacher training programmes. I have enjoyed seeing the whole process, especially how the students were interviewed for the programmes.

Alongside the opportunities for development identified in Case study 19.1, mentors require understanding from the university that the school mentor role is at times taken on over and above their already heavy workload, and they may already be mentoring their beginning teachers. Although there are many similarities between the mentee of a beginning teacher and a trainee teacher, it is important to recognise the requirements set by the university in terms of the time and space the mentor needs. This may be on top of your mentoring duties with your beginning teacher.

You could consider how you could involve your beginning teacher within such activities as:

- weekly meetings
- lesson observations
- verbal feedback
- writing up lesson observations
- writing interim and final reports for trainee teachers
- liaising with class teachers
- organising development time with other members of staff
- day-to-day chats and support.

Philosophical approaches to successful partnership

Van Ginkel et al. (2016) undertook research into what teacher mentors and trainee teachers believed formed a successful partnership working within their teacher training programme.

These philosophical approaches could also be considered within your role as mentor for your beginning teacher. Van Ginkel et al. (2016) proposed that the philosophical approach to the partnership had fundamental implications for the success of the mentee (student teacher). The two approaches identified were instrumental versus developmental. Instrumental approaches focused on preparing the trainee teacher to attain certain professional standards, whereas the developmental approaches focused on helping the individual on their personal developmental trajectory. The developmental approach adopts a description of 'growing a teacher', whereas the instrumental one often focuses on judgements about the suitability of a person to be in the profession based on the day-to-day practicalities. Therefore, these two philosophies can often be at the root of tensions between academic institutions and school-based practitioners. Table 19.1 has been designed as a self-audit tool for you to consider and evaluate your own philosophy and the resulting frameworks, processes and relationships. Complete the table as part of Task 19.3.

Task 19.3 Reflect on your mentoring philosophy

Use Table 19.1 for this task.

- What frameworks and processes are in place?
- How do these enable you to be an effective mentor?
- What other frameworks or processes might be supportive?

Researchers such as Spendlove, Howes and Wake (2010) focus on the tensions between schools and higher education institutions within teacher education partnerships. They consider that views from both school and higher education institutions can be polarised, with school focused on the 'day-to-day pragmatics of working in school classrooms', whereas higher education institution tutors seek to support the trainee teachers' interpretation of those events through theory. Spendlove, Howes and Wake (2010, p. 65) refer to the observation of Hodkinson and Hodkinson (1999, p. 275), who note that during the school experience part of the programme, the main focus was the practical implementation of government

Table 19.1 Self-audit tool

	Instrumental	*Developmental*
Frameworks: What framework exists in your partnership to support the communication between partners?		
Processes: What processes exist in your partnership to support the development of all partners?		
Relationships: How are relationships developed in your partnership?		
Is there a place for both instrumental and developmental philosophies in successful partnerships?		

policy and national politics instead of reflecting upon pedagogical approaches. You as a mentor could help to reduce any tensions by discussing the philosophy of your school with both your link tutor from the university and your trainee teacher while they are on placement with you. It might also be suitable for you to discuss the philosophy of your school with your beginning teacher when they first start with you, and how they will embed the philosophy into their teaching and learning with the children.

Rowland et al.'s (2018) research considered what school-based mentors perceived as enabling or acting as barriers to mentoring trainee teachers. This research was commissioned by a higher education institution that had recently made substantial changes to their partnership. The significant change was that the university tutors, instead of working with the trainee teachers alongside the mentors, decided to develop the university tutor role so that they mentored the mentors to enable stronger mentoring of the students. The focus of the research was to explore the impact these changes had on the partnership. Findings showed that school mentors believed their relationship with the university tutor was key. Enablers to mentor development included the opportunity to conduct joint lesson observations of trainee teachers with the tutor and being able to call on the support of the tutor as needed.

However, a barrier was identified when mentors perceived that university tutors did not recognise their expertise. Bullough and Draper (2004b) present a case study where the relationship between a school-based mentor and a university tutor breaks down, resulting in the trainee teacher having to decide which party to align herself with in order to complete a successful school placement. This dysfunctional relationship between a school-based mentor and a member of staff from a teacher education provider could stem from a deep-rooted conception that school mentors base their teaching practice on practical experience rather than academic knowledge. Yet, as we saw in Chapter 18, the importance of research and using research is key for both mentors and beginning teachers to continue to enhance their teaching and learning.

Zeichner (2010) believes it is important that the divides between academic knowledge and practitioner knowledge are bridged. Butler and Cuenca (2012) also highlight the importance of school-based mentors and university tutors having a common language, including a shared understanding of the goals of teacher education: 'Teacher learning is transformative for student teachers when the goals and expectations of campus and field-based teacher educators are closely aligned and readily understood' (Butler and Cuenac, 2012, p.303). This alignment can be built with time as well as the consistency of having the same combination of mentor and link tutor working together, which can help to enhance the partnership. Task 19.4 asks you to consider your experiences of working with others.

Task 19.4 Working with others

- What positive successes have you experienced when you and your beginning teacher or trainee teacher have had the same expectations? How did you continue to develop these?

- Have you experienced a situation where different individuals have had different expectations of a trainee teacher or beginning teacher? If so, how did you manage this?
- How can partnership relationships support trainee teachers and beginning teachers to value both types of knowledge - academic knowledge and practitioner knowledge?
- What are the enablers and barriers to these types of relationships flourishing?

The secrets of successful partnerships

Researchers have focused on the features of partnership that ultimately enable success for their trainee teachers, and therefore could also be useful when you mentor beginning teachers. The research conducted by van Ginkel et al. (2016) focused on 726 secondary school mentors in the Netherlands who completed surveys. They found that an important aspect of the partnership identified was how mentors conceptualised their roles. It may be important for you to consider for a moment how you conceptualise your own mentoring role: is it different when you mentor your beginning teacher versus a trainee teacher? The secret of a successful partnership - whether with your beginning teacher or with trainee teachers - can be applied to both situations. A body of research focuses on successful partnerships from researchers, including Hargreaves and Fullen (2000); Butler and Cuenca, (2012) and Kemmis et al. (2014). Conceptualisations have encompassed ideas of nurturing, clarifying, supervising or collaborative self-development. Two conceptions explored by van Ginkel et al. (2016) were that mentors were motivated by personal self-development and by contributing to the teaching profession. Although small in scale, Aitken et al.'s (2017) study drew on these ideas and identified that some mentors positioned themselves as instrumental, while others considered themselves developmental. It would be worth pausing to consider how you position yourself with your mentees. These positions had distinct implications for how mentors interacted within the partnerships, either positioning themselves as enforcing the requirements of the placement or developing the capacity of the trainee teachers to meet the requirements. Additionally, their research from 2016 built on previous research themes emerging from mentor conversations about the partnership, whereas earlier findings in 2014, when the partnership was newly implemented, showed that the themes were relationships, communication, investment and interdependence (Aiken et al., 2017). In 2016, the four key emergent themes were relationships, communication, commitment and collaboration (2017). The shift in thematic identification could relate to the partnership becoming more established, so that the investment during the beginning of the partnership had manifested into commitment and interdependence into collaboration.

Aitkin et al. (2017) analysed the discourses used to describe the mentor role, with the aim of providing insight into how the mentors assigned different aspects of their roles. Seven factors were identified. Unsurprisingly, a number of these were focused on building relationships and supporting partnerships. However, two key aspects of their role were described in terms of interacting with the structures implemented by the institution. One of these themes was about 'adhering' to the guidelines from the institution. Another referred to clarifying expectations (Aitken et al., 2017, p. 38). This is particularly important in a school where you may mentor different types of trainee teachers within one academic year, as well as your beginning teachers.

It is important that the partnership builds the relationships between the mentor and the institution. The supporting aspect of the mentor role needs to be structured around shared goals and expectations. These, in turn, are structured around the frameworks and processes that are implemented by the institution. A specific example was a 'planning booklet' given to mentors by the institution, which provided a structure upon which to develop the ongoing communication between the mentor and the higher education institution. One mentor participant said, 'brilliant, they're the best things invented, I reckon' (Aitken et al., 2017, p. 37). Although the authors do not detail the content of this planning booklet, it is clear that the institution had created a document in which expectations were explicit. For Task 19.5, read Case study 19.2, which focuses on how a university in the Netherlands works with local primary schools.

Task 19.5 Partnerships between school staff and university tutors

Consider the partnership that exists between the school staff and the university tutors in Case study 19.2, and assess the impact of these partnerships on the mentoring of both the teacher trainee and the beginning teacher.

Case study 19.2 A mentoring partnership in the Netherlands

Schools in this area of the Netherlands can apply to become 'Teaching Schools' and are selected by School Boards according to whether the school can demonstrate a high quality of teaching and innovation and in line with the number of university students requiring placements. The university also has a say in which schools are chosen. The Teaching Schools agree to take on at least eight trainee teachers, who are at various stages of their four-year degrees. Trainee teachers are placed in classes, and the class teacher acts as their mentor by giving daily support. Trainee teachers usually spend two days a week in their placement schools as well as having block placements at various times throughout the year.

Each Teaching School has a coach who oversees all the trainees and all the mentors (illustrated in Figure19.1). The coach has one day out of the classroom each week to take on this role. The coach supports mentors in their support of the trainee teachers, for example, by being present when mentors give feedback to trainee teachers following observation of teaching. Each coach is supported by a tutor from the university.

The coaches encourage an 'investigative attitude' from the trainees. They encourage the trainees in the school to reflect on their progress. Trainees set their own targets

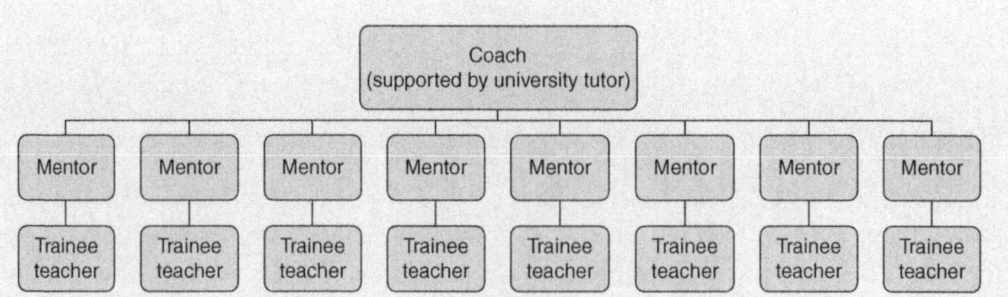

Figure 19.1 The coach-mentor-trainee relationship

and the coaches support the mentors (class teachers) to guide the trainees to achieve them. Mentors tend to help trainees with small, day-to-day targets, whereas school coaches and university tutors support trainees in achieving their main overarching targets.

Groups of schools that work with this university use different initiatives to support the development of all teaching staff. Some schools use Tweets and Facebook to spread news of the initiatives of which they are proud. One group of schools gathers coaches and school leaders together in a pub to share initiatives. In this way, schools are encouraged to 'give it a go' and learn by doing, recognising the importance of theory being brought together with practice. Another group of schools has put together training for beginning teachers. These beginning teachers spend Fridays out of the classroom to take part in training. The schools are hoping to align this 'curriculum' even more closely to the training of trainee teachers, and are using the standards for trainee teachers when working with beginning teachers. The plan is that these beginning teachers will take the ideas they meet on these training days and implement them in their classrooms, then other teachers in the schools will ask the beginning teachers about these methods, spreading these ideas across schools. In this way, the schools intend to use new teachers to transform the practice of current teachers.

As you can see in Case study 19.2, a strong relationship exists between the university tutors and school based mentors in the Netherlands. Consider how the example in Case study 19.2 could be applied to your setting in Task 19.6.

Task 19.6 Types of relationships

- Which of the relationships described in Case study 19.2 resonate with relationships you have in your mentoring role and how could these support you in your mentoring of beginning teachers?
- How are these schools in the Netherlands using partnerships to support the development of trainee and beginning teachers? Would any of these strategies translate into the settings in which you operate?
- How do you support your mentees with reflecting on their own practice and engaging in research (also refer to Chapter 18)? Could you foster relationships with mentoring partners to support you in this role?

Summary

This chapter has explained a range of international partnerships between higher education institutions and schools supporting trainee teachers on placement and how these could also be utilised by your mentoring philosophy of all your mentees including your beginning teachers within your school. Initial teacher education partnerships can be conceptualised as the roles and relationships that enable successful joint working between higher education institutions and schools to support trainee teachers. Philosophical approaches, either developmental or instrumental, can impact your mentoring approaches - the frameworks, processes and relationships within the partnerships. The instrumental approach focuses on meeting course requirements related to policy and practice, achieving standards in a 'tick box' style interaction. Developmental approaches, however, focus on the personal professional development of the mentees. Research has shown that open communication and developing a community of practice can help with shared goals and processes. Case studies from a mentor working in England and a partnership in the Netherlands demonstrated how the secrets of partnerships include frameworks, processes and relationships that are collaborative between all partners, including the trainee teacher, as well as established beginning teachers situated within the schools, so all can flourish through your support as a mentor.

Further reading

Aitken, V., Corkery, F. and Jones, K. (2017) Positions, storylines and speech acts: How five mentor teachers from EIT's Bachelor of Teaching (Primary) conceptualise their role in the partnership, *Waikato Journal of Education*, 22(3), pp. 33-46.

Rowland, G., King, H., Webb, P., Cogger, A. and Vincent, K. (2018) Fishing for evidence of impact, *Professional Development Today*, 19(3/4), pp.76-85.

Spendlove, D., Howes, A. and Wake, G. (2010) Partnerships in pedagogy: Refocusing of classroom lenses, *European Journal of Teacher Education*, 33(1), pp.65-77.

REFERENCES

Adams, E. (2016) *Agent of Change: In Art, Design and Environmental Education,* Shepshed: Loughborough Design Press.

Aitken, V., Corkery, F. and Jones, K. (2017) Positions, storylines and speech acts: How five mentor teachers from EIT's Bachelor of Teaching (Primary) conceptualise their role in the partnership, *Waikato Journal of Education*, 22(3), pp. 33–46.

AITSL (Australian Institute for Teaching and School Leadership) (2011) *The Australian Professional Standards for Teachers,* Melbourne: AITSL. Available at: www.aitsl.edu.au/teach/standards. Accessed 25 January 2018.

Ambrosetti, A. (2010) Mentoring and learning to teach: What do pre-service teachers expect to learn from their mentor teachers?, *The International Journal of Learning,* 17(9), pp. 117–32.

Archer, L., Dawson, E., DeWitt, J., Seakins, A. and Wong, B. (2015) 'Science capital': A conceptual, methodological, and empirical argument for extending Bourdieusian notions of capital beyond the arts, *Journal of Research in Science Teaching*, 52, pp. 922–48.

Askew, M. (2012) *Transforming Primary Mathematics,* Abingdon: Routledge.

Askew, M., Brown, M., Rhodes, V., William, D. & Johnson, D. (1997) *Effective Teachers of Numeracy: Report of a Study Carried Out for the Teacher Training Agency*, London: King's College, University of London.

Aspfors, J. and Fransson, G. (2015) Research on mentor education for mentors of newly qualified teachers: A qualitative meta-synthesis, *Teaching and Teacher Education*, 48, pp. 75–86.

Atkinson, M., Lord, P. and Mitchell, H. (2008) *Mentoring and Coaching for Professionals: A Study of the Research Evidence*. Available at: www.nfer.ac.uk/nfer/publications/MCM01/MCM01.pdf Accessed 12 December 2018.

Aubrey, K. and Riley, A., (2017) *Understanding and Using Challenging Educational Theories*, London: Sage.

Bailey, R., Howells, K. and Glibo, I. (2018) Physical activity and mental health of school-aged children and adolescents: A rapid review, *International Journal of Physical Education*, 55(1), pp. 1–14.

Baker, W. and McNicoll, A. (2006) I can get by with a little help from my friends: Peer mentoring – critical friends for the reflective practitioner, in *Critical Visions, Proceedings of the 29th HERDSA Annual Conference, Western Australia, 10–12 July 2006*, pp. 28–34.

Barrett, L., Mazerolle, S.M. and Nottingham, S.L. (2017) Attributes of effective mentoring relationships for novice faculty members: Perspectives of mentors and mentees, *Athletic Training Educational Journal*, 12(2), pp. 152–62.

Barrett, P., Zhang, Y., Davies, F. and Barrett, L. (2015) *Clever Classrooms*. Available at: www.salford.ac.uk/cleverclassrooms/1503-Salford-Uni-Report-DIGITAL.pdf. Accessed: 11 January 2019.

Bassot, B. (2013) *The Reflective Journal*, London: Palgrave Macmillan

Bearne, E. and Reedy, D. (2018) *Teaching Primary English: Subject Knowledge and Classroom Practice*, London: Routledge.

Berry, B., Hopkins-Thompson, T. and Hoke, M. (2002) *Assessing and Supporting New Teachers: Lessons from the Southeast*. Chapel Hill, NC: The Southeast Center for Teaching Quality at the University of North Carolina.

Beutel, D. and Spooner-Lane, R. (2009) Building mentoring capacities in experienced teachers, *The International Journal of Learning*, 16(4), pp. 351–60.

Birenbaum, M., DeLuca, C., Earl, L., Heritage, M., Klenowski, V., Looney, A., Smith, K., Timperley, H., Volante, L. and Wyatt-Smith, C. (2015) International trends in the implementation of assessment for learning: Implications for policy and practice, *Policy Futures in Education*, 13(1), pp. 117–40.

Black, P. (2003) The nature and value of formative assessment for learning, *Improving Schools*, 6(3), pp. 7–22.

Black, P. (2007) *Formative Assessment: Promises or Problems?*, London: King's College, University of London.

Black, P. and Wiliam, D. (1998) *Inside the Black Box: Raising Standards Through Classroom Assessment*, London: King's College, University of London.

Black, P. and Wiliam D. (2009) Developing the theory of formative assessment, *Educational Assessment, Evaluation and Accountability*, 21(1), pp. 5–31.

Bleach, K. (1997) The importance of critical self-reflection in mentoring newly qualified teachers, *Mentoring & Tutoring*, 4(3), pp. 19–24.

Bloom, B.S. (1969) Some theoretical issues relating to educational evaluation. In R.W. Taylor (ed.), *Educational Evaluation: New Roles, New Means: The 68th Yearbook of the National Society for the Study of Evaluation*, Part II, Chicago, IL: University of Chicago Press, pp. 26–50.

Boaler, J. (2016) *Mathematical Mindsets*, San Francisco: Jossey-Bass.

Bobek, B.L. (2002) Teacher resiliency: A key to career longevity, *The Clearing House*, 75(4), pp. 202–05.

Boing, Boing (2018) *Resilience Framework (Adults)*. Available at: www.boingboing.org.uk. Accessed 6 August 2018.

Bower, M. (1966) *Will to Manage*, New York: McGraw Hill.

Bowlby, J. (1969) *Attachment and Loss, Vol. 1: Attachment*, New York: Basic Books.

Bowtell, J., Holding, S. and Bearne, E. (2014) Early reading, in T. Cremim and J. Arthur (eds), *Learning to Teach in the Primary School*, 3rd ed., London: Routledge, pp. 527–40.

Breiner, J.M., Johnson, C.C., Harkness, S.S. & Koehler, C.M. (2012) What is STEM? A discussion about conceptions of STEM in education and partnerships. *School Science and Mathematics*, 112(1), pp. 3-11.

Bressman, S., Winter, J.S. and Efron, S.E. (2018) Next generation mentoring: Supporting teachers beyond induction, *Teaching and Teacher Education*, 73, pp.162-70.

Brookfield, S. (2012) *Teaching for Critical Thinking: Tools and Techniques to Help Students Question Their Assumptions*, San Francisco: Jossey-Bass.

Brookfield, S. (2017) *Becoming a Critically Reflective Teacher*, New York: John Wiley & Sons.

Brown, G. and Wragg, E.C. (1993) *Questioning*, London: Routledge.

Bruner, J. (1966) *Toward a Theory of Instruction*, Cambridge, MA: The Belknap Press.

Bryk, A.S. and Schneider, B.L. (2002) *Trust in Schools: A Core Resource for Improvement*, New York: Russell Sage Foundation.

Bullough, R.V. Jr and Draper, R.J. (2004a) Making sense of a failed triad: Mentors, university supervisors, and positioning theory, *Journal of Teacher Education*, 55(5), pp. 407-20.

Bullough, R.V. Jr and Draper, R.J. (2004b) Mentoring and the emotions, *Journal of Education for Teaching: International Research and Pedagogy*, 30(3), pp. 271-88.

Burnett, C., Davies, J., Merchant, G. and Rowsell, J. (2014) *New Literacies Around the Globe*, New York: Routledge.

Burnett, C. and Merchant, G. (2018) Affective encounters: enchantment and the possibility of reading for pleasure, *Literacy*, 52(2), pp. 62-69.

Burton, L. (2017) *Mentor Awards*, Canterbury: Canterbury Christ Church University.

Butler, B. and Cuenca, A. (2012) Conceptualising the roles of mentor teachers during student teaching, *Action in Teacher Education*, 34(4), pp. 296-308.

Cain, T. (2009) Mentoring trainee teachers: How can mentors use research? *Mentoring and Tutoring*, 17(1), pp. 53-66.

Cameron-Jones, M. and O'Hara, P. (1997) Support and challenge in teacher education, *British Educational Research Journal*, 23(1), pp.15-25.

Carnell, E., MacDonald, J., and Askew, S. (2006) *Coaching and Mentoring in Higher Education: A Learning-centred Approach*, London: Institute of Education.

Castro, A.J., Kelly, J. and Shih, M. (2010) Resilience strategies for new teachers in high-needs areas. *Teaching and Teacher Education*, 26(3), 622-29.

Cayley, R. (2011) Using writing to clarify your own thinking, *Explorations of Style* (blog). Available at: https://explorationsofstyle.com/2011/01/12/using-writing-to-clarify-your-own-thinking. Accessed 12 December 2019.

CBI (2015) *Tomorrow's World: Inspiring Primary Scientists*, London: CBI. Available at: https://www.stem.org.uk/resources/elibrary/resource/35987/tomorrows-world-inspiring-primary-scientists#&gid=undefined&pid=1. Accessed 5 March 2017.

Cheng, M.M.H. and Tang, S.Y.-F. (2008) The dilemma of field experience assessment: Enhancing professional development or fulfilling a gate-keeping function?, *Teacher Development*, 12(3), pp. 223-36.

Child, A. and Merrill, S. (2005) *Developing as a Secondary School Mentor: A Case Study Approach for Trainee Mentors and their Tutors*, Exeter: Learning Matters.

Cho, C., Ramanan, R. and Feldman, M. (2011) Defining the ideal qualities of mentorship: A qualitative analysis of the characteristics of outstanding mentors, *The American Journal of Medicine*, 124(5), 453–58.

Christie, D. (2008) Professional studies in initial teacher education. In T.G.K. Bryce and W. Humes (eds), *Scottish Education: Education Beyond Devolution,* 3rd ed., Edinburgh: Edinburgh University Press.

CIPD (Chartered Institute of Personnel and Development) (2012) *Coaching and Mentoring Fact Sheet*. Available at: www.cipd.ae/knowledge/factsheets/coaching-mentoring. Accessed 12 December 2019.

Cliff-Hodges, G. (2010) Reasons for reading: why literature matters, Literacy 44(2), pp.60–68.

Clutterbuck, D. (2004) *Everyone Needs a Mentor: Fostering Talent in Your Organisation*, London: Chartered Institute of Personnel and Development (CIPD).

Clutterbuck, D. (2014) *Everyone Needs a Mentor*, 4th ed., London: Chartered Institute of Personnel and Development (CIPD).

Cochran-Smith, M. & Lytle, S.L. (1999) Relationships of knowledge and practice: Teacher learning in communities, *Review of Research in Education* 24, pp. 249–305.

Cochran-Smith, M. and Lytle, S. (2009) *Inquiry as Stance: Practitioner Research for the Next Generation*, New York: Teachers College Press.

Coldwell, M., Greany, T., Higgins, S., Brown, C., Maxwell, B., Stiell, B., Stoll, L. Willis, B. & Burns, H. (2017) *Evidence-informed Teaching: An Evaluation of Progress in England,* London: Department for Education.

Comber, B., Nixon, H. and Reid, J.A. (2007) *Literacies in Place: Teaching Environmental Communications*. Newton: Primary English Teaching Association.

CooperGibson Research (2018) *Factors Affecting Teacher Retention: Qualitative Investigation Research,* London: Department for Education.

Cordingley, P., Higgins, S., Greany, T., Buckler, N., Coles-Jordan, D., Crisp, B., Saunders, L. and Coe, R. (2015) *Developing Great Teaching: Lessons from the International Reviews into Effective Professional Development*, London: Teacher Development Trust.

Covey, S. (2015) *The 7 Habits of Highly Effective People: Powerful Lessons in Personal Change,* New York: FranklinCovey.

Covey, S. and Merill, R. (2006) *The Speed of Trust: The One Thing That Changes Everything,* New York: The Free Press.

Cowan, E.M. (2009) Implementing formative assessment: student teachers' experiences on placements, *Teacher Development,* 13(1), pp. 71–84.

Cox, E., Bachkirova, T. and Clutterbuck, D. (2014) *The Complete Handbook of Coaching*, 2nd ed., London: Sage.

Crasborn, F., Hennison, P., Brouwer, N., Korthagen, F. and Bergen, T. (2011) Exploring a two-dimensional model of mentor teacher roles in mentoring dialogues, *Teaching and Teacher Education,* 27, pp. 320–31.

CUREE (2007) *National Framework for Mentoring and Coaching*, Coventry: CUREE. Available at: www.curee.co.uk/files/publication/1219313968/mentoring_and_coaching_national_framework.pdf. Accessed 8 November 2018.

Daloz, L.A. (2012) *Mentor: Guiding the Journey of Adult Learners*, New York: Wiley.

Darling-Hammond, L. (2003) Keeping good teachers: Why it matters, what leaders can do, *Educational Leadership*, 60(8), pp. 6–13.

Day, C. (2004) *A Passion for Teaching*, London: Routledge Falmer.

Day, C., Edwards, A., Griffiths, A. and Gu, Q. (2011) *Beyond Survival: Teachers and Resilience*, Nottingham: University of Nottingham. Available at: www.nottingham.ac.uk/research/groups/crelm/documents/teachers-resilience/teachers-resilience.pdf. Accessed 2 February 2020.

Deal T.E. and Peterson K.D. (1999) *Shaping School Culture: The Heart of Leadership*, San Francisco: Jossey-Bass.

Department for Education (DfE) (2011) *Teachers' Standards: Guidance for School Leaders, School Staff and Governing Bodies* , London: Crown Copyright.

Department for Education (DfE) (2013a) *The National Curriculum in England:Key Stages 1 and 2 Framework Document*, London: Crown Copyright.

Department for Education (DfE) (2013b) *The National Curriculum in England: Mathematics Programmes of Study*. Available at: www.gov.uk/government/publications/national-curriculum-in-england-mathematics-programmes-of-study (Accessed:29 June 2018).

Department for Education (DfE) (2014) *Statutory Framework for the Early Years Foundation Stage: Setting the Standards for Learning, Development and Care for Children from Birth to Five*, London:Crown Copyright.

Department for Education (DfE) (2016a) *National Standards for School-based Initial Teacher Training (ITT) Mentors*, London: Crown Copyright. Available at: https://assets.publishing.service.gov.uk/government/uploads/system/uploads/attachment_data/file/536891/Mentor_standards_report_Final.pdf. Accessed 20 September 2019.

Department for Education (DfE) (2016b) *A Framework of Core Content for Initial Teacher Training (ITT)*, London: Crown Copyright. Available at: www.gov.uk/government/uploads/system/uploads/attachment_data/file/536890/Framework_Report_11_July_2016_Final.pdf. Accessed 25 January 2018.

Department for Education (DfE) (2018) Induction for NQTs:*Statutory Guidance for Appropriate Bodies, Headteachers, School Staff and Governing Bodies*, London:Crown Copyright.

Department for Education (DfE) (2019) *Teacher Recruitment and Retention Strategy*, London:Crown Copyright. Available at:https://assets.publishing.service.gov.uk/government/uploads/system/uploads/attachment_data/file/786856/DFE_Teacher_Retention_Strategy_Report.pdf Accessed 2 February 2019.

Department of Education and Science (1988) *Task Group on Assessment and Testing: A Report*, London:Department of Education and Science and the Welsh Office.

Department of Education and Skills and Welsh Office (1989) *Science in the National Curriculum*. London:Her Majesty's Stationery Office.

Department of Education and Training (2004) *Competency Framework for Teachers*, East Perth: Department of Education and Training.

Dewey, J. (1938) *Experience and Education*, New York:Collier Books.

Diener, E., Helliwell, J.F. and Kahneman, D. (eds) (2010) *International Differences in Wellbeing*, Oxford:Oxford University Press.

Driscoll, L.G., Parkes, K.A., Tilley-Lubbs, G.A., Brill, J.M. and Pitts Bannister, V.R. (2009) Navigating the lonely sea:Peer mentoring and collaboration among aspiring women scholars, *Mentoring and Tutoring:Partnership in Learning*, 17, pp.5–21.

Durlak, J.A., Weissberg, R.P., Dymnicki, A.B., Taylor, R.D. and Schellinger, K.B. (2011) The impact of enhancing students' social and emotional learning: A meta-analysis of school-based universal interventions, *Child Development*, 82(1), pp. 405–32.

Dweck, C. (2007) *Mindset: The New Psychology of Success*, New York: Ballantine Books.

Earl, L. and Timperley, H. (2009) *Professional Learning Conversations: Challenges in Using Evidence for Improvement*, New York: Springer.

Eby, L.T., McManus, S.E., Simon, S.A. and Russell, J.E. (2000) The protégé's perspective regarding negative mentoring experiences: The development of a taxonomy, *Journal of Vocational Behavior*, 57, pp. 1–21.

Education Endowment Foundation (2018) *Within-class Attainment Grouping*. Available at: https://educationendowmentfoundation.org.uk/pdf/generate/?u=https://educationendowmentfoundation.org.uk/pdf/toolkit/?id=2618&t=Teaching%20and%20Learning%20Toolkit&e=2618&s=. Accessed 30 January 2019.

Egan, G. (1975) *The Skilled Helper: A Systematic Approach to Effective Helping*, Pacific Grove, CA: Brooks/Cole.

Egan, G. (2002) *The Skilled Helper: A Problem Management and Opportunity Development Approach to Helping*, 7th ed., Pacific Grove, CA: Brooks Cole.

Egan, G. (2006) *Essentials of Skilled Helping: Managing Problems, Developing Opportunities*, Pacific Grove, CA: Brooks Cole.

Eisner, E.W. (2002) *The Arts and the Creation of the Mind*, Chicago, IL: Donnelley and Sons.

Ehri, L.C. (1987) Learning to read and spell words, *Journal of Reading Behaviour*, 19, pp. 5–31.

Ehri, L.C. (1995) Phases of development in learning to read words by sight, *Journal of Research in Reading*, 18(2), pp. 116–25.

Eriksson, A. (2017) Pre-service teachers' questions about the profession during mentoring group conversations. *European Journal of Teacher Education* 40(1), pp. 76–90.

Evans C., Waring, M. and Christodou, A. (2017) Building teachers' research literacy: Integrating practice and research. *Research Papers in Education*, 32(4), pp. 403–23.

Ewing, R.A. and Smith, D.L. (2003) Retaining quality beginning teachers in the profession, *English Teaching: Practice and Critique*, 2, pp. 15–32.

Fairbanks, M., Freedman, D. and Kahn, C. (2000) The role of effective mentors in learning to teach, *The Journal of Teacher Education*, 51(1), pp. 102–12.

Fairholm, G.W. (1994) *Leadership and the Culture of Trust*, Westport, CT: Praeger.

Family Links (2015) *The Teaching Puzzle: Your Guide to Social and Emotional Learning*, Oxford: Family Links: The Centre for Emotional Health.

Family Links (2018) *Emotional Health at School*, Oxford: Family Links: The Centre for Emotional Health.

Farber, K. (2015) *Why Great Teachers Quit and How We Might Stop the Exodus*, New York: Simon and Schuster.

Feiman-Nemser, S. (2012) *Teachers as Learners*, Cambridge, MA: Harvard University Press.

Feyerabend, P. (1993) *Against Method*, 3rd ed., London: Verso.

Fletcher, S.J. and Mullen, C.A. (eds) (2012) *The Sage Handbook of Mentoring and Coaching in Education*, London: Sage.

Fletcher-Wood, H. (2015) *What Underpins an Outlier's Success*? Available at: www.teachfirst.org.uk/stories/what-underpins-outliers-success. Accessed 6 August 2018.

Forde, C., McMahon, M., McPhee, A.D. and Patrick, F. (2006) *Professional Development, Reflection and Enquiry*, London: Paul Chapman.

Foster, D. (2018) *Teacher Recruitment and Retention in England*, House of Commons Briefing Paper No. 7222, London: UK Parliament.

Foster, D. (2019) *Initial Teacher Training in England*, House of Commons Briefing Paper No. 6710, London: UK Parliament.

Fransson, G. (2010) Mentors assessing mentees? An overview and analyses of the mentorship role concerning newly qualified teachers, *European Journal of Teacher Education*, 33(4), pp. 375–90.

Friesen, S. and Scott, D. (2013) Inquiry-based learning: A review of the research literature, paper prepared for the Alberta Ministry of Education. Available at: http://galileo.org/focus-on-inquiry-lit-review.pdf. Accessed 6 August 2017.

Fullan, M.G. and Hargreaves, A. (1996) *What's Worth Fighting for in Your School*, New York: Teachers College Press.

Furlong, J. (2005) New Labour and teacher education: The end of an era, *Oxford Review of Education*, 31(1), pp. 119–34.

Furlong, J. and Maynard, T. (1995) *Mentoring Student Teachers: The Growth of Professional Knowledge*, London: Routledge.

Gallant, A. and Riley, P. (2014) Early career teacher attrition: new thoughts on an intractable problem, *Teacher Development*, 18(4), pp. 562–80.

Gallwey, W.T. (1974) *The Inner Game of Tennis*, New York: Random House.

Garvey, B., Stokes, P. and Megginson, D. (2014) *Coaching and Mentoring: Theory and Practice*, London: Sage.

Geiger, T. and Pivovarova, M. (2018) The effects of working conditions on teacher retention, *Teachers and Teaching: Theory and Practice*, 24(6), pp. 1–22.

General Teaching Council (2004) *The Learning Conversation, Talking Together for Professional Development*, Available at: http://dera.ioe.ac.uk/8254/1/tplf_learncon_plcon0904.pdf. Accessed 11 February 2019.

General Teaching Council Scotland (2019) In2Teaching, Blogspot. Available at: http://in2teaching.org.uk/Blogspot/View/880Meandmymentor.aspx. Accessed 11 February 2019.

GTCS (2012) *Teacher Journey*. Available at: www.gtcs.org.uk/TeacherJourney/teacher-journey.aspx. Accessed 11 February 2018.

Gibbs, G. (1988) *Learning by Doing: A Guide to Reaching and Learning Methods*. Oxford: Further Education Unit, Oxford Polytechnic.

Gilbert, P. (2009) *The Compassionate Mind: A New Approach to the Challenge of Life*, London: Constable and Robinson.

Ghosh, R. and Reio, T.G. (2013) Career benefits associated with mentoring for mentors: A meta-analysis, *Journal of Vocational Behavior*, 83, pp. 106–16.

Goodman, A., Joshi, H., Nasim, B. and Tyler, C. (2015) *Social and Emotional Skills in Childhood and Their Long-term Effects on Adult Life*, London: EIF. Available at: www.eif.org.uk/wp-content/uploads/2015/03/EIF-Strand-1-Report-FINAL1.pdf Accessed 18 April 2018.

Graham, P. (1999) Powerful influences: A case of one student teacher renegotiating his perceptions of power relations, *Teaching and Teacher Education*, 15(5), pp. 523–40.

Gravells, J. (2017) *Mentoring in a Week*, St Albans: Critical Publishing.

Gregory, P., March, C. and Tutchell, S. (2020) *Mastering Primary Art and Design*, London: Bloomsbury.

Gruenert, S. and Whitaker, T. (2015) *School Culture Rewired: How to Define, Assess, and Transform It*, Alexandria VA: ASCD.

Haggard, D.L., Dougherty, T.W., Turban, D.B. and Wilbanks, J.E. (2011) Who is a mentor? A review of evolving definitions and implications for research, *Journal of Management*, 37, pp. 280-304.

Hall, E.T. (1976) *Beyond Culture*, New York: Doubleday.

Hall, K. (2003) *Listening to Stephen Read:Multiple Perspectives on Literacy*. Maidenhead:Open University Press.

Hargreaves, A. (1992) Cultures of teaching: A focus for change, in A. Hargreaves, and M. Fullan, *Understanding Teacher Development,* London: Cassell.

Hargreaves, A. and Fullan, M. (2000) Mentoring in the new millennium, *Theory into Practice*, 39(1), pp. 50–56.

Hargreaves, E. (2007) The validity of collaborative assessment for learning, *Assessment in Education*, 14(2), pp. 185–99.

Harlen, W. (2005) Teachers' summative practices and assessment for learning – tensions and synergies, *The Curriculum Journal*, 16(2), pp. 207-23.

Harrison, J.K., Lawson, T. and Wortley, A. (2005) Mentoring the beginning teacher:developing professional autonomy through critical reflection on practice, *Reflective Practice*, 6(3), pp. 419–41.

Hawkins P. (1985) *CLEAR Coaching model.* Available at: www.personal-coaching-information.com/clear-coaching-model.html. Accessed 23 September 2019.

Hawkey, K. (1997) Roles, responsibilities and relationships in mentoring: A literature review and agenda for research, *Journal of Teacher Education*, 48(5), pp. 325–35.

Hayward, L. and Spencer, E. (2010) The complexities of change: Formative assessment in Scotland, *Curriculum Journal*, 21(2), pp. 161–77.

Hazell, W. (2018) Reasons to worry: 5 new facts about teacher retention, *Times Education Supplement*. Available at: www.tes.com/news/reasons-worry-5-new-facts-about-teacher-retention, 27 September. Accessed 20 January 2019.

Headspace (2018) *Headspace App.* Available at www.headspace.com. Accessed 6 August 2018.

Hegarty, S. (2000) Teaching as a knowledge-based activity, *Oxford Review of Education*, 26, pp. 451-65.

Hempel-Jorgensen, A., Cremin, T., Harris, T. and Chamberlain, L. (2018) Pedagogy for reading for pleasure in low socio-economic primary schools: Beyond 'pedagogy of poverty'?, *Literacy* 52(2), pp. 86–94.

Hendrick, C. and Macpherson, R. (2017) *What Does This Look Like in the Classroom?* Woodbridge: John Catt Educational.

Hennissen, P., Crasborn, F., Brouwer, N., Korthagen, F. and Bergen, T. (2008) Mapping mentor teachers' roles in mentoring dialogues, *Educational Research Review*, 3, pp. 168–86.

Hewlett, C. (2013) Can we use the built environment to support children's learning?, in M. Sangster (ed.), *Developing Teacher Expertise*, London: Bloomsbury, pp. 19–22.

Hickman, R. (2014) *Why We Make Art: And Why It is Taught*, 2nd ed., Bristol: Intellect.

Hiebert, J. and Carpenter, T. (1992) Learning and teaching with understanding, in D.A. Grouws (ed.), *Handbook of Research on Mathematics Teaching and Learning: A Project of the National Council of Teachers of Mathematics*, New York: Macmillan, pp. 65–97.

Higgins, M.C. and Thomas, D.A. (2001) Constellations and careers: Toward understanding the effects of multiple developmental relationships, *Journal of Organisational Behavior*, 22, pp. 223–47.

Higgins, R., Hartley, P. & Skelton, A. (2001) Getting the message across: The problem of communicating assessment feedback, *Teaching in Higher Education*, 6(2), pp. 269–74.

HMIe (2008) *Mentoring in Teacher Education*, Livingston: HMIe. Available at: https://dera.ioe.ac.uk/998/7/mite_Redacted.pdf. Accessed 23 September 2019.

HMIe (2011) *Research Summary - assessment for learning*, Livingston: HMIe.

Hobson, A.J. (2003) Student teachers' conceptions and evaluations of 'theory' in initial teacher training (ITT), *Mentoring & Tutoring: Partnership in Learning*, 11(3), pp. 245–61.

Hobson, A.J. (2016) Judgementoring and how to avert it: Introducing ONSIDE mentoring for beginning teachers, *International Journal of Mentoring and Coaching in Education*, 5(2), pp. 87–110.

Hobson, A.J., Ashby, P., Malderez, A. and Tomlinson, P.D. (2009) Mentoring beginning teachers: What we know and what we don't. *Teaching and Teacher Education: An International Journal of Research and Studies*, 25(1), pp. 207–19.

Hobson, A.J. and Malderez, A. (2013) Judgementoring and other threats to realizing the potential of school-based mentoring in teacher education. *International Journal of Mentoring and Coaching in Education*, 2(2), pp. 89–108.

Hodkinson, H. and Hodkinson, P. (1999) Teaching to learn, learning to teach? School-based non-teaching activity in an initial teacher education and training partnership scheme, *Teaching and Teacher Education*, 15(3), pp. 273–86.

Hodson, D. (1985) Philosophy of science, science and science education, *Studies in Science Education*, 12, pp. 25–57.

Hoffman, J.V., Wetzel, M.M., Maloch, B., Greeter, E., Taylor, L., DeJulio, S. and Khan Vlach, S. (2015) What can we learn from studying the coaching interactions between cooperating teachers and preservice teachers? A literature review, *Teaching and Teacher Education*, 52, pp. 99–112.

Hofstede, G. (1980) *Culture's Consequences: International Differences in Work-Related Values*, London: Sage.

Howells, K. (2012) Pacing an importance on health and physical activity', in G. Griggs (ed.), *An Introduction to Primary Physical Education*, London: Routledge, pp. 207–20.

Howells K. (2015) Physical education planning in the National Curriculum, in K. Sewell (ed.), *Planning the Primary National Curriculum: A Complete Guide for Trainees and Teachers*, London: Sage, pp. 262–76.

Howells, K. (2017) Developing physical curiosity and physical development in K. Howells with A. Carney, N. Castle and R. Little (eds), *Mastering Primary Physical Education*, London: Bloomsbury.

Howells, K. (2018) Physical education planning in the National Curriculum in in K. Sewell (ed.), *Planning the Primary National Curriculum: A Complete Guide for Trainees and Teachers*, 2nd ed., London: Sage, pp. 266–80.

Howells, K. (2019) International perspectives of 'the A,B,Cs of physical activity, play and motor learning, paper presented at AIESEP International Conference Building Bridges for Physical Activity and Sport, New York, June 2019.

Howells, K. and Bowen, J. (2016) Physical activity and self-esteem: 'Jonny's story'. *Education 3-13: International Journal of Primary, Elementary and Early Years Education*, 44(5), pp. 577–90.

Howells, K. with Carney, A., Castle, N. and Little, R. (2017) *Mastering Primary Physical Education*, London: Bloomsbury.

Howes, A., Davies, S.M.B. and Fox, S. (2009) *Improving the Context for Inclusion: Personalising Teacher Development Through Collaborative Action Research*, London: Routledge.

Hoyle, E. and John, P. (1995) *Professional Knowledge and Professional Practice*, London: Cassell.

Hudson, P. (2016) Forming the mentor-mentee relationship, mentoring & tutoring, *Partnership in Learning*, 24(1), pp. 30–43.

Huppert, F.A. and So, T.T. (2013) Flourishing across Europe: Application of a new conceptual framework for defining well-being, *Social Indicators Research*, 110(3), pp. 837–61.

Jennings, P.A. and Greenberg, M.T. (2009) The prosocial classroom: Teacher social and emotional competence in relation to student and classroom outcomes. *Review of Educational Research*, 79(1), pp. 491–525.

Jerrim, J. and Vignoles, A. (2016) The link between East Asian 'mastery' teaching methods and English children's mathematics skills. *Economics of Education Review*, 50, pp. 29–44.

Jewett, P. and Smith, K. (2003) Becoming critical: moving toward a critical pedagogy: An argument for critical literacy, *Action in Teacher Education*, 25(3), pp. 69–77.

Johnson, B., Down, B., Le Cornu, R., Peters, J., Sullivan, A., Pearce, J. and Hunter, J. (2014) Promoting early career teacher resilience: A framework for understanding and acting, *Teachers and Teaching*, 20(5), pp. 530–46.

Jones, M. and Straker, K. (2006) What informs mentors' practice when working with trainees and newly qualified teachers? An investigation into mentors' professional knowledge base, *Journal of Education for Teaching*, 32(2), pp. 165–84.

Kardos, S. and Johnson, S. (2010) New teachers' experiences of mentoring: The good, the bad, and the inequity, *Journal of Educational Change*, 11, pp. 23–44.

Katz, L.G. (1995) *Talks with Teachers: A Collection*, Norwood, NJ: Ablex.

Kemmis, S., Heikkinen, H.L.T., Fransson, G., Aspfors, J. and Edwards-Groves, C. (2014) Mentoring of new teachers as contested practice: Supervision, support and collaborative self-development, *Teaching and Teacher Education*, 43, pp. 154–64.

Kime, S. (2017) Four pillars of assessment. Available at: https://evidencebased.education/pillars-assessment-purpose. Accessed March 2020.

King, H. (2013) Learning from each other in every lesson: How can a Year 3 class help each other to learn, whatever the subject?, in Canterbury Christ Church University (ed.), *Mobilising Pupil Agency in School Development.* Available at: www.canterbury.ac.uk/ education/our-work/research-knowledge-exchange/docs/ActionResearch-Barham-Primary.pdf. Accessed 6 March 2019.

Kirk, D. (1993) Curriculum work in physical education: Beyond the objectives approach? *Journal of Teaching in Physical Education,* 12(3), pp. 244-65.

Kirk, G. (2000) *Quality Assurance in Initial Teacher Education*, Edinburgh: Dunedin Press.

Kline, N. (2009) *Time to Think: Listening to Ignite the Human Mind*, London: Ward Lock.

Kolb, D.A. (1984) *Experiential Learning: Experience as the Source of Learning and Development*, Vol. 1. Englewood Cliffs, NJ: Prentice-Hall.

Korthagen, F. and Vasalos, A. (2005) Levels in reflection: Core reflection as a means to enhance professional growth. *Teachers and teaching: Theory and practice*, 11(1), pp. 47-71.

Kress, G. (2010) *Multimodality: A Social Semiotic Approach to Contemporary Communication*, New York: Routledge.

Kritcher, P. (1998) Nothing endures but change: Ecology's newly emerging paradigm, *Northeastern Naturalist*, 5, pp. 165-74.

Kroll, J. (2016) What is meant by the term group mentoring? *Mentoring and Tutoring: Partnership in Learning*, 24, pp. 44-58.

Krueger P.J. (2000) Beginning music teachers: Will they leave the profession? *Update Applications of Research in Music Education,* 19(1), pp. 22-26.

Laker, A. (2000) *Beyond the Boundaries of Physical Education: Educating Young People for Citizenship and Social Responsibility,* London: Routledge.

Langdon, F. and Ward, L. (2015) Educative mentoring: A way forward, *International Journal of Mentoring and Coaching in Education,* 4(4), pp. 240-54.

Larson, J. and Marsh, J. (2015) *Making Literacy Real: Theories and Practices for Learning and Teaching,* 2nd ed., London: Sage.

Lawrence, D. (2014) *The Socratic Method: The Key to Effective Mentoring,* Available at: http:// mentoringassociation.org. Accessed September 2018

Lawrence, J. (2018) Reflective practice in primary schools, in A. Hansen (ed.), *Primary Professional Studies,* London: Sage, pp. 203-14.

Lawrence, J. (2019) Holding pre- and post-lesson discussions, in S. Capel and J. Lawrence (eds), *Mentoring Physical Education Teachers in the Secondary School*, Abingdon: Routledge, pp. 207-20.

Lawrence, J. and Mellor, P. (2011) The review process, unpublished manuscript, Leeds Metropolitan University.

Lawrence, J. and Woolliscroft, J. (2019) 'What knowledge, understanding and skills does a mentor of beginning physical education teachers need?' In S. Capel and J. Lawrence *Mentoring Physical Education Teachers in the Secondary School*, Abingdon: Routledge, pp. 111-34.

Learning & Teaching Scotland (2008) Assessment for learning. Available at: www.ltscotland.org.uk/assess/for/intro.asp. Accessed 15 August 2010.

Leland, C.H., Harste, J.C. and Huber, K.R. (2005) 'Out of the box: critical literacy in a first-grade classroom', *Language Arts*, 82(4), pp. 257-68.

Lieberman, A. and Pointer Mace, D.H. (2009) The role of 'accomplished teachers' in professional learning communities: uncovering practice and enabling leadership, *Teachers and Teaching: Theory and Practice*, 15(4), pp. 459-70.

Lofthouse, R.M. (2018) Re-imagining mentoring as a dynamic hub in the transformation of initial teacher education: The role of mentors and teacher educators, *International Journal of Mentoring and Coaching in Education*, 7(3), pp. 248-60.

Lofthouse, R.M., Leat, D. and Towler, C. (2010) *Improving Teacher Coaching in Schools: A Practical Guide - Project Report*, London: National College for Teaching and Leadership.

Lortie, D.C. (1975) *Schoolteacher: A Sociological Study.* Chicago, IL: University of Chicago Press

Luthar, S.S. (2006) Resilience in development: A synthesis of research across five decades, in D. Cicchetti and D.J. Cohen (eds), *Developmental Psychopathology: Risk, Disorder, and Adaptation* (pp. 740-95). New York: Wiley.

Mackie, L. (2020, forthcoming) *Perceptions of the Use of Formative Assessment Within the Mentoring Process.*

Marshall, B., and Drummond, M.J. (2006) How teachers engage with Assessment for Learning: lessons from the classroom, *Research Papers in Education*, 21(2), pp.133-49.

Maynard, T. and Furlong, J. (1995) 'Learning to teach and models of mentoring', in T. Kerry and A. Shelton-Mayes (eds), *Issues in Mentoring*, London: Routledge, pp. 10-14.

McDermott, K., Henchy, D., Meade, D. and Golden, K. (2007) Exploring who we are in the context of global reforms in education: The second level support service in conversation, *Irish Educational Studies*, 26(3), pp. 239-52.

Meijer, M.-J., Kuijpers, M., Boei, F., Vrieling, E. and Geijsel, F. (2017) Professional development of teacher-educators towards transformative learning. *Professional Development in Education*, 43(5), pp. 819-40.

Menter, I., Brisard, E. and Smith, I. (2006) Making teachers in Britain: Professional knowledge for initial teacher education in England and Scotland, *Educational Philosophy and Theory*, 38(3), pp. 269-86.

Mikulincer, M. and Shaver, P.R. (2007) *Attachment Patterns in Adulthood: Structure, Dynamics and Change*, New York: The Guilford Press.

Ministry of Education and Research (2010) *Differentiated Primary and Lower Secondary Teacher Education Programmes for Years 1-7 and Years 5-10*, Oslo: Swedish Ministry of Education and Research.

Moberg, D. and Velasquez, M. (2004) Ethics of mentoring. *Business Ethics Quarterly*, 14(1), pp. 95-122.

Montgomery, B.L. (2017) Mapping a mentoring roadmap and developing a supportive network for strategic career advancement, *SAGE Open*, April-June. Available at: https://journals.sagepub.com/doi/10.1177/2158244017710288. Accessed 24 September 2020.

Mowbray, D. (2008). Building resilience: An organisational cultural approach to mental health and well-being at work - a primary prevention programme. In A. Kinder, R. Hughes and C.L. Cooper (eds), *Employee Well-being Support: A Workplace Resource.* Chichester: John Wiley & Sons, pp. 309-21.

Mowbray, D. (2011) *Resilience and Strengthening Resilience in Individuals,* London: Management Advisory Service.

Mowbray, D. (2012) *RAQ8*, London: Management Advisory Service.

Mowbray, D. (2018) *Guide to Personal Resilience*, 3rd ed., London: Management Advisory Service.

Muijs, D. and Reynolds, D. (2017) *Effective Teaching: Evidence and Practice*, London: Sage.

Murphy, C. (2016) *Coteaching in Teacher Education: Innovative Pedagogy for Excellence*, St Albans: Critical Publishing.

Murray, J. (2002) Between the chalkface and the ivory tower, PhD thesis, Institute of Education, University of London.

NASUWT (2018) Student voice. Available at: www.nasuwt.org.uk/advice/in-the-classroom/children-and-young-people/student-voice. Accessed 6 August 2018.

National College for Teaching and Leadership (2016) Women leading in education: Get leadership coaching. Available at: www.gov.uk/guidance/women-leading-in-education-get-leadership-coaching. Accessed 1 March 2018.

National Education Union (2018) Teachers and workload. Available at: https://neu.org.uk/policy/teachers-workload. Accessed 22 January 2019.

Neacşu, I. (2010) *Introduction in Psychology of Education and Development*, Iasi: Polirom.

Neenan, G. (2009) Using Socratic questioning in coaching, *Journal of Rational-Emotive and Cognitive-Behavior Therapy,* 27(4), pp. 249–64.

Neff, K. and Germer, C. (2018) *The Mindful Self-Compassion Workbook,* New York: The Guildford Press.

Nesta Policy and Research Unit (2006) *The Innovation Gap: Why Policy Needs to Reflect the Reality of Innovation in the UK*. Available at: www.nesta.org.uk/report/innovation-gap-policy-briefing. Accessed 23 September 2017.

New Teacher Center (2011) *NTC Continuum of Mentoring Practice,* Santa Cruz, CA: New Teacher Center.

NICE (2018) *Social and Emotional Wellbeing for Children and Young People*. Available at: www.nice.org.uk. Accessed 6 August 2018.

Nicol, D.J. and MacFarlane-Dick, D. (2006) Formative assessment and self-regulated learning: A model and seven principles of good feedback practice, *Studies in Higher Education*, 31(2), pp. 199–218.

Norton, S.J. (2017) Primary mathematics trainee teacher confidence and its relationship to mathematical knowledge, *Australian Journal of Teacher Education*, 42(2), pp. 46–61.

Nunes, T., Carraher, D. and Schliemann, A. (1993) *Street Mathematics and School Mathematics (Learning in Doing: Social, Cognitive and Computational Perspectives),* Cambridge: Cambridge University Press.

NUT/YouGov (2015) *Teacher Survey on Government Education Policy*, Available at: www.teachers.org.uk/news-events/press-releases-england/nutyougov-teacher-survey-government-education-policy. Accessed 23 September 2019.

O'Brien, J., Christie, F. and Draper, J. (2007) Induction standards and the assessment of beginning teacher competence: A UK Perspective, in M. Valencic-Zuljan and J. Vogrinc (eds), *Professional inductions of Teachers in Europe and Elsewhere*, Ljubijana: European Social Fund and Ministry of Education, Slovenia, pp. 289–308.

Oates, T. (2011) Could do better: Using international comparisons to refine the National Curriculum in England, *Curriculum Journal,* 22(2), pp. 121–50.

OECD (2007) *Education at a Glance 2007: OECD Indicators.* Available at: www.oecd.org/education/skills-beyond-school/39313286.pdf. Accessed 22 January 2019.

OECD (2008) *Assessment for Learning: Formative Assessment,* Paris: OECD.

OECD (2017), *PISA 2015 Results (Volume III): Students' Well-Being, PISA,* Paris: OECD.

Office for Standards in Education (2013) *Promoting Improvement in Initial Teacher Education (ITE) Primary Mathematics.* Available at: https://www.gov.uk/government/publications/promoting-improvement-in-initial-teacher-education-primary-mathematics. Accessed 6 June 2018.

Ogier, S. (2017) *Teaching Primary Art and Design,* London: Sage.

Ohio Department for Education (2015) *Ohio Standards for Professional Development,* Columbus, OH: Department for Education. Available at: http://education.ohio.gov/Topics/Teaching/Professional-Development/Organising-for-High-Quality-Professional-Development. Accessed 27 October 2018.

Opie, C. (2004) *Doing Educational Research,* London: Sage.

Orland-Barack, L. and Yinon, H. (2007) When theory meets practice: What student teachers learn from guided reflection on their own classroom discourse, *Teaching and Teacher Education,* 23, pp. 957–69.

Osborne, J.F. (1996) Beyond constructivism, *Science Education,* 80(1), pp. 53–82.

Parsloe, E. and Wray, M. (2005) *Coaching and Mentoring: Practical Methods to Improve Learning,* London: Kogan Page.

Pate, R.R., O'Neill, J.R. and McIver, K.L. (2011) Physical activity and health: Does physical education matter?, *Quest,* 63(1), pp. 19–36.

Patrick, F., Forde, C. and McPhee, A. (2003) Challenging the 'new professionalism': From managerialism to pedagogy?, *Journal of In-Service Education,* 29(2), pp. 237–54.

Peiser, P., Duncalf, D. and Mallaburn, A. (2019) 'The role of the mentor in an increasingly school-led English initial teacher education policy context', *Professional Development in Education,* doi:10.1080/19415257.2019.1694053.

Pemberton, C. (2006) *Coaching to Solutions: A Manager's Tool Kit for Performance Delivery,* Oxford: Butterworth Heinemann.

Pemberton, C. (2015) *Resilience: A Practical Guide for Coaches,* Berkshire: Open University Press.

Perkins, D. (2009) *Making Learning Whole: How Seven Principles of Teaching Can Transform Education,* San Francisco: Jossey-Bass.

Perkins, J. (2009) *Review of Engineering Skills,* London: Department for Business Innovation and Skills. Available at: www.raeng.org.uk/publications/other/perkins-review-of-engineering-skills Accessed 23 January 2020.

Peters, J. and Pearce, J. (2012). Relationships and early career teacher resilience: A role for school principals, *Teachers and Teaching: Theory and Practice,* 18(2), pp. 249–62.

Pickup, I., Price, L., Shaughnessey, J., Spence, J. and Trace, M. (2008) *Learning to Teach Primary PE,* London: Sage.

Pollard, A. (2014) *Reflective Teaching in Schools,* 4th ed., London: Bloomsbury

Pollard, A., Black-Hawkins, K., Hodges, G.C., Dudley, P., James, M., Linklater, H., Swaffield, S., Swann, M., Turner, F. and Warwick, P. (2014). *Reflective Teaching in Schools*, London: Bloomsbury.

Pollard, A., and Tann, S. (1993) *Reflective Teaching in the Primary School: A Handbook for the Classroom*, 2nd ed., London: Continuum.

Portner, H. (ed.) (2005) *Teacher Mentoring and Induction: The State of the Art and Beyond,* Thousand Oak, CA: Corwin Press.

Pound, L. and Lee, T. (2011) *Teaching Mathematics Creatively,* London: Routledge.

Public Health England (2015) *Promoting Children and Young People's Emotional Health and Wellbeing: A Whole School and College Approach.* Available at: https://assets.publishing.service.gov.uk/government/uploads/system/uploads/attachment_data/file/414908/Final_EHWB_draft_20_03_15.pdf. Accessed 23 January 2020.

Quality Assurance Agency (2006) *Quality Assurance in Initial Teacher Education: The Standard for Initial Teacher Education in Scotland: Benchmark Information*, Gloucester: QAA.

Ragins, B. (2016) From the ordinary to the extraordinary: High quality mentoring relationships at work, *Organisational Dynamics* 45, pp. 228–44.

Ranting Teacher (2005) *Everything You Need to Know to Survive Teaching*, London: Continuum.

Remnant, H. (2019) Stories of science: An auto/biographical study in primary science, PhD thesis, Canterbury Christ Church University. Available at: https://repository.canterbury.ac.uk/item/88z10/stories-of-science-an-auto-biographical-study-in-primary-science. Accessed 12 December 2019.

Rhodes, C., Stokes, M. and Hampton, G. (2004) *A Practical Guide to Mentoring, Coaching and Peer-networking*. London: RoutledgeFalmer.

Rippon, J. and Martin, M. (2003) Supporting induction: Relationships count, *Mentoring and Tutoring*, 11(2), pp. 212–25.

Roberts, A. (2000) Mentoring revisited: A phenomenological reading of the literature, *Mentoring and Tutoring*, 8, pp. 145–70.

Roberts, D.A. (1982) Developing the Concept of 'Curriculum Emphases' in Science Education, *Science Education*, 66 (2), pp.243-260.

Roberts, D.A. (2007) 'Scientific Literacy/Science Literacy', in Abell, S.K. and Lederman, N.G. (eds.) *Handbook of Research on Science Education*, Mahwah, NJ: Lawrence Erlbaum, pp. 729–80.

Roberts, G. (2002) *SET for Success: The Supply of People with Science, Technology, Engineering and Mathematics, Skills*, London: HM Treasury.

Robinson, V., Hohepa, M. and Lloyd, C. (2009) *School Leadership and Student Outcomes: Identifying What Works and Why: Best Evidence Synthesis Iteration (BES)*. Available at: https://www.educationcounts.govt.nz/__data/assets/pdf_file/0015/60180/BES-Leadership-Web-updated-foreword-2015.pdf. Accessed August 2019.

Roche, M. (2015) *Developing Children's Critical Thinking Through Picture Books*, London: Routledge.

Rogers, A., Luksyte, A. and Spitzmueller, C. (2016) Predictors of effective formal mentoring: Is the mentor's commitment all that matters? *Human Performance*, 29(3), pp. 209–25.

Rogers, C. (1961) *On Becoming a Person*, Boston: Houghton Mifflin.

Rogers, J. (2004) *Coaching Skills: A Handbook*, Maidenhead: Open University Press.

Rogoff, B. (2003) *The Cultural Nature of Human Development,* Oxford:Oxford University Press.

Rolfe, G., Freshwater, D. and Jasper, M. (2001) *Critical Reflection in Nursing and the Helping Professions: A User's Guide*, Basingstoke: Palgrave Macmillan.

Rose, N. and Eriksson-Lee, S. (2017) *Putting Evidence to Work:How Can We Help New Teachers Use Research Evidence to Inform Their Teaching?* Available at: https://www.teachfirst.org.uk/sites/default/files/2017-10/Putting_Evidence_to_work_2017.pdf. Accessed 16 September 2019.

Rosenthal, R. and Jacobsen L. (1968) *Pygmalion in the Classroom: Teacher Expectation and Pupils' Intellectual Development*, New York: Holt, Rinehart and Winston.

Rowland, G., King, H., Webb, P., Cogger, A. and Vincent, K. (2018) Fishing for evidence of impact, *Professional Development Today,* 19(3/4), pp. 76–85.

Rowland, T., Turner, F., Thwaites, A. and Huckstep, P. (2009) *Developing Primary Mathematics Teaching: Reflecting on Practice with the Knowledge Quartet,* London: Sage.

The Royal Society (2010) *State of the Nation Report on 5–14 Science and Mathematics Education*, London: Royal Society. Available at: https://royalsociety.org/~/media/Royal_Society_Content/education/policy/state-of-nation/2010-07-07-SNR3-Fullreport.pdf. Accessed 30 January 2020.

Rudolph, J.L. (2014) Dewey's 'science as method' a century later: Reviving science education for civic ends', *American Educational Research Journal*, 51(6), pp.1056–83.

Russell, S. (2000) Developing computational fluency with whole numbers in the elementary grades, in B. Ferrucci and K. Heid (eds), Millennium Focus Issue: Perspectives on Principles and Standards, *The New England Math Journal,* 32(2), pp. 40–54.

Sach, E. (2015) An exploration of teachers' narratives: What are the facilitators and constraints which promote or inhibit 'good' formative assessment practices in schools?, *Education 3–13,* 43(3), pp. 322–35.

Sachs, J. (2001) Teacher professional identity: Competing discourses, competing outcomes, *Journal of Education Policy,* 16(2), pp. 149–61.

Sachs, J. (2003) *The Activist Teaching Profession,* Maidenhead: Open University Press.

Schein, E.H. (1985) *Organisational Culture and Leadership*, San Francisco: Jossey-Bass.

Schön, D.A. (1983) *The Reflective Practitioner: How Professionals Think in Action*, New York: Basic Books.

Scottish Government (2011) *Teaching Scotland's Future*, Edinburgh: Scottish Government.

Scriven, M. (1967) The methodology of evaluation. In R.W. Tyler, R.M. Gagne and M. Scriven (eds), *Perspectives of Curriculum Evaluation*, Vol. I, Chicago, IL: Rand McNally, pp. 39–83.

Seligman, M.E.P. (2002) *Authentic Happiness: Using the New Positive Psychology to Realize Your Potential for Lasting Fulfilment*, New York: The Free Press.

Seligman, M.E.P. (2011) *Flourish: A Visionary New Understanding of Happiness and Well-being*, New York: The Free Press.

Serafini, F. (2001) Three paradigms of assessment: measurement, procedure, and inquiry, *The Reading Teacher,* 54(4), pp. 384–93.

Sewell K. (ed.) (2018) *Planning the Primary National Curriculum: A Complete Guide for Trainees and Teachers*, 2nd ed., London: Sage, pp. 266–80.

Shulman, L.S. (1986) Those who understand: Knowledge growth in teaching, *Educational Researcher*, 15(2), pp. 4-14.

Shulman, L.S. (1987) Knowledge and teaching: Foundations of the new reform, *Harvard Educational Review*, 57(1), pp. 1-21.

Sims, S. and Allen, R. (2018). Identifying schools with high usage and high loss of newly qualified teachers, *National Institute Economic Review*, 243(1), pp. R27-R36.

Skemp, R. (1989) *Mathematics in the Primary School*, London: Routledge.

Smith, P. and West-Burnham, J. (1993) *Mentoring in the Effective School*, Harlow: Longman.

Smyth, J. and Shacklock, G. (1998) *Remaking Teaching: Ideology, Policy and Practice*, London: Routledge.

Spendlove, D., Howes, A. and Wake, G (2010) 'Partnerships in pedagogy: Refocusing of classroom lenses', *European Journal of Teacher Education*, 33(1), pp. 65-77.

Spooner-Lane, R. (2016) Mentoring beginning teachers in primary schools: Research review, *Professional Development in Education*, 43(2), pp. 253-73.

State Education Department and University of the State of New York (2011) *The New York State Mentoring Standards*, Albany, NY: State Education Department and University of The State of New York. Available at: http://usny.nysed.gov/rttt/docs/MentoringStandards.pdf. Accessed 25 January 2018.

Strauss, A. and Corbin, J. (1990). *Basics of Qualitative Research: Grounded Theory Procedures and Techniques*. Thousand Oaks, CA: Sage.

Stevenson, D. and Farmer, P. (2017) *Thriving at Work: A Review of Mental Health and Employers*, London: UK Government. Available at: https://www.gov.uk/government/publications/thriving-at-work-a-review-of-mental-health-and-employers. Accessed 6 August 2018.

Stirling, S. and Emery, H. (2015) *A Whole School Framework for Emotional Wellbeing and Mental Health*, London: National Children's Bureau. Available at: https://www.ncb.org.uk/resources-publications/resources/whole-school-framework-emotional-well-being-and-mental-health. Accessed 12 December 2017.

Stone, R. (2018) A Study of primary school teachers' understandings and perceptions of teaching reading, EdD thesis, Canterbury Christ Church University.

Sundli, L. (2007) Mentoring: A new mantra for education? *Teaching and Teacher Education*, 23, pp. 201-14.

Struthers, D. (2018) Professional resilience and wellbeing, in J.-L. Dutaut & L. Rycroft-Smith (eds), *Flip the System UK: A Teachers' Manifesto*, London: Routledge.

Talbot, D., Denny, J. and Henderson, S. (2018) 'Trying to decide ... what sort of teacher I wanted to be': Mentoring as a dialogic practice, *Teaching Education*, 29(1), pp. 47-60.

Tang, S.Y.F. (2008) Issues in field experience assessment in teacher education in a standards-based context, *Journal of Education for Teaching: International Research and Pedagogy*, 34(1), pp. 17-32.

Tanner, J., Yeo, A. and McManus, S. (2018) *Emotional Health at Work: Why It Matters and How You Can Support It*, London: Institute for Public Policy Research. Available at: https://www.ippr.org/files/2018-03/emotional-health-at-work-march18.pdf. Accessed 6 August 2018.

Taylor D. and Hamdy, H. (2013) Adult learning theories: Implications for learning and teaching in medical education: AMEE Guide No. 83, *Medical Teacher,* 35(11), pp. 1561-72.

Teaching Schools Council (2016) *National Standards for School-based Initial Teacher Training (ITT) Mentors,* London: Teaching Schools Council. Available at: https://www.gov.uk/government/uploads/system/uploads. Accessed 12 September 2019.

Thompson, S. and Thompson, N. (2018) *The Critically Reflective Practitioner*. London: Macmillan.

Tillema, H.H. and Smith, K. (2009) Assessment orientation in formative assessment of learning to teach, *Teachers and Teaching*, 15(3), pp. 391-405.

Timperley, H. (2009) *Professional Learning and Development in Schools and Higher Education,* Toronto: Springer.

Timperley, H. (2020) *Enablers for Effective Professional Conversations*, Auckland: AITSL. Available at: https://www.aitsl.edu.au/docs/default-source/default-document-library/professional-conversations-a3.pdf?sfvrsn=b0c1ec3c_2. Accessed 12 December 2019.

Timperley, H., Wilson, A., Barrar, H. and Fung, I. (2007) *Teacher Professional Learning and Development: Best Evidence Synthesis Iteration*, Wellington: Ministry of Education (NZ).

Tytler, R., Osborne, J., Williams, G., Tytler, K., Cripps, J. (2008) *Opening Up Pathways: Engagement in STEM Across the Primary-Secondary School Transition*. Available at: https://pdfs.semanticscholar.org/26d3/9dde4d8dcb50de6855a3a4f229649dcce104.pdf. Accessed 12 January 2020.

Van Ginkel, G., Oolbekkink, H., Meijer, P.C. & Verloop, N. (2016) Adapting mentoring to individual differences in novice teacher learning: The mentor's viewpoint, *Teachers and Teaching*, 22(2), pp. 198-218.

Vincent, K. (2018) Researching the impact of changes to mentoring approaches within a large initial teacher education partnership, *CollectivED*, 4, pp. 18-24. Available at: http://leedsbeckett.ac.uk/-/media/files/research/collectived-june-2018-issue-4.pdf?la=en. Accessed 16 December 2019.

Vincent, K., King, H. and Webb, P. (2018) Researching the impact of ambitious changes to mentoring within in a large initial teacher education partnership, paper presented at the Teacher Education Advancement Network (TEAN) 9th annual conference, Birmingham, 10 May.

Vygotsky L.S. (1978) *Mind in Society: The Development of Higher Psychological Processes*, Cambridge, MA: Harvard University Press.

Walker-Smith, E. (2017) Facilitated learning conversations model, unpublished manuscript.

Wang, J. and Odell, S.J. (2002) Mentoring learning to teach according to standards-based reform: A critical review, *Review of Educational Research,* 72(3), pp. 481-546.

Wasconga, C.O., Wanzare Z.O. and Dawo, J.I. (2015) Mentoring beginning teachers: Bridging the gap between pre-service training and in-practice realities, *Journal of International Education and Leadership*, 5(2), pp. 1-11.

Watkins, C. (2010) Learning, performance and improvement, *Research Matters,* 34, pp. 1-16.

Watts, R. (2019) Drawing inspiration from children's visual culture, in S. Ogier (ed.), *A Broad and Balanced Curriculum in Primary Schools: Educating the Whole Child,* London, Sage, pp. 118-32.

Wellcome Trust (2011) *Exploring Young People's Views on Science Education*, London: NFER. Available at: https://wellcome.ac.uk/sites/default/files/wtvm052732_0.pdf. Accessed 6 June 2016.

White, E. (2014) Being a teacher and a teacher educator: Developing a new identity?, *Professional Development in Education*, 40(3), pp. 436–49.

Whitmore, J. (1998) *Coaching for Performance: GROWing People, Performance and Purpose*, London: Nicholas Brealey.

Whitmore, J. (2002) *Coaching for Performance: GROWing People, Performance and Purpose*, 2nd ed., London: Nicholas Brealey.

Whitty, G. and Willmott, E. (1991) Competence-based teacher education: Approaches and issues, *Cambridge Journal of Education*, 21(3), pp. 309–18.

Wiliam, D. (2014) Formative assessment and contingency in the regulation of learning processes, paper presented at Toward a Theory of Classroom Assessment as the Regulation of Learning, Philadelphia, PA.

Yeomans, J. and Sampson, R. (eds) (1994) *Mentorship in the Primary School*, London: Falmer Press.

Yorke, M. (2003) Formative assessment in higher education: Moves towards theory and the enhancement of pedagogic practice, *Higher Education*, 45, pp. 477–501.

Young, J.R., Bullough, R.V. Jr., Draper, R.J., Smith, L.K. and Erickson, L.B. (2005) Novice teacher growth and personal models of mentoring: Choosing compassion over inquiry, *Mentoring & Tutoring: Partnership in Learning*, 13(2), pp. 169–88.

Young Minds (2018) *360° Schools Community*. Available at: www.youngminds.org.uk/what-we-do/360-schools-hub/360-schools-community. Accessed 6 August 2018.

Zeichner, K. (2010) Rethinking the connections between campus courses and field experiences in college- and university-based teacher education. *Journal of Teacher Education*, 61(1/2), pp. 89–99.

Ziman, J.M. (1978) *Reliable Knowledge: An Exploration of the Grounds for Belief in Science*, Cambridge: Cambridge University Press.

INDEX

Printed in Great Britain
by Amazon